Critical Race Theory Perspectives
on the Social Studies

The Profession, Policies, and Curriculum

A volume in
Research in Social Education
Series Editor: Merry M. Merryfield, *The Ohio State University*

Critical Race Theory Perspectives on the Social Studies

The Profession, Policies, and Curriculum

Edited by

Gloria Ladson-Billings
University of Wisconsin–Madison

INFORMATION AGE
PUBLISHING

80 Mason Street • Greenwich, Connecticut 06830 • www.infoagepub.com

Library of Congress Cataloging-in-Publication Data

Critical race theory perspectives on the social studies : the
profession, policies, and curriculum / edited by Gloria Ladson-Billings.

    p. cm. – (Research in social education)
Includes index.
 ISBN 1-59311-034-0 (pbk.) – ISBN 1-59311-035-9 (hardcover)
 1. Social sciences–Study and teaching. 2. Race–Study and teaching.
I. Ladson-Billings, Gloria, 1947- II. Series.
 H62.C69743 2003
 305.8'0071'273–dc22

                                        2003016124

Printed in the United States of America

CONTENTS

Part III
The Curriculum

Part IV
The Technology

CHAPTER 1

LIES MY TEACHER STILL TELLS

Developing a Critical Race Perspective Toward the Social Studies

Gloria Ladson-Billings

In his widely read book, *Lies My Teacher Told Me*, author Jim Loewen (1996) argues that high school students hate history. When they list their favorite subject, history always comes in last. They consider it the most irrelevant of twenty-one school subjects; "boring" is the adjective most often applied to history as a school subject. Loewen spent two years at the Smithsonian Institution surveying twelve leading high school textbooks of American History. What he found was an embarrassing amalgam of bland optimism, blind patriotism, and misinformation pure and simple, weighing in at an average of four-and-a-half pounds and 888 pages.

In response, he wrote *Lies My Teacher Told Me*, in part a telling critique of existing books but, more important, a wonderful retelling of American history as it should—and could—be taught to American students. But, despite Loewen's brilliant critique of the high school history curriculum (and the social studies curriculum in general), we continue to tell our students lies about our history, our world views, and our culture. In this chapter I want to argue that one of the central concepts that we predicate many of our

Critical Race Theory Perspectives on the Social Studies, pages 1–11
Copyright © 2003 by Information Age Publishing

1

social lies on is the concept of race. And, for the purpose of this discussion I want to suggest that race is an ever-present concept in the social studies—in the curriculum, the profession, and its policies and practices.

What is race? The question invariably creates a sense of discomfort. No one wants to talk about it since it represents such a contradiction of American life. We like to talk about having transcended race or at least having gotten past it. But, we still have a contradictory and intertwined stance toward it.

In its 1998 statement on race the American Anthropological Association asserted that:

> In the United States both scholars and the general public have been conditioned to viewing human races as natural and separate divisions within the human species based on visible physical differences. With the vast expansion of scientific knowledge in this century, however, it has become clear that human populations are not unambiguous, clearly demarcated, biologically distinct groups. Evidence from the analysis of genetics (e.g., DNA) indicates that most physical variation, about 94%, lies within so-called racial groups. Conventional geographic "racial" groupings differ from one another only in about 6% of their genes. This means that there is greater variation within "racial" groups than between them. In neighboring populations there is much overlapping of genes and their phenotypic (physical) expressions. Throughout history whenever different groups have come into contact, they have interbred. The continued sharing of genetic materials has maintained all of humankind as a single species. (see: www.aaanet.org)

This assertion that science no longer recognizes the concept of race baffles us because we have organized so much of our society around the concept. Nobel Laureate Toni Morrison (1992) suggests that:

> Race has become metaphorical—a way of referring to and disguising forces, events, classes, and expressions of social decay and economic division far more threatening to the body politic than biological "race" ever was.

> Expensively kept, economically unsound, a spurious and useless political asset in election campaigns, racism is as healthy today as it was during the Enlightenment. It seems that it has a utility far beyond economy, beyond the sequestering of classes from one another, and has assumed a metaphorical life so completely embedded in daily discourse that it is perhaps more necessary and more on display than ever before. (p. 63)

So, if race does not exist from a scientific perspective, but is ever present from a social perspective, what do we teach our students about race? On one level we might argue that we teach them nothing about race. Most social studies and history textbooks avoid the term "race" altogether. Psychologists tell us that children develop awareness of skin color differences as early as 3 years old. That awareness is not unlike the awareness that children develop as they select a red shirt over a yellow one. However, it is the meaning that others ascribe to these differences that begin to shape how children perceive themselves and others.

Olneck (1995) points out that "ethnic identities are not inheritances or preservations but are, rather, on going active constructions that emerge out of interactions among groups within social-political and symbolic contexts. The nature of those identities depends upon the interpretations parties make of their interactions" (pp. 318–319).

RACE AND THE CURRICULUM

One of the places that race still operates is in the social studies curriculum. If one were to attempt to construct the history of African Americans based on the information presented in a typical U.S. History textbook that history might consist of the following: Africans were first brought to the Americas in the early 1600s as slaves and indentured servants. Some fought for the British in the American Revolution because King George offered freedom from bondage to those who fought on the British side. One notable African American who died protesting Britain's colonial rule was Crispus Attucks. In the 1800s African Americans were responsible for the economic prosperity of the nation—particularly that of the South. In the mid 1800s tensions between the North and South over slavery led to the Civil War. After the North won the war the Reconstruction period was a difficult time for the South and many restrictive laws were enacted to subvert the new amendments to the Constitution that guaranteed Black rights. Black people fought for their civil rights in the 1960s.

Sprinkled in this history students might encounter the names of people such as Harriet Tubman, Nat Turner, Frederick Douglass, and Martin Luther King, Jr. However, they will not leave their history course with any sense of a coherent history of Africans in the Americas. In social studies courses other than history, African Americans are virtually invisible.

In the case of American Indians a similar erasure occurs (see Rains chapter in this volume). We see them as welcoming European settlers, joining them in a Thanksgiving celebration, guiding them as they explore the west, being massacred as settlers push westward, and finally being removed and subdued by Andrew Jackson. After the "Trail of Tears" American Indians disappear from the pages of our textbooks and the curriculum. For our students American Indians are museum exhibits. No discussion of the ongoing plight of Indians in America is available to most students in our schools. The contemporary Indian rarely emerges in the classroom. At most, our national discussion of American Indians focuses on gambling casinos and alcoholism. We rarely configure race into our discussion of American Indians.

This discourse of invisibility is true of every non-European group of people who constitute our nation. Asian Americans appear in our discussion of the Chinese participation in the building of the transcontinental railroad and the Japanese-American internment during World War II. Latinos appear briefly in the Battle of Guadalupe Hidalgo and the United Farm Workers formation and protests. Throughout our history we present an incoherent, disjointed picture of those who are not White.

Perhaps this erasure would not be as damaging to the body politic if it were merely a matter of not seeing the other in our courses and curriculum. However, this erasure is compounded by a societal curriculum (Cortés, 1979) that operates within and beyond the school and classroom. This is the hidden curriculum that articulates social locations and social meanings. Students have access to this curriculum whenever they turn on their evening news and see people of color as menacing, dangerous social outcasts. They have access to this curriculum when they see inverse relationships between who the student population is and who the teachers and administrators are. If the people who look like them occupy the lowest skilled jobs in the school—janitors, cafeteria workers, instructional aids—then they begin to calculate their own understanding of people. The official curriculum only serves to reinforce what the societal curriculum suggests, i.e., people of color are relatively insignificant to the growth and development of our democracy and our nation and they represent a drain on the resources and values.

RACE AND THE SOCIAL STUDIES PROFESSION

In addition to the curriculum shortcomings regarding race, the social studies profession itself continues to exclude race as a part of its focus. Despite the salience of history and social issues to people of color, the profession has done little to recruit and retain teachers of diverse backgrounds. While this lack of diversity among social studies teachers is symptomatic of the overall teaching profession, the social studies seem to be a place of curious absence for such teachers. Some of the nation's most eminent historians and social scientists are people of color—John Hope Franklin, Kenneth Clark, Clayborn Carson, Ronald Takaki, Gary Otero, Nell Painter, Sterling Stuckey, Manning Marable, Robin D.G. Kelley, Darlene Clark Hine, William Julius Wilson, and Elsa Barkely Brown are but a few of those whose work has shaped our perspectives on American history, life and culture. Their work has documented the way life in our nation is a complex contradiction of traditions, customs, laws, and practices, and how people of various races have used the tenets of the nation to challenge injustice and inequity. Surely such a noble work should draw other people to a field that holds such promise for human liberation.

To be sure, I am not suggesting that having teachers of color would be the remedy for the myriad problems that plague education in the United States. Indeed, there is no empirical evidence to support such a claim. Rather, I argue that diversity is always a valued added phenomenon. It is a linchpin of democracy, for without diversity there is no need for democracy. If we are all the same—we look, think, act, and believe the same things—we can be governed by consensus or acclamation. But democracy insists on different ideas, dissent, and failure to acquiesce to majority power.

The social studies profession should be the most overt of the school subjects to insist upon the recruitment, training, and retention of a diverse professional teaching force. My own experience as a social studies teacher is instructive as to the way schools as organizations actively discourage new professionals and their new perspectives. As the only woman and only African American in my department my views were regularly challenged. To some degree I chalked this up as my running counter to the "old boys network." However, by the time I became a part of the academy and was considered a scholar of some import, I thought that some of that might change. I am sad to report that at the college and university level, social studies education remains as frozen in its old paradigms as it was in the late 1960s. The governance, research agenda, knowledge production, and demographics of college level teaching in social studies education look very much like it looked more than 30 years ago when I was preparing to teach. Of course, some faculty have included "diversity" topics in their syllabi but much of it remains the same. Social studies educators continue to debate the definition of social studies. They continue to argue over the need for single discipline study versus integrated social sciences. They continue to fight about depth versus coverage. They pay almost no attention to their complete failure to nurture a new cadre of social studies educators who can move us past these old debates.

In contrast to the social studies professional organization, my "adopted" professional association, the National Council of Teachers of English has been explicit in its attempt to address issues of diversity and social justice in its programming, teacher recruitment, and research agenda. The winter 2003 NCTE Homepage (www.ncte.org) advertises a summer workshop titled, "Teaching multiAmerica: Redefining multiculturalism and U.S. Literature" with noted authors Maxine Hong Kingston and Ishmael Reed. It also contains a link to something it calls the "African American Read-In" that is sponsored by the Black Caucus of NCTE and NCTE. There is also a link to something called the "Langston Hughes Poetry Circles." In the Winter 2003 Mid-Year Research Forum, which is one of the major research activities of the organization, NCTE focused exclusively on race. When I have attended NCTE annual meetings the number of people of color who attend and participate on the program has pleasantly surprised me. NCTE seems to always incorporate people from the community in which it holds its annual meeting. At a meeting in Nashville, Tennessee NCTE invited in a group from Fisk University and a group from Tennessee State University, two Historically Black Colleges/Universities, to showcase aspects of their program and simultaneously get to know the professional organization. When I attended the NCSS annual meeting in Nashville (located in the same hotel), it seemed as if the conference attendees were in a hermetically sealed bubble, untouched by the Nashville community.

I do not mean to idealize NCTE. Clearly it has its own set of professional challenges. However, it is amazing that the social studies organization with its expressed mission toward citizenship and democracy cannot seem to seriously engage issues of diversity and social justice *within* the profession. My decision to leave the social studies professional organization came as a result of the clear message the organization sent regarding its lack of commitment to issues of diversity and social justice. For three years running, the organization held meetings in cities serving large communities of color (Detroit, Washington, DC, Cincinnati) and did almost nothing to engage the larger community. Our meeting rooms and programs were so culturally exclusive it was stifling.

At the Cincinnati meeting, a Black Heritage Tour was scheduled and was later cancelled, "for lack of interest"—how apropos! As we sat in those meetings watching our chairs set up, our water glasses filled, and our trash removed by low paid people of color, my colleagues seemed untroubled by the growing distance between the organization and the social conditions in which we found ourselves. My own conscience made my participation in this situation intolerable. I could no longer financially and politically support the hypocrisy. From time to time I receive messages from my graduate students that someone in the organization has inquired as to whether or not I would consider rejoining the group. I always ask, "How have they changed?" This question typically is met with a blank stare. That stare is my answer. The profession continues to ignore one of the more pressing social issues of our day—race (and social justice).

RACE AND SOCIAL STUDIES POLICIES

In addition to the curriculum and the profession, the social studies rely on a set of policies that define what it is and what it stands for. These policies can influence curriculum, instruction, and assessment. Most social studies policies are developed and enacted under the aegis of the National Council for the Social Studies (NCSS). For example, in the 1990s NCSS decided to appoint a task force[1] to develop a set of curriculum standards so that social studies could be better aligned with the national call for higher standards. Rather than acquiescence to the pressure to create narrowly prescriptive standards, the task force opted for a broader, more flexible set of standards that left maximum responsibility in the hands of local school districts, schools, and individual teachers. The NCSS Standards entitled, *Expectations for Excellence* (1996), were ten thematic strands:

- Culture;
- Time, continuity, and change;
- People, places, and environments;
- Individual development and identity;
- Individuals, groups, and institutions;
- Power, authority, and governance;
- Production, consumption, and distribution;
- Science, technology, and society;
- Global connections;
- Civic ideals and practices.

While these strands are broad enough to allow for the academic freedom and ingenuity of teachers, they may also suggest that issues of race and racism are not particularly urgent in the social studies. No statement regarding race and racism was incorporated into the standards. Ongoing social problems such as environmental degradation, poverty, and maintaining national security are directly addressed. However, race and racism are submerged under the more palatable rubrics of "prejudice" and "discrimination." This strategy reinforces the idea that attitudes and behaviors need to be changed without addressing the structural and ideological foundations from which these attitudes and behaviors emerge.

NCSS has adopted a range of policy and position statements (see NCSS website at: www.ncss.org) including statements on early childhood education, ability grouping, academic freedom, character education, the Columbian Quincentenary, testing, and sexism. The organization's statement on "Curriculum guidelines for multicultural education" represents a 1991 revision of a document adopted in 1976. However, there is little evidence that such policy and position statements have had any significant impact on social studies practice. The typical K–12 social studies curriculum has changed very little in the past thirty years. Many elementary schools continue to use the expanding horizons approach starting with family and moving to school, community, state or region, nation, and world history. Secondary schools (from grades 7–12) continue to offer two years of U.S. History (typically grade 8 and grades 10 or 11), a civics or U.S. Government course, and a world history course. Depending on the size of the high school, a wide range of social studies electives might be offered. The national association's policies have done little to impact course offerings and no evidence exists to suggest that the association impacts course content.

Given its lack of impact on practice, one might presume that the association would take greater liberty in expressing its opinion. Since no one seems to listen, why not speak with a more forceful voice? Instead, the association seems to have responded in just the opposite way. During the mid 1990s reorganization of committee structure, NCSS saw fit to eliminate its committee on race and racism. With the exception of the multicultural education curriculum guidelines, almost nothing about race and/or racism is featured in NCSS policy and position statements.

BREAKING THE RACIAL SILENCE[2]

The failure of the social studies to meaningfully engage in dialogue about one of the nation's persistent social justice issues is not surprising. However, it is disappointing. The historical, social, economic, and political records provide compelling blueprints for the way the nation has recruited the concept of race to justify hierarchy, inequity, and oppression. The social studies can serve as a curricular home for unlearning the racism that has confounded us a nation. Yet, we still find teachers continuing to tell us lies.

This volume is designed to make race a centerpiece of our understanding about social studies. The contributors discuss the way the curriculum, the profession, the policies, and even the new embrace of technology conform to a racial script. By employing critical race theory, the contributing authors prevent readers from casting their gaze is some other direction to explain the persistent inequities we find in our schools and in the society.

Critical race theory sprang up in the mid-1970s with the early work of legal scholar Derrick Bell and Alan Freeman, both of whom were distressed over the slow pace of racial reform in the United States. They, along with other scholars, formed alternate civil rights legal perspectives. The first attempt at this alternate theoretical lens was something termed, "Critical legal studies" (CLS) which drew heavily on Gramsci's (1971) notion of "hegemony" to describe the continued legitimacy of oppressive structures in American society. CLS scholars critiqued mainstream legal ideology for its portrayal of U.S. society as a meritocracy but failed to include racism in their critique. Thus, Critical race theory (CRT) was a logical outgrowth of the discontent of legal scholars of color.

CRT begins with the notion that racism is "normal, not aberrant, in American society" (Delgado, 1995, p. xiv), and, because it is so enmeshed in the fabric of our social order, it appears both normal and natural to people in this culture. Derrick Bell (1992) argues that racism is a permanent fixture of American life. Thus, the strategy of critical race theorists is one of unmasking and exposing racism in its various permutations.

Second, CRT departs from mainstream legal scholarship by sometimes employing storytelling to "analyze the myths, presuppositions, and received wisdoms that make up the common culture about race and that invariably render blacks and other minorities one-down" (Delgado, 1995, p. xiv). Critical race theorists ... "integrate their experiential knowledge, drawn from a shared history as 'other' with their ongoing struggles to transform a world deteriorating under the albatross of racial hegemony" (Barnes, 1990, pp. 1864–1865). Thus, the experience of oppressions such as racism or sexism is an important aspect of developing a CRT analytic standpoint.

Third, CRT insists on a critique of liberalism. Crenshaw (1988) argues that the liberal perspective of the "civil rights crusade as a long, slow, but always upward pull" (p. 1334) is flawed because it fails to understand the limits of current legal paradigms to serve as catalysts for social change and its emphasis on incrementalism. CRT argues that racism requires sweeping changes but liberalism has no mechanism for any such cataclysmic change. Rather, liberal legal practices support the painstakingly slow process of arguing legal precedence to gain citizen rights for people of color.

Fourth, and related to the liberal perspective, is the argument posed by CRT that Whites have been the primary beneficiaries of civil rights legislation. For example, while Whites decry the policy of affirmative action, they regularly benefit from it since White women are its biggest beneficiaries. White women are more likely to live in households with other Whites and share those benefits (income, occupational prestige, and status) with those in their households.

In the case of social studies, CRT examines the way racism is made invisible through the curriculum, participation in the profession, and its policies. CRT can serve as an analytic tool to explain the systematic omissions, distortions, and lies that plague the field. Rather than search for a "multicultural palliative" to suggest that the field is changing, CRT points to the way such inclusions always come at a cost. For example, the increased "multicultural presence" in many social studies textbooks typically represents what King (1995) terms, "marginalizing knowledge" (p. 274). This is a "form of curriculum transformation that can include selected 'multicultural' curriculum that simultaneously distorts both the historical and social reality that people actually experienced" (p. 274). Social studies textbooks exhibit this marginalization by including people of color in "features" that literally adorn the margins of the text while leaving the monocultural, exclusive narrative undisturbed.

CRT's analysis of the social studies profession helps to uncover the systematic way that people of color are discouraged from pursuing careers in the social studies. If, for example, people are mentored into professions, what is the likelihood that students of color are actively encouraged to participate in classes and activities that feed into the social sciences? How do the students access history and geography bees? How are their questions about their missing stories addressed in classrooms? In addition to drawing students into the social studies, what professional initiatives exist to support those teachers of color who are already in the profession? How are they made aware of the opportunities for professional growth and career advancement? How are the stories of teachers of color incorporated into our understanding of the profession? What specific obstacles and challenges do they face? How might new professionals avoid them?

CRT's analysis of the social studies policy and position statements calls for a textual deciphering, not unlike that of Morrison (1992) that requires us to look, not only at what is present in these documents, but to ask pointed questions about what is missing. This analysis would also raise questions about how such documents are formulated. Who is asked to serve on committees and task forces that formulate such policies? What are the rules of governance that move position statements from individuals to committees to association?

The role of this volume is to begin to pry open some of the silences that have defined the social studies. This text is deliberate in its move to include "race talk" in the study of history and the social sciences in our schools. Rather than pretend that we live in a society and world where social justice and equity prevail, the contributors to this volume understand the urgency with which we must address the disconnect between the artificial life of the classroom and the real lives of the students who attend our schools.

NOTES

1. I was a member of the NCSS National Standards Task Force.
2. Portions of this section adapted from, Ladson-Billings, G. (1998). Just what is critical race theory and what's it doing in a nice field like education? *Qualitative Studies in Education, 11*(1), 7–24.

REFERENCES

Barnes, R. (1990). Race consciousness: The thematic content of racial distinctiveness in critical race scholarship. *Harvard Law Review, 103*, 1864–1871.

Bell, D. (1992). *Faces at the bottom of the well.* New York: Basic Books.

Cortés, C. (1979, April). The societal curriculum and the school curriculum: Allies or antagonists? *Educational Leadership, 36*(7), 475–479.

Crenshaw, K. (1988). Race, reform, and retrenchment: Transformation and legiti-mation in antidiscrimination law. *Harvard Law Review, 101,* 1331–1387.

Delgado, R. (Ed.). (1995). *Critical race theory: The cutting edge.* Philadelphia, PA: Temple University Press.

Gramsci, A. (1971). *Selections from the prison notebooks.* Q. Hoare & G. N. Smith (Eds. & Trans.) New York: International Publishers.

King, J.E. (1995). Culture-centered knowledge: Black studies, curriculum transfor-mation, and social action. In J.A. Banks & C.M. Banks (Eds.), *Handbook of research on multicultural education* (pp. 265–290). New York: Macmillan.

Loewen, J. (1996). *Lies my teacher told me: Everything your American history textbook got wrong.* New York: Touchstone Books.

Morrison, T. (1992). *Playing in the dark: Whiteness and the literary imagination.* Cam-bridge, MA: Harvard University Press.

National Council for the Social Studies. (1996). *Expectations for excellence.* Washing-ton, DC: Author.

Olneck, M. (1995). Immigrants and education. In J.A. Banks & C.M. Banks (Eds.), *Handbook of research on multicultural education* (pp. 310–327). New York: Mac-millan.

part I

THE PROFESSION

CHAPTER 2

A BRIDGE OVER
TROUBLED WATER

Social Studies, Civic Education,
and Critical Race Theory

Cynthia A. Tyson

INTRODUCTION

. . . like a bridge over trouble water . . .

—Simon & Garfunkel

Social Studies cannot disconnect from societal "troubled waters" of institutionalized inequities enacted in racist ways. If we as teachers and researchers of the social sciences continue on what has become a patriotic and
nationalistic trajectory toward civic competence, we are left with the
dilemma of how to successfully build a "bridge" over the troubled waters of
racism that have become an integral part of American civic ideals and principles. As educators, we sometimes have ignored how race as an institutionalized politically oppressive construction can continue to shape American
life. This shaping occurs in ways that are expressly evident in social studies

Critical Race Theory Perspectives on the Social Studies, pages 15–25
Copyright © 2003 by Information Age Publishing
15

curriculum (Hahn, 1991,1996; Miller & Singleton, 1997; Parker, 1996; Ross, 2001) in general and civic education (Barber, 1989; Hahn, 1998) in particular.

We cannot "overcome" the history of racial oppression rooted in our nationhood without understanding and speaking to the insidious ways race continues to be a destructive in our lives. We must begin theorizing race in the social studies and begin to delineate strategies for societal transformation. Critical race theory (CRT) as a theoretical perspective can provide a lens to critique the social studies in an attempt to move beyond the traditional boundaries of history, geography, anthropology, political science and economics education. Although CRT began as a movement in American jurisprudence, CRT is theoretically situated in activism. It not only endeavors to understand our social and political locations, it sets out to analyze how society sanctions as the norm racial categories and hierarchies, and then proposes (re) vision (Crenshaw, 1995; Bell, 1995; Delgado, 1995, 1998; Parker, 1998). This (re) visioning—how we have standardized the concepts of civic participation and responsibilities in a racialized society, moves discussions (Barber, 1989) of race and racism from the margins to the essence of citizenship education in the social studies. CRT therefore places race as a unit of analysis becoming instrumental in discussing the roles of race, racism, and power.

In civics education we have traditionally and conservatively focused too narrowly on civic competencies (Torney-Purta & Hahn & Amadeo, 2000) in curriculum standards and pedagogy. With a broader view that explores beyond a list of proposed civic competencies, we define being a "good" citizen as a concept that must include addressing the inequities that are the byproduct of endemic racism. In this chapter I suggest CRT as a framework for critiquing that full view of citizenship education.

CIVIC EDUCATION AND CRITICAL RACE THEORY: A (RE) VISIONING

Using CRT as a framework in the critical examination of social studies civic education allows the existing gaps in the national and local curriculum standards and in the pedagogy of classroom teachers and university educators, to become more visible. As we begin to develop new standards and teach the curriculum that results from those standards we can begin to introduce a look at race like we have not done before.

To that end the National Council of Social Studies (NCSS) announced a position statement prepared by the NCSS Task Force on Revitalizing Citizenship Education, a position approved by the NCSS Board of Directors in May 2001. This position reveals a commitment to the revitalization of citizenship education in our schools and provides a perfect "site" to challenge the exclusion of racialized hegemony as a fundamental component of education for civic participation (Parker, 1996). NCSS has taken the position that the basic objective of public education is to "prepare students to be engaged and effective citizens" (NCSS, 2001). This preparation will help students acquire the knowledge, skills and attitudes requisite to assume the "office of citizen" in our democracy.

What does it mean to be an effective citizen? As we examine the documented and undocumented histories of this nation, we should not ignore that not so long ago, part of being a good citizen was to embrace economic tenets that supported the enslavement of Africans; political tenets that supported the internment of Japanese; geographical tenets that supported the decimation of sacred burial grounds and ceremonial sites and historical tenets that supported the legalized denial of civil rights (Bennett, 1962; Zinn, 1999). NCSS believes an effective citizen:

- Embraces core democratic values and strives to live by them.
- Accepts responsibility for the well being of oneself, one's family and the community.
- Has knowledge of the people, history, and traditions that have shaped our local communities, our nation and the world.
- Has knowledge of our nations founding documents, civic institutions and political processes.
- Is aware of issues and events that have an impact on people at local, state, national and global levels.
- Seeks information from varied sources and perspectives to develop informed opinions and creative solutions.
- Asks meaningful questions and is able to analyze and evaluate information and ideas.
- Uses effective decision-making and problem-solving skills in public and private life.
- Has the ability to collaborate effectively as a member of a group.
- Actively participates in civic and community life (NCSS, 2001, p. 319).

The recommendation that citizenship education become a part of the core in social studies (NAEP, 1999) also leads to the delineation of the characteristics of effective citizenship education programs. That is, a civic education program should ensure that:

- Civic knowledge, skill and values are taught explicitly and a systematically at every grade level.
- School and classroom management and culture exemplify and demonstrate core democratic values.

- Citizenship education is integrated throughout and cross the curriculum.
- Students have meaningful opportunities to participate in class and school governance.
- All students at every grade level are provided with opportunities to participate in the civic life of their school and community.
- Learning activities extend beyond the school and invite parents and the community to participate and work with students.
- Student are provided with opportunities to participate in simulation, service learning projects, conflict resolution programs, and other activities that encourage the application of civic knowledge, skills and values.
- All students are provided with instruction on out nations' founding documents, civic institution ad political processes.
- All students are provided with instruction on the people history and traditions that have shaped our local communities, our nation and the world.
- Preparing students to be effective citizens is explicitly recognized as an important part of the school mission (NCSS, 2001, p. 319).

Before every student at every grade level is able to take the "office of citizen," attention must be given to the cultural and legal foundations that underpin what it historically and contemporarily means to be American. What it means to be American, post 9–11 for example, is that in many classrooms prepared unit or lesson plans gave way to the consummate "teachable moment." This facilitates a departure from the traditional ways we may impart citizenship knowledge with respect to what it means to be patriotic, to a "hot bed" of racialized social and political topics. Even with a renewed wave of classroom discussions, curriculum development, and national media attention on the social studies, the (re) conceptualization of civic education to facilitate discourse about the invisibility of race/racism in the social studies was intimated but not explicitly endorsed.

How we set up the terms for a conversation of racial issues—via civics education in the social studies can shape student perceptions and responses to the issues. The use of principles found in critical race theory can assist. One fundamental principle of critical race theory is that racism is pervasive and endemic in all aspects of our society. While critical race theory is an outgrowth of the critical legal studies movement, the attempt to demonstrate how legal ideology has helped to create, support, and legitimatize, civic values that later translated into what it means to be an effective citizen, often while simultaneous oppressing others, is important. As critical race theory departed from traditional legal scholarship, it created a particular space for storytelling to describe the racial and social realities of

American society (Ladson-Billings, 1998). Ladson-Billings notes that the narratives (counter stories) add "necessary contextual contours" (p. 11). Critical race theory also maintains that the limitations of American jurisprudence to bring about social change is found in the hegemonic power structures of society that were legally in place to act as beneficiary for some and oppressive for others. When it is not explicitly stated, the context of citizenship (the legal rights and privileges of being a citizen) is left as a social construction that can reify an ideology that maintains hegemony (Omi & Winant, 1993). Much like the subtle syncopation of musical instruments in a jazz arrangement, racism is embedded within our lives and our theory and praxis related to the civic education.

Each of the tenets of what it means to be an effective citizen speaks to embracing democratic values. These values when juxtaposed with explicitly challenging injustices and self-conscious activism as civic participation can become the cornerstone of students' examination of privilege and power. More important, as students "take the office of citizen" the need to be morally and ethically responsible shifts us away from blaming the victim to seeking constructive ways to develop and support public policy that keeps the issues out in the open. We then can make steady progress in efforts of social reform.

How can the use of critical race theory in the development of civic education begin to re(vision) becoming an effective decision-maker and active participant in civic and community life? To see how this can be, we must look at schools in the context of a society governed by class, caste, and entitlement and examine the role race plays in inculcating and endorsing the values of the dominant society. We must examine in depth the social reality for many Americans who in our not so distant past were denied basic civic (citizen) rights. For example, Europeans that arrived on the American scene after the Civil War encountered a legal and political system that on the whole excluded them due to socioeconomic barriers. If you were poor and immigrant, you were denied civic participation. However, with naturalization laws, the Irish, Italian, Germans, and other European groups received the vote. With that vote they organized neighborhoods and communities, voting as blocs, exchanging the votes for alliances with established centers of power. The personal stories of these lived experiences when analyzed from a CRT perspective would include more than a study of the voting rights. The use of CRT would lead students and teachers to ask, what are the stories and counter stories of the people? There was no naturalization process for the "freed" slave, no citizenship, and no granting of political power, not even the right to vote. While laws were later passed and policies were established, CRT leads us to ask: What impact did the Ku Klux Klan, poll taxes, literacy test, Constitution tests, and Grandfather clauses have on the voting disenfranchisement of Black "citizens" who were freed from chattel slavery without money, land and education?

While there are still very broad gaps between the perception of what is needed and the activity taken to achieve those goals, CRT can facilitate a retooling of what it means to be an effective citizen to include the explicit critique and to challenge societal barriers to access, particularly in the area of race. Notably, this would add social activism, a tenet of CRT, definitively to the knowledge, skills, and values of civic education.

Social studies education with a strong civic education component would include lessons about power, about intellectual frameworks that are analytical, critical, and action oriented. This is not a new concept. In the summer of 1963, a family member, living in Greenwood, Mississippi, attended the Mississippi Freedom School. The Mississippi Freedom Schools were created by members of the Student Nonviolent Coordination Committee (SNCC) working in collaboration with the Council of Federated Organizations (COFC). SNCC worked under the tutelage of Charles Cobb to create an educational experience that would teach lessons in Black history and citizenship education. I wish I could say that I was attentive to the stories she often told about her experiences, but as immaturity would have it, the stories my cousin shared during my youth were not of interest to me at the time. Attention to the critical race narratives from the Mississippi Freedom Schools, Septima Clark, and Fannie Lou Hammer, can reinforce that for most citizens living in what had been labeled the "Johannesburg of America," there was little connection to being provided the same opportunities as their white counterparts to participate in the democracy.

Critical race theory can operate as a tool to fill in the gaps in the collective memory of civic knowledge. The integration of narratives of those enslaved juxtaposed, for example, with the many founding documents would facilitate a critique of power and the role of oppression and empowerment in what it means to be citizen in a democracy. As a fourth grade teacher in a public school (Tyson, 1997) I knew students were required to read a primary source document, to answer questions on a standardized measure of assessment, and more importantly become engaged with civic education (Sansone, 1999). I gave each student a copy of the Constitution and subsequent amendments. We read portions of the document each day coupled with slave narratives (Taylor, 1999) from the same time period. After several days a student recorded in her journal:

> The constitution is cool and everything, but the founding fathers seem to forget they had *found* some land and *found* some Africans to buy to pick the cotton on the land, and *found* mo [sic] money an mo money in they pockets because of it (italics added).

Some would suggest that the while "best citizens" of this democracy crafted the Constitution, they did so without attention to the racial liberation of enslaved Africans that could have been accomplished by extending it to included the conferring of citizenship. The use of slave narratives provided the students the opportunity to critique the evolution of democratic freedoms at the intersection of racialized inequities. The use of the slave narratives became a pedagogical strategy for reading the primary source documents (Krug, 1970) through a racialized lens. Similarly, teachers who then use CRT as an influence in the creation of pedagogical strategies will provide for their students opportunities to critique democracy and citizenship (Tyson, 2001, 2002) from multiple perspectives, "through different lenses ... different properties than the ones deeply established in the consciousness of American society. These different perspectives engender many possibilities, particularly opportunities to transform an ideology of enslavement and oppression, to one of economic, political and social equality" (Tyson, 2002). If teachers are a part of this equation, then it makes sense that a closer look at teacher education in pre-service teacher preparation.

CIVIC EDUCATION, RACE, AND TEACHER EDUCATION

"Social studies educators," NCSS further states, "teach students the content knowledge, intellectual skills, and civic values necessary for fulfilling the duties of citizenship in a participatory democracy" (NCSS, 2001). Many pre-teachers embrace this position theoretically as it is introduced in their social studies methods courses. At times, the sense of teaching about a basic set of beliefs that guide action in this case civic beliefs and participatory action, is in direct conflict with the unique histories, value systems, social and educational goals of teachers and their students. How so? Most often, successful public school educators have been indoctrinated in an educational system K–12 that perpetuates racism, sexism, classism, homophobia and other forms of oppression. This is exacerbated as they matriculate through a post-secondary system in preparation as classroom teachers to transmit the values and the culture of the dominant society to schoolchildren. In reality, it is through this system that educators learn to support the status quo. Public schools were not designed to stimulate controversy, and classroom teachers are not expected to teach students to question and challenge authority.

Pre-service teachers' use of critical race theory in the social studies can serve to help them address issues of equity and race, and "bridge" power differentials, assumptions, and historical contexts of racism to develop critical civic consciousness in them and their students. In doing this, pre-service teachers in the social studies should become attentive to the historical periods and the ways that consciousness about racism has changed (Goodman & Adler, 1985). For example the legal and social addressing of state laws and practices in the South were deeply entrenched in the varieties of racism that chartered early times. Southern officials resolutely prosecuted and convicted civil rights activist for disorderly conduct and disturbing of the peace while ignoring the violent acts against demonstrators committed by white segregationist. Although most of the convictions were later overturned by the Supreme Court, Southern judges operated to effectively discourage nonviolent protests by holding demonstrators under exorbitant bail, requiring surety bonds, imposing harsh sentences for frivolous changes and subjecting protestors to intolerable jail conditions (U.S. Commission on Civil Rights, 1964, p. 12). Even challenges to the Constitution and later amendments were only yielding returns that were reflective of the earlier system from which they grew. If pre-service teachers in social studies methods courses use critical race theory when teaching a unit for example, on the Jim Crow years or exercising the right to vote, they can begin to deconstruct the mainstream legal ideologies (Irvine, 1997; Ladson-Billings & Tate, 1995; Parker, 1998) that support institutionalized enactment of racism. This ideology ignored racial oppression and placed at its center the examination of the endemic racism in law and society that is often devoid of contextual and historical examinations. These pedagogical moves create a space to address the disparity between the American credo [liberty and justice for all] and the pervasiveness of racism the American experience.

Correspondingly, pre-service teachers would need to be engaged in ongoing professional development activities (see Figure 2.1) that support the essential elements of developing strategies for applying CRT in their teaching.

There have been pilot and existing teacher preparation programs (Ladson-Billings, 2001) that provide a template for "novice teachers" to work with students from diverse cultural, ethnic, linguistic and ability groups in urban centers. However, few provide the comprehensive coursework and professional development support to use CRT as a lens to explore issues of curriculum development and pedagogical strategies that transform theory into more generative praxis.

The tragedy of our condition is that many social studies educators—pre-service, in-service and educator teacher educators—have ignored how race continues to shape the American story in ways that are expressly racist in our nation's schools and curriculum. Critical race theory acknowledges racialized structures that are limited by a dominant construction of reality that perpetuates racial oppression. These structures create a reality and relationship to what it means to be a citizen and participate in American democracy. Educators' approach to the teachings of civic education should

Professional Development Activities	Examples
• Reading research and primary source documents	• Join professional organizations and read journals and reports distributed by the American Memory Project, NAACP, and local grassroots organizations
• Cross cultural field experiences	• Participating in tutoring at area community centers, churches, mosques, and synagogues
• Reflective action research	• Participation in "Critical Friends" support groups, to collect and analyze data of their pedagogy
• Critical service learning initiatives.	• Participate in an education community programs(Aids or Substance Abuse Programs, Neighborhood Watch)
• Social Action	• Develop sense of political identity, monitor and lobby for local education legislative actions,

Figure 2.1.

be with an intention to: transform civic education; revitalize citizenship participation; and answer the call of a democratic imperative.

CONCLUSION

In 1952, when novelist Ralph Ellison wrote, "I am invisible, understand, simply because people refuse to see me" (Ellison, 1935, p. 3) he illustrated how his racialized identity made him an invisible man. The absence of race in our curriculum standards and position statements (NCSS, 1994) makes race social studies' invisible man.

This invisibility is accentuated in our primary, secondary, and post-secondary schools with the use of textbooks and professional journals in the social studies that are written, refereed, edited, published, selected (Schneider & VanSickle, 1979) and taught by those who in theory and praxis often present a distorted view of the historical and contemporary power relationships between whites and non whites in the world. Our education systems like our society in general, fail to recognize that the ideals of justice and equity for all cannot be achieved without fundamental change in the standing institution of America.

To that end, educators must engage in deeper explorations of the relationship of becoming an effective citizen and race. As educators continue to develop critical pedagogies, they can also view teaching as a political act. Education has found itself in troubled waters in an effort to improve what can be viewed in some cases as a dismal record in the many attempts to educate for democracy. Social studies can be counted among many factors that contribute to a more informed citizenry. New situated pedagogies that integrate the theory of critical race theory may not "still the troubled water" but could create "bridges" for teachers and students alike to understand what it means in a racialized society to be effective citizens.

REFERENCES

Barber R.B. (1989). Public talk and civic action: Education for participation in a strong democracy. *Social Education, 53*, 355–356, 370.

Bell D. (1995). Racial realism—after we're gone: Prudent speculations on America in a post-racial epoch. In R. Delgado (Ed.), *Critical race theory: The cutting edge* (pp. 2–8). Philadelphia, PA: Temple University Press.

Bennett, L. (1962) *Before the Mayflower: A history of Black America.* Chicago: Johnson Publishing Co.

Crenshaw, K. (1995). Race, reform and retrenchment: Transformation and legitimization in anti- discrimination law. In K. Crenshaw, N. Gotanda, B. Peller, & K. Thomas (Eds.), *Critical race theory: Key writing that formed the movement* (pp. 103–122). New York: The New Press.

Delgado, R. (1995a). *Critical race theory: The cutting edge.* Philadelphia, PA: Temple University Press.

Delgado, R. (1995b). The imperial scholar. In K. Crenshaw, N. Gotanda, B. Peller, & K. Thomas (Eds.), *Critical race theory: Key writing that formed the movement* (pp. 46–57). New York: The New Press.

Delgado Bernal, D. (1998). Using a Chicana feminist epistemology in educational research. *Harvard Educational Review, 68*(4), 555–582.

Ellison, R. (1935) *The invisible man.* Grove Press, New York.

Goodman, J., & Adler, S. (1985). Becoming an elementary social studies teacher: A study of perspective. *Theory and Research in Social Education, 13*(2),1–20.

Hahn, C.L. (1991). Controversial issues in social studies. In J. Shaver (Ed.), *Handbook of research on social studies teaching learning* (pp. 470–480). New York: Macmillan.

Hahn, C. (1996). Research on issues-centered social studies. In. R.W. Evan & D. W. Sace (Eds.), *Handbook on teaching social issues* (pp. 26–39).

Hahn, C. (1998). *Becoming political: Comparative perspective on citizenship education.* Albany: State University of New York Press.

Irvine, J. (1997). *Critical knowledge for diverse teachers & learners.* Washington, DC: AACTE NCSS.

Krug, M.M. (1970). Primary sources in teaching history. *The History Teacher, 3*(3), 401–411.

Ladson-Billings, G. (1995). Just what is critical race theory and what is it doing in a nice field like education? *International Journal of Qualitative Studies in Education, 11*(1), 7–24.

Ladson-Billings, G., & Tate, W. (1995). Toward a critical race theory of education. *Teachers College Record, 97*, 47–68.

Ladson-Billings, G. (2001). *Crossing over Canaan: The journey of new teachers in diverse classrooms.* San Francisco: Jossey-Bass.

Miller, B., & Singleton, L. (1977). *Preparing citizens: Linking authentic assessment and instruction in civic/law related education*. Boulder, CO: Social Science Education Consortium.

National Council for the Social Studies. (1994). *Expectations of excellence: Curriculum standards for social studies teaching*. Washington, DC: National council for the Social Studies.

National Center for Education Statistics. (1999). *NAEP 1998 civics report card for the nation*. Washington, DC: U.S. Department of Education.

Parker. L. (1998). Race is . . . race ain't: An exploration of the utility of critical race theory in qualitative research in education. *International Journal of Qualitative Studies in Education, 11*, 43–55.

Parker, W.C. (1996). Curriculum for democracy. In R. Soder (Ed.), *Democracy education and the schools* (pp.182–210). San Francisco: Jossey-Bass Publishers.

Parker, W. (1989). Participatory citizenship: Civics in the strong sense. *Social Education, 53*, 353–354.

Omi, M., & Winant, H. (1993). On the theoretical status of the concept of race. In C. McCarthy & W. Crinchlow (Eds.), *Race, identity, and representation in education* (pp. 3–10). New York: Routledge.

Sansone, S.C. (1999). Get your students involved in civics. *Social Education, 63*(4), 228–232.

Torney-Purta, J., Hahn, C., & Amadeo, J., (2000). Principles of subject specific instruction in education for citizenship. In J. Brophy (Ed.), *Subject specific instructional methods and activities* (pp. 271–408). Stamford, CT: JAI Press.

Taylor, I. (1999). *I was born a slave: An anthology of classic slave narratives*. IL: Lawrence Hill Books.

Tyson, C., & Kenreich, T. (2001, September-October). Social studies, social action, and realistic fiction. *Social Studies and the Young Learner*, pp. 22–26.

Tyson, C (2002). Get up off that thing: African American middle school students respond to literature to develop a framework for understanding social action. *Theory in Social Studies Education, 30*(1), 42–65.

Tyson, C. (1999). Shut my mouth wide open: Realistic fiction and social action. *Theory into Practice, 38*(3), 155–159.

U.S. Commission on Civil Rights. (1964). *Law enforcement* (pp. 12–13). Washington, DC: Government Printing Office.

Zinn, H. (1999). *A people's history of the United States: 1492- present* (20th anniversary ed.). New York: HarperCollins.

CHAPTER 3

THE DIS(G)RACE OF THE SOCIAL STUDIES

The Need for Racial Dialogue in the Social Studies

Tyrone Howard

ABSTRACT

Social studies education has been viewed as the primary subject matter in U.S. schools concerned with the development of democratic citizens in a racially and culturally diverse society. However, a historical examination of the theory, research, and practice in the field of social studies shows very little attention given to race and racism in the conception of democratic citizenship. This chapter attempts to place the social studies in a critical race theory framework, in which race and racism are at the center of the discussion of the work of social studies education. This chapter will examine critical race theory in the social studies, and provide transformative ways of conceptualizing more race-conscious social studies theory and research.

Critical Race Theory Perspectives on the Social Studies, pages 27–43
Copyright © 2003 by Information Age Publishing

INTRODUCTION

The social studies have long been viewed through a multitude of lenses according to scholars in the field (Barth, 1996; Davis, 1991; Hertzberg, 1971; Saxe, 1992). Over the past eight decades a number of theorists have attempted to bring clarity to a subject matter that remains in a state of flux (Barr, Barth, & Shermis, 1978; Dougan, 1985; Ross, 1997). Amidst all of the debates on the purpose and mission of the social studies, one of the central tenets of the field has been to improve human relations and develop civic competence in the pursuit of a democratic and just society (Dewey, 1933; Parker, 1991; Saxe, 1997; Shaver, 1977, 1991).

The quest for democratic citizenship is tied to the idea that individual differences such as race, culture, and ethnicity are to be recognized, respected, and embraced in a multiracial and multicultural society. Yet, history is replete with widespread accounts of racial oppression under the guise of "democratic citizenship" (Banks, 1997; Crocco & Davis, 2002; Manning, 2002; Parker, 1997). Ideally, any threat to democracy should warrant immediate interrogation from social studies educators to eliminate malevolent attempts to disrupt core democratic ideas, particularly within K–12 education. In many cases, social studies educators have heeded the call to investigate important issues including, but not limited to, democratic suppression (Morse, 2001), violence in schools (Hinds, 2000), historical revisionism (VanSledright & Afflerbach, 2000; VanSledright, 2002), technology (Merryfield, 2000; Mason & Berson, 2000), gender equity (Crocco & Davis, 2002; Tetreault, 1987), and homophobia and sexual identity (Bickmore, 2002; Crocco, 2002). Nonetheless, issues pertaining to race and more importantly racism have been conspicuously absent from most of the discourse, research, and scholarship within the social studies. This chapter will attempt to develop a conceptualization of social studies education that provides much needed attention to race and racism.

One of the more disturbing realities about the absence of race in social studies discourse is the notion that social studies education, and social studies scholars should assume a leading role in helping educators to examine, comprehend, and combat racial oppression within schools and society. Issues such as racism and discrimination are central features of the nation's social economic, and political fabric (Bell, 1992; Robinson, 2000). Who would be better suited to theorize about how to eliminate discriminatory practices and racist attitudes than social studies educators? In an attempt to gain a better grasp on the role of race, or lack thereof it has played in social studies research, scholarship, and practice, this chapter will have three primary goals; (1) to discuss how the social studies as a profession have blatantly ignored race in its conception of democratic citizenship, cultural pluralism, and the pursuit of an egalitarian nation state, (2) to examine and critique the research and scholarship in social studies' major journals, and (3) attempt to center the social studies in a critical race framework, in order to offer recommendations for proactive strategies that will move race to the center of social studies research and scholarship.

WHY RACE MATTERS

This chapter is situated within a critical race framework, as it places race at the center of the discussion of social studies education. Critical race theory is a movement borne out of critical legal studies that seeks to address issues of racial inequality, and the overlooked role that race and racism have played in the construction of the legal foundation (Crenshaw, 1988, Harris, 1994; Matsuda, 1991). As critical race theory has emerged in the field of education, it has sought to move the dialogue about race and racism from the realm of the experiential to the realm of the ideological (Ladson-Billings, 2000; Parker & Lynn, 2002; Tate, 1997). Leading critical race theorists have argued that the marginalization of race and consequently racism are interwoven into the historical conscious and ideological framework of the U.S. legal system (Bell, 1992; Delgado, 1989). Consequently, critical race theorists would argue that a thorough examination of race within the legal context is desperately needed.

Critical race theory within education seeks to give much needed attention to the role that race plays in educational research, scholarship, and practice (Ladson-Billings, 2000; Solarzano, 1998; Solorzano & Yosso, 2002). The inclusion of a critical race framework is warranted in education when one considers the perennial underachievement of African American, Latino/Latina, Native American, and certain Asian American students in U.S. schools (National Assessment of Educational Progress, 1994, 1996, 1998, 2000). Educators can ill-afford to subscribe to the notion that mere coincidence explains the perpetual school failure of students of color. At some point, the question must be posed, "What's race got to do with it?" (Parker & Lynn, 2002). Critical race theory within education is an evolving methodological, conceptual, and theoretical construct that attempts to disrupt race and racism in education (Solarzano, 1998). It enables scholars to ask the important question of what racism has to do with inequities in education in unique ways. Critical race theory examines racial inequities in educational achievement in a more critical framework than multicultural education or achievement gap theorists by centering the discussion within the context of racism. Thus, the question from a critical race standpoint is not, "Does racism play a role in educational disparities?" but it acknowledges the historical and contemporary role that racism plays, and has played in education, and asks a more pene-

trating question, "How has racism contributed to the educational disparities, and how can it be dismantled?"

Critical race theorists anchor their interrogation of racism in education
in four primary ways; (1) by theorizing about race along with the intersectionality of racism, classism, sexism, and other forms of oppression in
school curriculum, (2) by challenging dominant ideologies that call for
objectivity and neutrality in educational research; (3) they offer counter-
storytelling as a liberatory and credible methodological tool in examining
racial oppression; and (4) they incorporate transdisciplinary knowledge
from women's studies and ethnic studies to better understand various manifestations of discrimination (Smith-Maddox & Solarzano, 2002).

As explanations become clearer as to what race and racism have to do
with the widespread failure of students of color, we can begin to understand the wider societal influences of inequality, discrimination, and racism, which is where social studies educators can play a significant role. The
social studies can help students move away from viewing race solely in rigid
or fixed biological or genetic categories, but to contextualize race within
social, political, and economic constructions in the United States. Who is
better suited to facilitate this much-needed dialogue than leaders on the
development of democratic citizens within the field of education? The failure to engage in such a dialogue may have profound implications for all
U.S. citizens, regardless of their racial affiliation. Cornel West (1994) aptly
states, "The paradox of race in America is that our common destiny is
more pronounced and imperiled precisely when our divisions are deeper."
Moreover, he states that "interracial interdependence, yet enforced racial
hierarchy dooms us as a nation to collective paranoia and hysteria-the
unmaking of any democratic order" (p. 8).

The movement of race from the fringes to the heart of a critical dialogue of the social studies is important for numerous reasons. First and
foremost, what discipline would be better suited to carry out this discussion
of race and racism within schools and society other than the social studies?
As a discipline charged with preparing democratic citizens and promoting
civic interest in the pursuit of equality for all citizens, the social studies
would seem to be a "natural fit" to address the salience of race and racism
in the United States and throughout the world. The pursuit of a civic culture in the name of democracy must be cognizant of forces that pose
threats to its aims and goals. Race, in many ways, has been and remains the
single dynamic that has shaped United States history, its landscape, and the
overall way of life (Horsman, 1981; Marable, 2002; Oliver & Shapiro,
1997). Failure to engage in critical discussions about race will only further
polarize a nation with increasingly rich racial diversity. As Manning
Marable points out, "Instead of talking abstractly about race, we should be
theorizing about the social processes of racialization, of how certain groups

in U.S. society have been relegated to an oppressed status, by the weight of law, social policy, and economic exploitation" (p. 10). Manning's claim should serve as a resounding call to social studies educators to incorporate race as an essential ingredient of how we describe life in the United States, past, present, and future. Exploring race-related issues is difficult and complex. With much value confusion at the root of many social problems, schools can play a significant role in helping students clarify their values and make moral decisions. Unfortunately, many U.S. citizens are unaware of the implications that race has had, and continues to have, on the United States and its varying institutions. More important, race continues to play a cogent role in adverse intergroup relationships. In the United States it is apparent that the role of race, and how many citizens come to grips with it are still unsettling. Consider the data from the Federal Bureau of Investigations (FBI) hate crime statistics over the past decade. While registered hate crimes in the areas of national origin, religious affiliation, sexual orientation, and disabilities have increased sharply over the past decade, they still pale in comparison to the number of racial hate crimes committed in the United States (Federal Bureau of Investigation, 1998). According to FBI statistics, the number of registered racial hate crimes outnumber the second leading type of hate crime (religion) at a rate of three to one. Thus, it goes without saying that our refusal as a nation to explicitly talk about the meaning of race, individual and institutional racism, and its implications may contribute to the persistent disdain and continuous rage that many individuals still have toward members of racially diverse groups. As social educators concerned with how schools and society problematize issues that prohibit the full expression of democratic citizenship the challenge is clear. Social studies educators, particularly those involved in teaching, research, and scholarship have an opportunity to help actualize the tenets of the field by engaging in thoughtful dialogue, critical inquiry, and inclusive solution-seeking to address the role of race and racism in the pursuit of democratic citizenship. Unfortunately, up to this point, the social studies have not adequately addressed the role of race. While issues such as culture and ethnicity have a platform for exploration in schools and classrooms, race has remained largely underresearched, undertheorized and relatively untouched (Ladson-Billings & Tate, 1995).

DEMOCRACY AND CIVIC COMPETENCE
WITHIN A RACIAL CONTEXT

Although much of social studies theory and discourse is rooted in history and the social sciences, there is a considerable amount of the field that is concerned with citizenship education and democratic values (Hahn, 1991;

Saxe, 1997). The notion of citizenship education and democratic values calls into question among other things, the attitudes and behaviors displayed toward fellow citizens, especially those from diverse backgrounds, with different realities and histories (Banks, 1995, 1997; Merryfield, 1998). Key social studies themes such as recognizing common purposes, interdependence, informed decision-making, and democratic ideas provide a basis upon which a diverse society can solve problems and manage conflict. However, the realization of democratic values within a society requires full recognition of past deeds that have denied individuals the right to enjoy the benefits of democracy. Manning Marable (2002) poses the all too important question when he asks, "Can American democracy ever be more than an abstract ideal, when tens of millions of its citizens feel alienated and marginalized by what have become 'normal' and routine consequences of American racialization in daily life?" (p. 22).

Examinations of race are most critical within the domain of democracy in a multiracial nation such as the United States. Whether the case is the enslavement of Africans in the United States, and subsequent Jim Crow laws, the cruel and inhumane treatment of Japanese Americans in Internment camps during World War II, the geographical and cultural ramifications of the colonization of Mexico, or the displacement, disenfranchisement, and destruction of Native Americans, race has played a critical role in the evolution of democracy in the United States. Thus, critical dialogue about racial discrimination is warranted. James Baldwin often referred to the "rage of the disesteemed" as a result of the United States' refusal to acknowledge historical injustices. According to Balfour (2002), Baldwin implies that the United States is guilty of "innocence" or,

> a willful ignorance, a resistance to facing the horrors of the American past and present and their implications for the future. This unwillingness to confront these horrors accounts for the resistance of racial injustices to remedy by formal, legal measures. For innocence sustains a mind-set that can accommodate *both* an earnest commitment to the principles of equal rights and freedom regardless of race *and* a tacit acceptance of racial division and inequality as normal. (p. 27)

To examine the social studies in a critical race theory framework begs several questions, how do we interrogate the "innocence" that Baldwin refers to as a normative component of U.S. society? In addition, why have the effects of racial discrimination in a democratic society been under researched and largely ignored in social studies education? And, more important, to what extent are today's racial inequities a by-product of the long history of racism in the United States?

SOCIAL STUDIES AND DEMOCRATIC CITIZENSHIP:
WHAT'S RACE GOT TO DO WITH IT?

The effects of racial injustice are subject to multiple interpretations, however, most concerning is the fact that many of the conceptions of social studies theory have not posed examinations of race within historical or contemporary contexts (Howard, 2001). A perusal of major theoretical frameworks of the social studies pays little attention to race in the development of democratic citizenship, social studies curriculum, or civic education. As previously mentioned, the purpose of social studies education has been subject to many debates over the past century. Some have argued that the origins of contemporary social studies curricula has been a contesting of ideas for those advocating a history-centered social studies, and those calling for an interdisciplinary study of current social issues for the development of democratic citizens (Ross, 1997). An examination of each domain would suggest that race should still remain central to either argument. Dating back to the formation of the National Council for the Social Studies (NCSS) during the early 1920s, Lybarger (1991) provides a historical account of the curricular development of the social studies. Most germane to Lybarger's historical account is the influence of such scholars as Rolla Tryon, Henry Johnson, and Edgar Wesley. Lybarger suggests that the work of Tryon, Johnson, and Wesley were influential in the early formation of the field. He asserts that the threesome viewed a history-based conception of the social studies as a means to developing good citizenship. However, the irony in these earlier works is the huge void of critical examinations of the social, economic, and political conditions of non-Whites during this time. Lybarger makes note of the lack of consideration given to the social and political context of schools and society in earlier social studies frameworks. Banks (1997) makes a similar claim in his account of the social studies historical evolution. He maintains that the early focus of the social studies were primarily concerned with history and geography, and that social relations between citizens and marginalized groups were not a part of social studies content. The work of Banks (1997) and Lybarger (1991) helps call into question how the development of a field concerned with the preparation of democratic citizens and social education inexplicably omits race from its discussion. Lawrie Balfour (2001) in her examination of James Baldwin's work and the pursuit for democracy asks, "What could be more democratic than conversation among citizens about issues of national importance? What matter is in greater need of honest, thoughtful attention than the ongoing significance of *race* in American public life?" (p. 1).

Contemporary theorists of social studies suggest that the field is concerned with the preparation of young people with the knowledge, skills, and attitudes for active participation in an increasingly diverse society, or what some might refer to as citizenship education (Ross, 1997). The value of teaching citizenship education is one that is embraced by many social studies scholars (Banks, 1997; Crocco, 2002; Parker, 1997, 2001). However, what becomes more important, but is not quite thoroughly understood is what are the attributes of a "good citizen?" And more important, who defines the criteria? And, whose interests are best served by the construction of "good citizen?" Social studies within a critical race theory framework might ask the question, "Would the Founding Fathers of this country be considered 'good citizens,' despite their advocacy of slavery and racial oppression?" The answer is subject to multiple interpretations and could merit strong arguments from both sides of the continuum. Yet it requires theorists to acknowledge the racial sub-text that is a part of U.S. history, but is so frequently ignored. Social studies scholars have attempted to define the criteria of what constitutes a good citizen through a number of lines of inquiry, from advocating for effective decision making (Engle, 1963; Parker, 1991), to moral development (Kohlberg, 1973), active civic participation (Parker, 1997), to discussion of controversial issues (Hahn, 1991; Hess, 2001). While each of these areas offer promise, it is critical that scholars conducting research in these areas provide race as much credence in their analysis as they would gender, class, or any other variable. Failure to do so only ignores the social and historical importance of race. The effects of the omission of race become more troublesome in a race-conscious society such as the United States that insists on adopting a color-blind approach to human interactions (Schofield, 1986). At a time of unprecedented racial diversity, honest and critical conversations about race are desperately needed. Omi and Winant (1994) reiterate a need for examining U.S. history within a racial context by stating:

> A cursory glance at American history reveals that far from being color-blind, the United States has been an extremely "color-conscious" society. From the very inception of the Republic to the present moment, race has been a profound determinant of one's political rights, one's location in the labor market, and indeed one's sense of "identity." The hallmark of this history has been *racism*. (p. 1)

Over the last two decades a number of social studies theorists have written about issues that have historically been omitted from social studies discourse. For example, an increasing amount of scholarship has been devoted to women in the social studies (Bernard-Powers, 1997; Noddings, 1997; Crocco & Davis, 2002). This work has been desperately needed because it has provided women a more meaningful and deserving status in the social studies discussion. Furthermore, this work has provided a sounding board for the silenced voices of countless women who have made important contributions to the field of social studies education.

In addition to gender equity, multicultural education has gained a salient position in social studies discourse over the past three decades (Banks, 1997; Gay, 1997; Parker, 1997). The contributions of multicultural theorists have been equally as important as the gender influence in the social studies. Multicultural education has enabled the construction of knowledge to be called into question, the infusion of ethnic content into the curriculum, and challenged superficial methods of incorporating ethnicity, class, and gender into school curriculum (Banks, 1997). Yet, one of the frequent criticisms of multicultural education has been its failure to critically examine the concept of race in the unequal distribution of power in a democratic society (Ladson-Billings & Tate, 1995; McCarthy, 1990; Tiedt & Tiedt, 1986). According to radical critics of multicultural education, the discipline must call into question the absence of race when issues of equity and access are debated (Jackson & Solis, 1995; Mattai, 1992). Multicultural education theorists must examine the problematic nature of the continual conflation of race and ethnicity, and how conservatives are more apt to engage in discussions around ethnicity, yet refuse to examine race, racism, and racial hierarchies (Sleeter, 1995). The irony that exists is that many multicultural educators have embraced the idea of a pluralistic society under the guise of democratic principles (Banks, 1997; Sleeter & Grant, 1998). Despite years of oppression and exclusion in schools and society, a number of scholars have still sought to realize the goals and aims of an egalitarian society using multicultural education and ethnic studies as a vehicle (Banks, 1999; Pang, Gay, & Stanley, 1995). Yet, a historical peruse of the field of social studies prior to 1970 shows that social studies scholars theorized about the same type of egalitarian society that multicultural theorists speak of without any mention of racial equality, elimination of racism, and all other form of oppression (Wills, 2001). Given one of the goals of multicultural education is to acknowledge and actualize equality for all citizens, social studies educators can serve as leaders in schools in helping to explain how racial injustices and discrimination violate the promise of freedom and democracy which is the birthright of all U.S. citizens. In short, social studies educators must help call into question the role that race plays in helping or enabling citizens to experience democracy in its fullest manifestations.

RACE AND CONTEMPORARY WORK IN THE SOCIAL STUDIES

Though the social studies, much like many other fields of study have undertheorized race over the past century, in the past decade we have witnessed an increase in the number of theoretical constructs attempting to interrogate the importance of race historically and contemporarily (Omi & Winant, 1994; Feagin, & Vera, 1995). Evidence that social studies scholars have omitted the salience of race and racism is apparent within the primary research journal in the discipline. *Theory and Research in Social Education* (TRSE) is the premier research journal in the field of social studies. The journal's aim is to publish systemic research and thinking in social studies education which reflects major trends, issues, and topics in the field. In short, *TRSE* serves as an insightful lens for what types of research is being done in social studies education. Unfortunately, amidst the important work that has been covered in *TRSE* over the past three decades, there has been a glaring absence of research related to race and racism. A review of *TRSE* from 1973 to 1997 conducted by Ehman (1998) revealed that out of the 87 issues that were published from 1973 to 1997, 7% of the articles were centered on important topics such as global education, 5% on multicultural education. What Ehman's review did not mention is that there was not a single research study centered on issues explicitly concerned with race or racism and its effects on schools and society. My own examination of *TRSE* during the years Ehman covers uncovered similar findings. However, I would consider the 5% of articles that Ehman reports to be on or about multicultural education to be quite generous. My own analysis would suggest approximately 2–3% of the articles published in that time line could be considered work on multicultural education. Much of the work between 1973–1997 pays no attention to race, and only scant attention to multicultural issues. An investigation of *TRSE* editions published between 1997 and 2002 shows an emerging presence in the number of works involving issues of social justice, inequity, and discrimination but only one viewpoint article centered explicitly on race and racism. In the particular viewpoint article, Pang, Rivera, and Gillette (1998) pose the question of whether social studies educators can be leaders in the debate on racism. In a provocative and much needed challenge to social studies educators, Pang, Rivera, and Gillette "call upon social studies organizations like CUFA and NCSS to wake up and give a public accounting of where they stand on, and what they are doing to address, the issues of race and its negative impact on K–12 education and the quality of life in the U.S." (p. 431). The authors heed a call for social studies educators to take a leadership role in examining and eradicating racism in a democratic society. A historical review of the scope of work highlighted in *TRSE* is insightful because according to Ehman "the journal can serve as a mirror for social education researchers" (p. 2). In short, a look in the mirror would suggest that social studies researchers by and large have not been concerned with researching and discussing the effects of race and racism in a democratic society, or more important, how to dismantle racial inequities. Reviewing the works published in outlets such as *TRSE* is also critical because it underscores the predominate manner in which history, citizenship education, and economics have had on the field without any consideration of race or racism.

While the history of *TRSE* reveals the omission of race in social studies research, the oldest journal within the field, *Social Education*, does not fare much better in discussing race in social studies research and practice. Garcia and Buendia (1996) cite Chapin and Gross' review of the history of *Social Education* which reports that prior to 1960 articles focusing on cultural diversity were "nonexistent." They also report that the review of *Social Education* found that the first article addressing minority groups did not appear until 1971. An examination of issues of *Social Education* between 1971 and the present reveals that the journal has given cursory attention to ethnic minority groups in the United States. Most of this work was done within a historical context, and offers teachers strategies about how to teach various facets of history, such as the May/June 1999 issue that examined African Americans and using oral histories to teach about the civil rights movement. While issues of *Social Education* do show improvement in the treatment of culturally diverse groups, they still fail to explicitly address race and racism within the historical development of the United States. Thus, we see the incorporation of culturally and racially diverse groups appearing in the journals, but there still are no direct references to race and racism in the United States in any of these works.

Although history, civic education, and economics have been some of the most frequently researched topics covered in *TRSE, Social Education* and *The Social Studies* each of the areas mentioned have direct racial links to their development in this country. For example, U.S. history is filled with a plethora of accounts of various racial legacies that have not been critically examined. Issues including, but not limited to, slavery, immigration, U.S. colonization, public policy, social welfare, community redistricting, democratic citizenship and certain legislative agendas all have explicit and implicit historical racial implications, but have received scant attention from social studies researchers. The same can be stated for economics education. A critical look at economic development in the United States would not be complete without examining the establishment of the United States' capitalist structure, built on the free labor, exploitation, removal and displacement of a number of racial minority groups (Horsman, 1981; Manning, 2002; Robinson, 2000). Moreover, economic distribution, capital accumulation, and overall access to wealth speaks volumes about racial hierarchies that have existed within the United States and the world for more than four centuries (Oliver & Shapiro, 1996), however, very little discussion and research has investigated economic disparities among racial groups, how they evolved, and most important, how they can be absolved. As stated earlier, a critical race framework within the social studies would require researchers to make sense of the racial implications attached to all facets of work within social studies education.

Within the context of civic education, areas of inquiry such as issues-centered education are ideal for critical dialogues about race, just as areas such as the discussion of controversial issues, character development, and multicultural education. A critical race framework within the social studies would acknowledge the salient roles that race and racism continue to play in defining life in the United States. Moreover, a critical race framework within social studies research would allow an examination of race and racism to be discussed within the context of democratic citizenship both in its historical origins and its contemporary ramifications.

RACE IN THE SOCIAL STUDIES: WHERE DO WE GO FROM HERE?

One of the reasons for the lack of attention paid to race and racism in social studies research and practice could be that organizations such as the National Council of Social Studies (NCSS) and College University Faculty Assembly (CUFA), and many other social studies educators are predominately White, thus topics such as race are less likely to be broached. This reality should raise several questions. First and foremost, why are so few people of color actively involved in social studies organizations? A second, and more pressing question should probe "Why people of color are expected to be the primary persons concerned with initiating a critical dialogue around issues of race and racism?" Or in other words, what responsibilities do White educators have in initiating discussions concerned with interrogating race and racism? To be clear, all citizens should be engaged in the conversation about race. Moreover, critical race theory advocates for victims of racial oppression to offer their stories and experiences to illustrate the dehumanizing effects of racism. But equally important is the notion that race and racism must stop being viewed as a "people of color problem." I would argue that social studies educators have a civic responsibility and professional obligation to interrogate race and racism, particularly when issues such as democratic citizenship, U.S. history, and economics are at the center of the discussion, as is the case with much of social studies research. Social studies educators must come to the reality that where issues of racism and inequity are concerned, neutrality, silence, and inaction all serve as ringing endorsements for racial oppression and inequity, and reflect deep-seated hypocrisy in the tenets of what it means to be a good citizen. One of the essential tenets of democratic citizenship is the active participation in making informed decisions for the good of the polity (Banks, 1997; Gay, 1997). Interrogating race and racism requires all educators to be active participants, and the quest for greater understanding of race and racism does not benefit from silent or inactive educators. As Dr. Martin Luther King Jr. informed us, "the greatest sin of our time is not the few who have destroyed, but the vast majority who have sit by idly and watched."

In order to begin the dialogue on race related issues, students need to be given the opportunity to study race as a social construct, as well as the social, political, historical, geographical, cultural, and economic ramifications of racism. As advocates for students, social studies educators have a moral imperative to address racism for the sake of strengthening and preserving democracy. Racism not only affects people of color, but all people. As a matter of social justice and promoting equality in schools, social studies educators need to view the quest for racial equity as not a potential area of inquiry, but as a democratic obligation. Social studies educators can play a key role in helping to redefine and reconceptualize school knowledge, most of which remains free of critical dialogue about race and racism. According to Wills (2001) "school knowledge is a poor resource for enabling students to develop a discourse of contemporary race and ethnic relations that moves beyond psychological understandings of racism to structural understandings of racism" (p. 44). As racism is a learned phenomenon, it can also be unlearned. Social studies educators must begin to help students understand that race in the United States still remains tied to power and privilege (Bell, 1992, Manning, 2002). The sooner that social studies educators can begin to facilitate discussions around race and racism, the quicker old wounds begin to heal, honest dialogue occurs, and a more meaningful discussion can begin to take place about what it means to be a democratic citizen. Not only are our students in need of such a critical dialogue, but our future as a nation is dependent upon it as well.

REFERENCES

Balfour, L. (2001). *The evidence of things not said: James Baldwin and the promise of democracy*. Ithaca, NY: Cornell University Press.

Banks, J.A. (1995). Transformative challenges to the social science disciplines: Implications for social studies teaching and learning. *Theory Into Practice, 34*(1), 2–20.

Banks, J.A. (1997). *Educating citizens in a multicultural society*. New York: Teachers College Press.

Banks, J.A. (1999). *An introduction to multicultural education* (2nd ed.). Boston: Allyn & Bacon

Barr, R., Barth, J., & Shermis, S.S. (1978). *The nature of the social studies*. Palm Springs, CA: ETC Publications.

Barth, J.L. (1996). NCSS and the nature of the social studies. NCSS in retrospect, *Bulletin 92*. Washington, DC: National Council for the Social Studies.

Bell, D.A. (1992). *Faces at the bottom of the well: The permanence of racism*. New York: Basic Books.

Bernard-Powers, J. (1997). Gender in social education. In E.W. Ross (Ed.), *The social studies curriculum* (pp. 71–90) Albany: State University of New York Press.

Bickmore, K. (2002). How might social education resist heterosexism? facing the impact of gender and sexual ideology on citizenship. *Theory and Research in Social Education, 30*(2), 198–216.

Crenshaw, K.W. (1988). Race, reform and retrenchment: Transformation and anti-discrimination law. *Harvard Law Review, 101,* 1331–1387.

Crocco, M.S. (2002). Homophobic hallways: Is anyone listening? *Theory and Research in Social Education, 30*(2), 217–232.

Crocco, M., & Davis, O.L. (2002). Building a legacy: Women in social education 1784–1984. *NCSS Bulletin 100*. Washington, DC: National Council for the Social Studies.

Davis, O.L. (1991). Citizenship education as the central purpose of the social studies: The heavy load of a dead metaphor. *Social Studies as a Discipline. Special issue of The International Journal of Social Education.* 33–36.

Delgado, R. (1989). Storytelling for oppositionists and others: A plea for narrative. *Michigan Law Review, 87,* 2411–2441.

Dewey, J. (1933). *How we think*. Boston: D.C. Heath.

Dougan, A.M. (1985). The search for a definition of the social studies: A historical overview. *Indiana Journal of Social Education, 3,* 13–35.

Ehman, L.H. (1998). What theory and research in social education tells us about ourselves: Trends from 1973 to 1997. *Theory and Research in Social Education, 26*(2), 238–257.

Engle, S. (1963). Decision-making: The heart of social studies instruction. *Social Education, 24*(7), 301–304, 306.

Feagin, J.R., & Vera, H. (1995). *White racism*. New York: Routledge.

Federal Bureau of Investigation. (1998). Criminal Justice Information Services (CJIS) Division. Uniform Crime Reports. Hate Crime—1998. (http://www.fbi.gov/ucr.ucr.htm).

Garcia, J., & Buendia, E. (1996). NCSS and ethnic/cultural diversity. *NCSS in Retrospect. NCSS Bulletin 92.*

Gay, G. (1997). The relationship between multicultural and democratic education. *The Social Studies, 88*(1), 5–11.

Hahn, C.L. (1991). Controversial issues in social studies. In J.P. Shaver (Ed.). *Handbook of research on social studies teaching and learning* (pp. 470–480). New York: Macmillan.

Harris, A.P. (1994). Forward: The jurisprudence of reconstruction. *California Law Review, 82,* 741–785.

Hertzberg, H.W. (1981). *Social studies reform, 1880–1980. A project span report.* Boulder, CO: Social Studies Consortium.

Hess, D.E. (2002). Discussing controversial public issues in secondary social studies classrooms: Learning from skilled teachers. *Theory and Research in Social Education, 30*(1), 10–41.

Hinds, M. (2000). Violent kids: Can we solve the problem? *Social Education, 64*(4), 225–231.

Horsman, R. (1981). *Race and manifest destiny*. Cambridge, MA: Harvard University Press.

Howard, T.C. (2001). Connection and democracy. *Theory and Research in Social Education, 29*(3), 524–531.

Jackson, S., & Solis, J. (1995). *Beyond comfort zones in multicultualism: Confronting the politics of privilege*. Westport, CT: Bergin & Garvey.

Kohlberg, L. (1973). Moral development and the new social studies. *Social Education, 14*(1), 35–49.

Ladson-Billings, G (2000). Racialized discourses and ethnic epistemologies. In N.K. Denzin & Y.S. Lincoln (Eds.), *Handbook of qualitative research* (2nd ed., pp. 257–278). Thousand Oaks, CA: Sage.

Ladson-Billings, G., & Tate, W.R. (1995). Toward a critical race theory of education. *Teachers College Record, 97*, 47–68.

Lybarger, M.B. (1991). The historiography of social studies: Retrospect, circumspect, and prospect. In J.P. Shaver (Ed.). *Handbook of research on social studies teaching and learning* (pp. 3–15). New York: Macmillan.

Marable, M. (2002). *The great wells of democracy: The meaning of race in American life*. New York: BasicCivitas Books.

Mason, C.L., & Berson, M.J. (2000). Computer mediated communication in elementary social studies methods. *Theory and Research in Social Education. 28*(4), 527–545.

Matsuda, C. (1991). Voices of America: Accent, antidiscrimination law, and a jurisprudence for the last reconstruction. *Yale Law Journal, 100*, 1329–1407.

Mattai, P.R. (1992). Rethinking multicultural education: Has it lost its focus or is it being misused? *Journal of Negro Education, 61*(1), 65–77.

Merryfield, M. (2000). Using electronic technologies to promote equity and cultural diversity in social studies education. *Theory and Research in Social Education, 28*(4), 502–526.

Merryfield, M. (1998). Pedagogy for global perspectives in education: Studies of teachers' thinking and practice. *Theory and Research in Social Education, 26*, 342–379.

McCarthy, C. (1990). Race and education in the United States: The multicultural solution. *Interchange, 21*(3), 45–55.

Morse, D. (2001). Enemies of the people: Poetry and politics in the time of Stalin. *Social Education, 65*(4), 198–207.

National Assessment of Educational Progress. (1994). *Reading report card for the nation and states. Office of educational research and improvement*. Washington, DC: U.S.Department of Education.

National Assessment of Educational Progress. (1996). *Reading report card for the nation and states. Office of educational research and improvement*. Washington, DC: U.S. Department of Education.

National Assessment of Educational Progress. (1998). *Reading report card for the nation and states. Office of educational research and improvement*. Washington, DC: U.S. Department of Education.

National Assessment of Educational Progress. (2000). *Reading report card for the nation and states. Office of educational research and improvement.* Washington, DC: U.S. Department of Education.

Noddings, N. (1997). Social studies and feminism. In E.W. Ross (Ed.), *The social studies curriculum* (pp. 71–90). Albany: State University of New York Press.

Oliver, M.L., & Shapiro, T.M. (1997). *Black wealth, white wealth: A new perspective on racial inequality.* New York: Routledge.

Omi, M., & Winant, H. (1994). *Racial formation in the United States.* New York: Routledge.

Pang, V.O., Rivera, J., & Gillette, R. (1998). Can CUFA be a leader in the national debate on racism? *Theory and Research in Social Education.*

Pang, V.O., Gay, G., & Stanley, W.B. (1995). Expanding conceptions of community and civic competence and civic competence for a multicultural society. *Theory and Rearch in Social Education, 23,* 302–331.

Parker, W.C. (1991). Achieving thinking and decision-making objectives in the social studies. In J.P. Shaver (Ed.), *Handbook of research on social studies teaching and learning* (pp. 345–356). New York: Macmillan.

Parker, W.C. (1997). Democracy and difference. *Theory and Research in Social Education, 25*(2), 220–234.

Parker, W.C. (2001). Educating democratic citizens: A broad view. *Theory Into Practice, 40*(1), 6–13.

Parker, L., & Lynn, M. (2002). What's race got to do with it? Critical race theory's conflicts with and connections to qualitative research methodology and epistemology. *Qualitative Inquiry, 8*(1), 7–22.

Robinson, R. (2000). *The debt: What America owes to Blacks.* New York: Dutton.

Ross, E.W. (1997). The struggle for the social studies curriculum. In E.W. Ross (Ed.), *The social studies curriculum* (pp. 3–19). Albany: State University of New York Press.

Saxe, D.S. (1992). A history of the social studies: A prologue to reformation. Inquiry in social studies: curriculum, research and instruction. Special issue, *The Journal of the North Carolina Council for the Social Studies, 20,* 13–25.

Saxe, D.W. (1997). The unique mission of the social studies. In E.W. Ross (Ed.), *The social studies curriculum* (pp. 39–55). Albany: State University of New York Press.

Schofield, J.W. (1986). The colorblind perspective in school: Causes and consequences. In J.A. Banks & C.A.M. Banks (Eds.), *Multicultural education: Issues and perspectives* (4th ed., pp. 247–267). New York: Wiley & Sons.

Shaver, J.P. (1977). *Building rationales for citizenship education* (Bulletin 52). Washington, DC: National Council for the Social Studies.

Shaver, J.P. (1991). *Handbook of research on social studies teaching and learning.* New York: Macmillan.

Sleeter, C.E. (1995). An analysis of the critiques of multicultural education. In J.A. Banks & C.A.M. Banks (Eds.), *Handbook of research on multicultural education* (pp. 81–94). New York: Macmillan.

Sleeter, C.E., & Grant, C.A. (1998). *Making choices for multicultural education: Five approaches to race, class, and gender* (3rd ed.). New York: Wiley.

Smith-Maddox, R., & Solarzano, D.G. (2002). Using critical race theory, Paulo Freire's problem-posing method, and case study research to confront race and racism in education. *Qualitative Inquiry, 8*(1), 66–84.

Solarzano, D.G. (1998). Critical race theory, race and gender microaggressions, and the experience of Chicana and Chicano scholars. *International Journal of Qualitative Studies in Education, 11*(1), 121–136.

Solarzano, D.G., & Yosso, T.J. (2002). Critical race methodology: Counter-storytelling as an analytical framework for education research. *Qualitative Inquiry, 8*(1), 23–44.

Tate, W.G., IV (1997). Critical race theory and education: History, theory an implications. In M. Apple (Ed.), *Review of research in education* (pp. 191–243). Washington, DC: American Educational Research Association.

Tiedt, I., & Tiedt, P. (1986). *Multicultural teaching: A handbook of activities, information, and resources.* Boston: Allyn and Bacon.

West, C. (1994). *Race matters.* New York: Random House.

VanSledright, B. (2002). Confronting history's interpretive paradox while teaching fifth graders to investigate the past. *American Educational Research Journal, 39*(4), 1089–1115.

VanSledright, B., & Afflerbach, P. (2000). Reconstructing Andrew Jackson: Prospective elementary teachers' readings of revisionist history texts. *Theory and Research in Social Education, 28*(3),411–444.

Wills, J.S. (2001). Missing in interaction: Diversity, narrative, and critical multicultural social studies. *Theory and Research in Social Education, 29*(1), 43–64.

CHAPTER 4

FROM LIBERAL TEACHER TO LIBERATED TEACHER EDUCATOR

A Reflection on My Journey Through the Profession

Ceola Ross Baber

ABSTRACT

An ethnobiographical reflection on the author's journey as a social educator from classroom teacher to teacher educator including a description of the context that motivated her to choose social studies as a profession; an analysis of her teacher preparation and experiences as a secondary social studies teacher, including the challenges and triumphs of being Black and female in a profession dominated by White males; and a critique of her multicultural education approach to social studies. The chapter ends with thoughts on how social studies can move from a philosophy grounded in liberalism to one grounded in critical race theory.

Critical Race Theory Perspectives on the Social Studies, pages 45–68
Copyright © 2003 by Information Age Publishing

INTRODUCTION

I understood very early on that teaching was about the survival of our people and social justice.

—Frederick Douglas Ross, Sr. (2002)

As I come to the end of an almost thirty-year journey as a social studies teacher and teacher educator, I find myself growing weary of feeling marginalized and betrayed by a collective of professionals that has time and again failed to actualize its moral imperative and responsibility as social educators, especially when it comes to race matters. A specific case in point precipitated my alienation from and boycott of the National Council for the Social Studies (NCSS) annual meetings for three years.

At its 1994 business meeting in Phoenix, the NCSS College University Faculty Assembly (CUFA) passed a resolution to take action in protest of California's passage of Proposition 187 that denied access to schooling, health, and other services to immigrants and their children who happened to be people of color. The action was to refrain from holding meetings in California until Proposition 187 was repealed or nullified. At the meeting, members of CUFA engaged in a sometimes intellectual and sometimes emotional debate over the resolution, but one inclusive of multiple perspectives. It was not a select group of CUFA members who decided to refrain from meeting in California; rather, it was a majority of the members present who concluded that in its violation of several international articulations of children's rights, Proposition 187 was an attack on the general welfare of certain immigrant children and their teachers (Baber, 1997).

Immediately after passage of the resolution, some CUFA members began working to overturn it. When brought before the NCSS House of Delegates, the resolution failed to pass. CUFA then had to decide whether or not to meet independent of NCSS at the 1998 scheduled meeting in Anaheim, California. The CUFA Executive Board voted to uphold its resolution and began looking for alternative sites for the 1998 meeting. After the 1994 meeting CUFA members continued to discuss the resolution and as the Anaheim meeting grew nearer, the discussions became more heated. The central issue of the 1994 resolution—California's denial of access to schooling and other human services to a particular class of children and the role of social educators in responding to this assault on human dignity—became circumvented by both discussions concerning the politicalization of CUFA, the scholar-activist dichotomy, the nature of democracy, and the meaning of civic competency in a pluralistic society.

In the end, at its 1997 business meeting in Cincinnati, Ohio, a motion was passed that rescinded the 1994 boycott resolution, allowing CUFA to meet in Anaheim with NCSS. At that meeting, Gloria Ladson-Billings and I (both then members of the CUFA Executive Board) made impassioned arguments for rejection of the motion. Not only were we professionally "dissed" as multi-cultural-social educators, but we were also personally assaulted as women of color by the NCSS Executive Director's statement in favor of rescinding the original boycott: "we should not be sidetracked by seductive but not so important issues." From my perspective, the dignity and welfare of brown immigrant children was a very important issue. It was, in fact a moral impera-tive to see all children as precious, as mandated in the NCSS curriculum standards document, *Expectations of Excellence* (NCSS, 1994).

It was at this meeting that I realized CUFA and NCSS had no desire or plans to move beyond intellectual discussions of democracy and take social justice to the streets. It should be noted that as part of its strategy to per-suade CUFA from holding a separate meeting in 1998, the NCSS board of directors at its April 1997 meeting had passed a related resolution. The NCSS resolution (a) condemned California Propositions 187 and 209, (b) provided for a forum at the 1998 meeting that would educate the profes-sional community and public about the significant issues, and (c) refused to schedule future meetings in California while these propositions were in effect. As Jeff Passe noted in the Spring 1997 newsletter: "The resolution faced strong opposition. Some NCSS board members opposed what they considered a political stance for the organization, others preferred softer wording. The final vote was 9 to with 3 abstentions" (1997, p. 4).

I was born and breed in the Deep South during the fervor of the civil rights movement. Men and women who fought injustice and literally put their lives on the line on a daily basis surrounded me. I learned that all acts of social justice were valued and valuable, whether they took place in the schoolhouse or the church house, the kitchen or the streets. I also learned that education was critical to liberation. I choose the social studies profes-sion because I believed it was the vehicle through which I could actualize my commitment to social justice. The CUFA incident muted my belief in the profession as a catalyst for justice and social reconstruction. I am not the passionate social educator I was eight years ago. Though weary, I am not yet worn out and am now looking for ways to rekindle my passion through a reconstruction of the profession.

This chapter is an ethnobiographical reflection on my personal and pro-fessional journey as a social educator from classroom teacher to teacher educator. I begin with describing the context that motivated me to choose this profession—southern roots and three generations of teaching for social justice. I then analyze my teacher preparation at a liberal university and my experiences as a secondary social studies teacher, including the challenges and triumphs of being Black and female in a profession domi-nated by White males. Next I look at my transition from classroom teacher to teacher educator. Finally I present some thoughts on how the profession can move from a philosophy grounded in liberalism to one grounded in critical race theory (CRT), becoming a catalyst for change and social justice in preparing the next generation of social educators.

THREE GENERATIONS OF TEACHING FOR SOCIAL JUSTICE

I am a third generation teacher. My paternal grandmother taught in a one-room schoolhouse in rural Alabama during the 1930s and 40s. My father taught junior high school social studies in northern California, after completing a 20-year career in the military. Growing up, I had several other teacher models on both sides of my family. My father's aunt, his mother's younger sister, also taught in a one-room schoolhouse during the 1950s and 60s. My mother's aunt taught in segregated schools in Selma during the 1940s and 1950s. My mother's sister taught in segregated and desegregated schools in Selma from the late 1950s through the early 1990s. My father and I recently had a conversation about his schooling experiences growing up in rural Alabama and the motivation that has driven three generations of teachers in our family. The conversation affirmed what I observed while watching these teacher-activists as a child, adolescent, and young adult: for teachers in our family, as for most African American teachers, teaching is both a calling and an act of social justice.

My father attended one of those one-room schoolhouses and his first teacher was his Uncle Mose, his mother's older brother. Uncle Mose and Grandmother Willa were both trained in a normal school. Their teacher training emphasized that their job as a teacher was to prepare their students to first survive in a racist society and then to improve the quality of life for themselves and others. "Both 'life skills' and academic content were taught in the one-room segregated schools and schooling was a community enterprise"(F.D. Ross, Sr., personal communication, October 27, 2002). Males were taught agricultural skills and females were taught domestic skills. Lessons included hands-on projects. For example, my father recalls in the eighth grade having to build a chicken brooder from scratch, including rigging the brooder with kerosene lamps to keep the eggs warm at night. Parents paid tuition with loads of wood for the schoolhouse stove. Social studies included an emphasis on local history, the geography of Alabama, and the economy of all fifty states. Black history was taught through the oral tradition by community residents coming in and sharing their slavery and reconstruction experiences and challenging the students to take advantage of opportunities those of previous generations had been denied: "The past was connected to the present in order to change the future" (F.D. Ross, Sr., personal communication, October 27, 2002). History was also taught through primary sources that the teachers had collected and saved, such as news articles kept in scrapbooks and bibles. For example, my father remembers that his mother had kept an article about how Charles Drew bled to death from injuries sustained in an automobile accident after being refused treatment at a local White hospital. Teachers used the smarter students as teaching assistants or apprentices, thus preparing them for one of the few professional careers open to them at that time in history. Religious studies and praying were mandatory.

My grandmother Willa was a quiet, introspective person who loved to read and write. Grandmother taught at the elementary and junior high school levels while raising seven children. Although Grandmother was quiet, when she spoke my grandfather Albert and everyone else listened carefully. I like to think I got my no-nonsense "teacher look" from Grandmother and I know she inspired in me a love of literature and history. Grandmother also had a wry sense of humor and gift for storytelling. She was always writing poetry and short stories. I loved to hear her stories, history lessons really, about African American freedom fighters. She named one of her sons after Frederick Douglass, the great orator and abolitionist. She named another one after John Henry, that "steel driving man" who struggled to the death against machines' displacement of humans. Unfortunately, her writings and other memorabilia were destroyed when the Ku Klux Klan burned down the "home house" in the middle of the night during the 1960s civil rights struggle.

My father was one of those smart students used by the teachers as a teaching assistant. He knew he wanted to be a teacher from the moment his Uncle Mose let him teach his peers. He always understood that "teaching was an act of social justice" from watching his uncle, mother, and other teachers. He recalls one wet and cold morning when he and other "neighborhood" children were walking to school. The White school bus passed them on the road and the bus driver deliberately drove through a big puddle of water, splashing the Black children as the White students shouted racial epithets out of the bus windows. When the Black students got to school, their teacher calmed them down and used their experience as a teachable moment to talk about the coming changes and their responsibility in helping to dismantle Jim Crowism. "School was about survival and social justice and Sunday school was an extension of school—using the Bible to teach about social justice and develop academic skills" (F.D. Ross, Sr., personal communication, October 27, 2002). My father completed his bachelor's degree and teacher training during the last few years of a 20-year military career. After retiring from the military he taught junior high social studies.

I knew from a very young age that I would become a teacher. After my first year in high school, I knew that I wanted to teach social studies and English at the junior high school level. I attended California State University at Sacramento where I completed a bachelor's degree in history with a minor in English and the social sciences. I then pursued the Master of Arts degree in secondary education at Stanford University. Here is an excerpt from the statement of purpose submitted with my application for admission to Stanford:

> My ultimate career goal has always been to teach. All of my academic energies have been geared to obtain this objective. The basic assumption behind this desire to teach is that education is vital to the survival of a society and consequently to the survival of a person (or people) in that society. Hopefully my M.A. program will revolve around the Afro-American experience in the American educational system. It seems evident that the Afro-American is not really surviving in this society and basic to this failure are his problems in the American school system. I hope my research will provide, at least in part, some answers to why schools are failing Afro-Americans in our society and how we can remedy this situation.

LIBERAL SOCIAL STUDIES TEACHER

The completion of a Master of Arts degree in Stanford University's Secondary Teacher Education Program prepared me to teach social studies at the junior and senior high school levels. While at Stanford, I studied with Richard E. Gross and Murry Nelson was my student teaching supervisor. During this early phase of my career I learned to work with students who were then defined as "low achievers."

My student teaching experience was a full-time internship with the Sequoia Union School District where I taught English and social studies at Ravenswood High School. Ravenswood was the school district's attempt to cope with desegregation by way of a voluntary transfer plan. Under this plan Black students could transfer to the more affluent White schools in the district and White students could transfer to the less affluent Black schools. In order to encourage White students to transfer, attractive courses were added to the curriculum at Ravenswood (e.g., courses in mountain climbing, "Women in Shakespeare," etc.). The purpose of the courses (to attract White students) determined their nature—White student-oriented. Ravenswood was located in East Palo Alto, a predominantly African American community, and a large percentage of the indigenous student population needed basic skills courses and needed a culturally relevant curriculum. The alternative curriculum was meeting neither their academic nor their sociocultural needs.

It was Professor St. Clair Drake, an anthropologist and sociologist at Stanford, who helped me to understand the extent to which low achievement of ethnic minority and poverty disadvantaged students is related to cultural diversity on the one hand and a culturally irrelevant curriculum on the other hand. I learned it was possible to dramatically increase the achievement level of "low achievers" by developing curricula that allowed these students to see reflections of themselves in the material that they were expected to learn. It is in this respect that I used social studies and English as content areas out of which I could easily produce relevant material for culturally diverse students. As an intern, I developed and taught several interdisciplinary units that met both the academic and sociocultural needs of the African American students at Ravenswood.

One of my first challenges at Ravenswood was to teach the general English curriculum to ninth grade students who were reading at the sixth grade level. Shakespeare was one of the literature units in the ninth grade general English curriculum. My students had not yet mastered standard American English and could care less about Shakespearean English. How could I begin where these students were academically and make the subject culturally relevant? I introduced them to Shakespeare's sonnets, using Sonnet #130 (also known as the "Dark Lady" Sonnet) and compared it to the Impressions' "The Woman Got Soul" (a hit rhythm and blues song at the time). The students immediately grasped that both were tributes to ladies who did not quite meet the ideal of physical beauty, but were deeply loved by their men anyway. This led to discussions of the constancy of love across time and space as well as the cultural standards of beauty. Here are excerpts from each love poem:

Shakespeare's Sonnet #130	Impressions' "The Woman Got Soul"
My mistress' eyes are nothing like the sun;	*She may not be the best looking woman I ever did see.*
If hairs be wires, black wires grow on her head;	*Nor have the charms of the ladies of high society.*
And yet, by heaven, I think my love as rare	*But the woman got soul worth all money and gold*
Any she belied with false compare.	*And all the love that I have belongs to the woman with soul.*

After our discussions my students agreed that Shakespeare might not be such a bad thing to study after all. We proceeded to his plays. For obvious reasons, I choose *Othello*. I gave the students a sound bite version of the play first: interracial relationship sabotaged by racism and jealously. I also gave them a "plain English" synopsis of each act before we read it aloud in class. By the second act, my "low achieving," poverty disadvantaged students were enacting scenes from *Othello* in the school courtyard, in Shakespearean English, and during lunchtime! My White colleagues were astounded and asked me how I had accomplished this academic "miracle." I had simply used the sociocultural context of my students' lives to make the curriculum relevant and obtainable for them. Twenty years later, Gloria Ladson-Billings (1995) named this approach to teaching and learning culturally relevant pedagogy.

After completing my master's degree and certification program, I was hired by the same school district to teach at San Carlos High School. By this time Ravenswood had been closed and the indigenous student population had been distributed to other schools in the district. At San Carlos, I was the coordinator of CORE, a special program funded by the federal government. CORE was designed to ensure the successful transition of sixty incoming ninth graders who had been diagnosed as "low achievers." These students were lower middle class and poverty disadvantaged African Americans, females of all ethnicities, and poverty disadvantaged White males. The CORE curriculum included courses in reading, mathematics, English, and social studies. The CORE program also had an advisor-advisee component and strong home-school linkages. As coordinator, I worked with the ESEA teacher to assist the teachers in adapting their materials and teaching styles to meet the needs of the CORE students. I was also the social studies teacher. In addition, I chaired the CORE team meetings and coordinated the home-school activities (home visits, parent-teacher-student conferences, etc.). This experience led to my first analysis of the leadership efficacy of African American women in a predominantly White workplace.

Work for most African American women, beginning with slavery and continuing through today, has taken place in predominantly White workplaces that is, workplaces owned and/or controlled by White women and/or men (Giddings, 1984; Jones, 1985) This work has taken place in a variety of settings including the mistress' kitchen or the master's fields; textile factories and the World War II munitions factories; Ms. Ann's house in the North, South, East and West United States; hospitals, schools, corporate offices, or even university halls. This situation has led to particular gender-race and race-gender relations between African American and White women and African American women and White men. The gender-race relationship, which has evolved, can be summed up as one grounded in a mistress-servant mentality that has severely constrained African American-White women's perceptions of and interactions with each other and has resulted in what I call gender-racism.

Gender-racism was the root of tension between African American and White women during the early stages of the Women's Liberation movement, including the development and implementation of (White) Women's Studies programs. Toni Morrison graphically describes this tension:

> [Black women] look at white [W]hite women and see them as the enemy—for they know that racism is not confined to white men and that there are more [W]hite women than men in this country, and that 53 per cent of the

population sustained an eloquent silence during times of greatest stress. The faces of those [W]hite women hovering behind that [B]lack girl at the Little Rock school in 1957 do not soon leave the retina of the mind. (1971, p. 14)

The mistress-servant mentality and its resultant gender-racism can be linked to the legacy of slave work especially in the "big house," the legacy of domestic work, and the legacy of White women upon-a-pedestalism. Over the past twenty-five years, the mutual concerns of balancing career and family faced by greater numbers of African American and White professional women as well as the multiculturalization of women's studies have helped to mitigate some of the hurt and distrust generated by gender-racism.

Race-sexism has its roots in the historical sexual and economic exploitation of African American women by White men. Contemporary race-sexism is manifested in sexual harassment and power games at the workplace. Francis Beal's (1970) article, "Double Jeopardy: To be Black and Female," Joyce Ladner's (1972) *Tomorrow's Tomorrow: The Black Woman*, Paula Giddings' (1984) *When and Where I Enter: The Impact of Black Women on Race and Sex in America*, Jacqueline Jones' (1985) *Labor of Love, Labor of Sorrow: Black Women, Work, and the Family from Slavery to the Present*, and Deborah King's (1988) "Multiple Jeopardy, Multiple Consciousness: The Context of a Black Feminist Ideology" offer stimulating critiques concerning the double discrimination African American women have historically faced and continue to face and the negative impact this has had on race and gender relations.

Gender-racism and race-sexism often converge around the myth of the advantaged status of African American women in the work place. While African American women perceive their race and gender as a "double whammy," White women, African American men, and White men have the opposite perception and see African American women as having a double bonus, especially in terms of affirmative action. The reality is that both White women and African American men have benefitted more from affirmation action than African American women (Federal Glass Ceiling Commission, 1995; Sokoloff, 1992). Sanchez-Huchs (1997) analyzes the deleterious effects of this myth thusly:

> The persistent myth of bonus status for Black women has continued to harm [B]lack women on multiple levels. The view that Black women are flourishing promotes a system where individuals continue to mentor and network with those most like themselves and thereby overlook Black women. The false perception of Black women's work experiences minimizes opportunities for them to collaborate with other women and minorities in the work force to overcome common obstacles. (p. 577)

As a neophyte social studies teacher back at San Carlos High School twenty-five years ago, I encountered both gender-racism and race-sexism. I was a twenty-six-year-old African American woman still new to the profession. My CORE colleagues were three middle-aged European American women who initially were not only unhappy with taking orders from me but were also outright skeptical of my competence in coordinating the program. My social studies colleagues were six middle-aged European American men. Half of them thought they were the epitome of 70s-style liberals. The other half tried to mask their racist and sexist tendencies in our team meetings and other interactions, while simultaneously telling ethnic jokes and making lewd sexual remarks. Both groups saw me as a token brought in to work with the African American students who were being bussed from East Palo Alto (with the closing of Ravenswood High School) and neither group mentored me as a new professional.

My early years in the profession can be summarized through the lens of multiculturalism as a reformist educational agenda. Multiculturalism is closely linked to the political philosophy of liberalism. In his acceptance of the New York Liberal Party nomination, then Senator John F. Kennedy defined liberalism as:

> not so much a party creed or set of fixed platform promises as it is an attitude of mind and heart, a faith in man's ability through the experiences of his reason and judgment to increase for himself and his fellow men the amount of justice and freedom and brotherhood which all human life deserves ().

Multiculturalism as manifested in multicultural education values diversity and upholds the worth and dignity of all collective and individual experiences. It is an inclusionary, emancipatory, liberatory, critical, and transformative approach to teaching and learning that is instrumental in helping us fully understand and appreciate our differences so that we can truly celebrate our differences (Baber, 1993, 2000; Banks, 1999; Crichlow, Goodwin, Shakes, & Swartz, 1990; Ladson-Billings & Henry, 1990; McCarthy, 1993; Nieto, 2000). Multicultural education aims for equity and excellence for students from all ethnic/racial, gender, and class groups. As a classroom teacher, I used multicultural education as a vehicle for teaching to *and* about cultural diversity by advocating for maximizing each of my student's potential while encouraging them to accept diversity in others. I did this while working within the institution of schooling in order to reform it.

LIBERATED SOCIAL STUDIES EDUCATOR

My action research as a classroom teacher and my attempts at teacher-leadership led me to believe that I needed to make a career change in order to be able to more effectively contribute to equity in education. I decided to pursue a doctorate in curriculum and administration at Purdue University where I worked with Geneva Gay. After earning my doctorate, I was appointed as director of Purdue's Afro-American Studies and Research Center with the primary responsibility of leadership and program development. I found myself in the leadership role of advocating for the academic legitimacy of what had become a very politicized program. The various program development activities associated with Afro-American Studies at Purdue helped me to better see the significance of a multicultural perspective (ethnic studies in this case) in achieving equity and excellence in education for all students at any level of instruction. Consequently, during this phase of my professional development most of my scholarship and teaching focused on the "at-riskness" of African American students and the relationship between academic performance and the exclusionary impact of a culturally irrelevant curriculum versus the inclusionary impact of multicultural education.

While I was very successful as a university administrator-scholar, my real concern remained with equity in education for K–12 students. I made another career shift into teacher education by way of an adjunct appointment in the Purdue University School of Education where I assisted James Barth in the methods course and supervision of social studies student teachers; I also taught a graduate course in multicultural education. I was later recruited by the University of North Carolina at Greensboro to strengthen the development of a multicultural perspective in the undergraduate teacher education curriculum.

During my first 15 years as a social studies educator I focused on (a) helping pre-service teachers develop a knowledge base and competencies for teaching middle school and secondary social studies or extending the knowledge base and competencies of in-service teachers in these areas; (b) helping pre-service teachers develop multicultural teaching competencies; and (c) extending the knowledge base, competencies, and curriculum development skills of in-service teachers in multicultural education. My underlying assumption has been that multicultural education and social studies are complementary components of a synergistic model for powerful teaching and learning.

The role of education in most societies has been that of socialization and cultural transmission. In theory, this role appears to be valid and viable. In practice, however it often deteriorates into sociopyschological control and political-economic dominance—or, controlling human potential rather than unleashing it. In discussions about educational philosophies, policies, and practices during the early 1990s this phenomenon was referred to as silencing the voices of marginalized members of our society, particularly in the process of knowledge construction (Baber, 1995; Cornbleth & Waugh, 1995; Crichlow et al., 1990; Greene, 1993; Nelson, 1991).

In 1993, the National Council for the Social Studies' vision of powerful social studies teaching and learning identified five principles critical to building civic understanding and civic efficacy for 21st century students and teachers:

Social studies teaching and learning is powerful when it is meaningful, integrative, value based, challenging, and active. This vision is based on the following assumptions about the nature of social studies education: (a) social studies is diverse; local curricula should reflect the essentials of social studies and NCSS principles, but their particular goals and objectives can and should vary; (b) *all* students should have access to the full richness of the social studies curriculum; (c) teachers need adequate time and resources to teach social studies well at every grade; and (d) social studies teachers need to treat the social world realistically as opposed to idealistically and they need to address its controversial aspects. (National Council for the Social Studies [NCSS], 1993, p. 215)

As a social studies educator, I have tried to demonstrate how multicultural education and social studies form a synergistic framework for powerful teaching and learning. The following four questions have guided my implementation of this synergistic framework: What are the dimensions of multicultural education? What values are central to a multicultural society? How does multicultural education support democratic values and commitment to social reconstruction? What are the benefits to involving local cultures and students' ethnic identities in social studies instruction?

Carter G. Woodson (1933/1969) maintained that the only way one can function effectively in society is to know oneself. Students need to understand the content of their own culture before they can fully appreciate the cultures of others. Woodson's basic tenet has been the essence of my mission as a social studies educator as reflected in the conceptualizations of multicultural education by three of the field's "founding" scholars: Christine Bennett, James Banks, and Geneva Gay.

Bennett's (1999) description of multicultural education is grounded in four values central to a multicultural society: acceptance and appreciation of cultural diversity, respect for human dignity and universal human rights, responsibility to a world community, and reverence for the earth. Bennett contends that multicultural education should help students develop multiple historical perspectives. Our world views are not universally shared, they are the product of our experiences, and others have views that may be profoundly different but are just as valid.

Banks (1999) outlines five dimensions of multicultural education. Equity pedagogy involves teachers modifying their teaching to facilitate the academic achievement of culturally diverse students. Empowerment is the deliberate promotion of gender, racial, and social class equality. Knowledge construction means teachers have to develop methods, activities, and questions that are designed to help students understand, investigate, and determine how the implicit cultural assumptions, perspectives, and biases within a discipline influence the ways in which meaning is constructed. In content integration, teachers use culturally diverse examples and content to illustrate key concepts, principles, generalizations, and theories in their subject area. Prejudice reduction teaching strategies help students to develop more positive attitudes about culturally diverse individuals and groups.

Gay (1994) contends that multicultural education is at the essence of learning. She presents multicultural translations of general educational principles related to human growth and development, democratic citizenship, and pedagogy. Themes associated with the multicultural translations include identity development, education as a basic right, conscience and community, representation and participation, universal literacy, scholarly truth, equity and excellence, and holistic instruction.

Bennett's goals, Banks' dimensions, and Gay's themes are embedded in the 1992 National Council for the Social Studies "Curriculum Guidelines for Multicultural Education." These guidelines reiterate the need for as well as the function of multicultural education in a culturally diverse society: "An important goal of multicultural education is to help students from diverse cultures learn *how* to transcend their cultural borders and engage in dialogue and action essential for the survival of our democratic political system and way of life" (NCSS, 1992, p. 274).

As a social studies educator I have sought to show how, on the basis of their common grounding in democratic ideals and principles, multicultural education and social studies have the potential for a synergistic relationship. Unfortunately, while multicultural education is deliberate in its aim of social reconstruction, social studies (in terms of citizenship education) has not traditionally sought to reconstruct society but rather to maintain the status quo. The National Council for the Social Studies' vision of powerful teaching and learning, however, offers an opportunity to bring multicultural and social studies together in a synergistic model of social education deliberately aimed at reconstructing society. Marshall and Bennett (1994) refer to this as social studies that is multicultural (SSM):

> Study of social studies that is multicultural, ultimately, should empower students to act in their daily lives in manners that are in accordance with democratic principles. As such, students should begin to examine issues related to diversity in a more substantive manner by acknowledging the prevailing inequities and forces of oppression that exist in society. (p. 23)

Powerful social studies teaching helps students to recognize that there are multiple historical, geographical, and cultural perspectives; thus expanding their world views, strengthening their social consciousness, and increasing their intercultural competence. Meaningful, integrative, values-based, challenging, and active social studies education builds the proactive social and civic education decision-making skills necessary for civic competency in a multicultural society. Table 4.1 presents a synergistic model of social studies that is multicultural. The model aligns four principles of powerful social studies teaching and learning with the NCSS curriculum guidelines for multicultural education, Banks' dimensions of multicultural education, Bennett's goals of multicultural education, and Gay's multicultural education themes.

There are numerous resources demonstrating how to make teaching to and about diversity *meaningful* for students (e.g., Davidman & Davidman, 2001; Gollnick & Chinn, 2002). Content integration, aimed at incorporating culturally pluralistic contributions and helping students to understand and accept multiple perspectives, has been the easiest and least threatening area of multicultural education for eliciting positive action from teachers. My experience in working with pre-service and in-service teachers indicates that they are increasingly moving away from the additive approach of including cultural contributions toward a truly integrative approach. Teachers perceive social studies and English as the most natural subjects for content integration. Indeed, this was my own experience as a classroom teacher as described in the previous section of this chapter.

A few years ago, I teamed with my English education and science education colleagues to develop and implement an interdisciplinary pre-service methods course with a heavy emphasis on multiculturalism. Students had to work in collaborative, interdisciplinary teams to develop units related to the theme of oceans. Integration of the authentic experiences of women and people of color had to be reflected in the learning experiences and the resources. *Integrative* teaching and learning in terms of knowledge construction to help students view and interpret events, situations, and conflict from culturally diverse perspectives and world views is one of the more controversial and less visible efforts in social studies. The diversity debates that raged on campuses of higher education during the early 1990s very graphically illustrated this controversy and struggle to pursue a genuine search for truth.

Banks' (1991) literature review concerning the effects of multicultural education on students' racial and gender role attitudes showed that *values-based* teaching and learning can be a powerful way to combat racism, prejudice, and discrimination. Using curriculum intervention strategies to help students develop, clarify, and reconsider their values and relate them to their understanding of ethnicity and cultural identity can increase their efficacy for interpersonal and intercultural group interactions. Since most of the studies reviewed by Banks were published in the 1960s and 1970s, he recommended that more current studies on the effects of curriculum interventions on racial gender role attitudes be conducted and they be more carefully designed. My doctoral students are pursuing such studies (e.g., Cooper, 1997).

Gay's (1991) review of research studies on the interaction of cultural diversity and learning addressed how studies of cultural diversity and the specific concerns of social studies educators can come together to make social studies *challenging* for culturally diverse students. Gay found that research on cultural diversity shows that (a) mismatches in the structural and procedural elements of teaching and learning can have negative effects on the academic achievement of culturally diverse students, (b) cultural discontinuities appear across the full range of teaching and learning interactions, (c) discontinuities between culturally different students and classroom teachers are especially evident in verbal interactions, and (d) ethnic minority and poverty disadvantaged students have to develop social and academic competence in order to succeed in school.

Social studies that is multicultural and approaches teaching and learning in meaningful, integrative, values-based, and challenging ways can only empower students to help build their social action skills while reaffirming equity and excellence, the basic right of education, and universal literacy. The following case of a multicultural teacher education project involving third grade students and teachers at a southeastern elementary school illustrates these points as they apply to the benefits of involving local cultures and students' ethnic identities.

A few years ago a colleague and I conducted a study of the impact of multicultural education on student achievement and motivation and teachers' ways of thinking about content and pedagogy. The study was carried out in collaboration with a Chapter I school that served students from African American, European American, Hispanic, and Native American heritages. At the time of the study, the student population was 92% ethnic minority and 8% White. Students and teachers from the four third grade classes at the school were selected to participate in the study that had three stages: (a) diagnosis of students' preferred learning styles, preassessment of student motivation and achievement, preassessment of teachers' thinking about content and pedagogy, preassessment of classroom curriculum and instruction; (b) intervention; and (c) post-assessments.

Students were interviewed, before and after the intervention, concerning their beliefs about their abilities to succeed in school. Teachers' lesson plans and student assignments were collected prior to and after the intervention. Information concerning the teachers' pre and post thinking about content and pedagogy was collected by way of concept maps. There were three treatment groups and one control group. One of the third grade teachers received both multicultural pedagogical and content treat-

Table 4.1. Synergistic Multicultural Model of Social Studies

NCSS (1993) Principles	NCSS (1992) Multicultural Education Guidelines	Banks (1999) Dimensions	Bennett's (1999) Goals	Gay's (1994) Themes
Meaningful	• Incorporated ethnic content and specific perspectives into all aspects of the curriculum • Utilizes instructional materials that treat racial, ethnic, and cultural differences and groups honestly, realistically, and sensitively • Offers a variety of materials on the histories, experiences, and cultures of many racial, ethnic, and cultural groups in libraries and resource centers	Content Integration	Multiple Perspectives	*Scholarly Truth* Education content and processes should incorporate culturally pluralistic contributions
Integrative	• Helps students identify and understand the value of conflicts inherent in a multicultural society • Helps students view and interpret events, situations, and conflict from diverse ethnic and cultural perspectives and points of view	Knowledge Construction	Strengthen Intercultural Competence Multiple Perspectives	*Scholarly Truth* Genuine search for truth is valid only if it includes cultural pluralism Conscience & Community Freedom, equality, and justice are applied to culturally pluralistic issues and experience

NCSS (1993) Principles	NCSS (1992) Multicultural Education Guidelines	Banks (1999) Dimensions	Bennett's (1999) Goals	Gray's (1994) Themes
Values-Based	• Helps students develop skills in clarifying and reconsidering their values and relating them to their understanding of ethnicity and cultural identity • Exhibits classrooms reflecting respect for and acceptance of ethnic and cultural differences • Helps students develop skills necessary for effective interpersonal and intercultural group interactions	Prejudice Reduction	Combat Racism, Prejudice, and Discrimination	*Conscience & Community* Community building requires knowing and valuing cultural diversity *Representation & Participation* Citizens combat racism and cultural hegemony Enfranchisement should be made available to oppressed and excluded groups *Equity & Excellence* Equity and excellence are impossible without sensitivity to cultural diversity
Challenging	• Reflects culturally diverse learning styles of students in the school • Provides continuous opportunities for student development of better sense of self	Equity Pedagogy	Strengthen Cultural Consciousness	*Identity Development* Ethnic identity is a major part of personal competence for culturally diverse students *Equity & Excellence* Positive ethnic identities have positive effects on achievement of culturally diverse students *Holistic Teaching* Many individual competencies are culturally contextual

ments; one received the content treatment only; one received pedagogical treatment only; and one received no treatment at all. The pedagogical treatment consisted of a staff development institute focusing on ethnic identity development, learning styles, evaluating children's literature for racism and sexism, and culturally relevant teaching strategies. The content treatment consisted of work sessions in which the teachers and university teacher educators collaboratively developed a three-week social studies and language arts content-based unit. The intervention was implementation of the unit in two of the third grade classes. During the intervention period, all four classes were observed and lessons videotaped; teachers also kept anecdotal records and reflective journals.

The intervention, a three-week unit on "Celebrating Our Heroes and Sheroes," was based on the assumption that content and pedagogy relevant to the cultural experiences of the students would motivate them to want to achieve. Our goals were to (a) increase the use of materials that reflect racially and ethnically diverse children and adults engaged in positive situations; (b) strengthen children's cultural consciousness, especially knowledge about and understanding of their cultural identity; (c) integrate literature and social studies to teach to and about cultural diversity; and (d) develop the children's intercultural competence through cooperative learning and sharing of cultural experiences.

The unit had several impacts on the students. It did increase their achievement motivation. That is, during the implementation phase, students' beliefs about their abilities to succeed in school and their attitudes about their schoolwork became more positive. We found that the unit also changed the students' sense of values, especially regarding the definition of hero and shero. They realized that heroes and sheroes are people who make a difference in the quality of living for those around them. They came to understand that (a) they have personal heroes and sheroes in their family, school, and community; and (b) famous heroes and sheroes are not limited to athletes and entertainers, but include educators, scientists, politicians, and freedom fighters. The most joyful, affective impact was on the self-concept of the students. In studying personal heroes and sheroes, the students realized that they themselves had positive qualities and the potential to make a difference in someone else's life.

Aaron, a nine-year-old African American male, was a very moving illustration of this impact on the students' self-concept and ethnic identity development. During the pre-interview session Aaron was an intensely serious and seemingly troubled young man. He came into the interview room with a no-nonsense and quietly hostile demeanor. He was respectful, but obviously did not like answering the questions, especially those on the achievement motivation instrument that seemed to question his ability and integrity. His responses were curt and to the point. The few extended responses he gave dealt with having to use violence in order to survive both in and out of school. He explained to me how he was new to this school because he and his mom had recently moved. According to Aaron, they had moved from a housing project mainly because his mom was afraid that he was going to kill someone or be killed himself. Aaron was struggling with violence in his life and very sincerely trying to control his violent tendencies in school so that he "wouldn't get into trouble" and could finish his work. Finally toward the end of the interview, in an attempt to engage him on a more personal and positive level, I asked him what he wanted to do when he grew up. He thought about this for a moment or two, and then looking frowningly at the floor he told me "You know, Dr. Baber, I'd better go into the marines because then I could kill people and not get into any trouble." Five weeks later, I interviewed a completely different young man. In contrast to his previous passive-aggressive mode, he was very excited about talking to me. He even came into the room with a new walk (head held high instead of bowed down) and a big smile. He could not wait to tell me about his hero assignment completed during the unit. He had chosen to research George Washington Carver for his public hero report. He was verbose in explaining what he had found out about Dr. Carver. The most important fact to Aaron was that Dr. Carver had accomplished many positive things by the time he was fourteen years old. Aaron energetically listed young Carver's accomplishments, and then he said to me, "You know, Dr. Baber, I still have time to do some of those things!" I then shared how that same Dr. Carver had taught my paternal grandfather, a peanut farmer in rural Alabama, during cooperative extension farming activities at Tuskegee Institute. My credibility really rose in Aaron's eyes when I told him that I had taught in Tuskegee for two years and had actually walked the same trails Dr. Carver had enjoyed on his nature walks—in a reverently impassioned voice, Aaron told me, "you're so lucky!" This story never fails to help the pre-service and in-service teachers with whom I work to understand the powerful connection between academic achievement and students' cultural experiences and ethnic identities.

My concern for equity in education means that I must take seriously the challenge to teach teachers how to develop multicultural perspectives based on self-awareness, knowledge acquisition about cultural diversity, and pedagogical competencies in multicultural education. My social studies courses and professional development workshops have been designed to facilitate pre-service and in-service teachers in their study and application of appropriate teaching practices by way of content knowledge, higher level thinking skills, reflective practices, and research. I have infused a multicultural perspective by raising the teachers' awareness of multiple ways of perceiving, knowing, and doing at the national and international levels. I have also emphasized the complementary, synergistic relationship of multiculturalism and civic efficacy vis-à-vis democratic values and beliefs.

UNLEARNING LIBERALISM AND UNSILENCING RACE IN THE PROFESSION

As a teacher and teacher educator I believe I have made valuable contributions to the social studies profession through involvement in the dialogue about the role of multicultural education (MCE) in citizenship education. However, over the past five years I have come to the conclusion that MCE is limited as a framework for honest and sustained dialogue concerning the impact of race in our society and our schools due to its appropriation as a paradigm to end all social inequities. MCE scholars, researchers, and practitioners are not in agreement regarding the clarity and scope of its focus in terms of the boundaries of cultural diversity and multivocality. For example, Banks and Banks (2001]) present social class, religion, gender, race/ ethnicity, language, and exceptionality as the scope of multicultural education while Gollnick and Chinn (2002) add differences in age and sexual orientation to this list. In addition, practitioners have transmuted the critical pedagogy potential of MCE into "superficial and trivial 'celebrations of diversity'" (Ladson-Billings, 1999, p. 26). Such diffusion and transmutation has silenced race as a key concept in MCE, thereby limiting its effectiveness as an empowering, critical, and transformative vehicle for social justice in educational reform.

As Gloria Ladson-Billings points out in the introduction to this book, there have been corollary silences surrounding race in the social studies. Critical race theory (CRT) offers a way for the profession to develop and sustain a visible, vocal, and vigilant dialogue on race and racism. Such a dialogue is imperative in a field that purports to be the standard bearer for citizenship education. CRT asserts that race still matters in our society and analyses of citizenship must be done within the context of historical racial hegemony (Bell, 1992; Crenshaw, 1988; Delgado, 1995; Ladson-Billings & Tate, 1995). According to Torres (1998):

> Racism is so deeply ingrained in the United States that a rethinking of citizenship needs to incorporate systematic challenges to the practice of racism in the legal system and, by extension, in the school system. Given the magnitude of the task, there are no naïve assumptions that antiracist positions can be easily organized in a coalition to challenge prevailing racist structures, sentiments, and values. By putting the question of race first, critical race theorists argue that the discussion of citizenship can no longer be treated as a homogeneous identity in search of the exercise of rights and obligations. (p. 430)

As social educators, we must move from a homogenized view of *e pluribus unum* toward an understanding of racialization as it affects the profession. This involves (a) the recognition that Whiteness continues to be the normative standard for political and pedagogical decision-making and (b) the will to not just desegregate the profession by providing equal access, but to truly integrate it through "descontruction of oppressive structures and discourses ... and construction of equitable and socially just relations of power" (Ladson-Billings, 1999, p. 10).

I do not mean to imply that there have not been progressive efforts in NCSS. Development and approval of the (1992) MCE Guildelines was one such progressive moment. However, as critical race theorists would point out, the MCE Guidelines were a manifestation of interest convergence rather than a transformation of NCSS. In addition, according to critical race theorists, times of progress are often followed by times of resistance and backlash with reassertion of White dominance (Taylor, 1999). So, while there may have been unity in diversity in developing the MCE Guidelines, when it came time to move from a theory of social justice to taking action and making full citizenship a reality for people of color vis-à-vis the 1998 meeting, "things fell apart."

Dinkelman (2001) describes what he calls two contemporary crosscurrents in social studies: conservative restorationists who are like a battering ram and radical/critical theorists (including CRT) who are like a whisper. The conservative restorationists certainly seemed to be in control at the 1997 CUFA business meeting. At the 1998 NCSS meeting, the whisper of CRT emerged with two young African American scholars in the forefront of leadership. Cynthia Tyson and Tyron Howard joined with Sue Noffke and other critical catalysts in establishing the CUFA Social Justice Committee at the 1998 NCSS annual meeting in Anaheim. In 2000, the Committee began sponsoring sessions and a Town Meeting at the NCSS annual meetings.

I returned to NCSS in 2001, attending the 2001 and 2002 Town Meetings sponsored by the Social Justice Committee. While the events were encouraging in that race and racism were explicitly discussed, the commitment to ending overt and subtle forms of racism remained at the theoretical and reflective levels. At neither meetings, however, were there actions taken related to social justice issues in the local schools of Washington, DC (2001) or Phoenix, Arizona (2002). My hope lies in the idea that reflective inquiry is both a pedagogical action and an antecedent to political action. Social studies educators who operate from a CRT paradigm are already bringing change to the scholarship of the profession by including not only their stories, but also the stories of the teachers and P–12 students with whom they work. They are reconstructing the social studies content and pedagogical knowledge bases. They are creating a new generation of scholars who are well grounded in CRT in order to institutionalize and continuously build these knowledge bases. They are challenging their White colleagues to reevaluate whiteness as the normative standard for inquiry and teaching.

In reflecting on my almost thirty years as a social studies educator, I realize that I have been consistently concerned with excellence and equity in education for students of color. Even within the constraints of a liberal multicultural perspective, I knew that race still mattered very much in our society and schools. Although I am still philosophically committed to an ideology of inclusivity, I now know that race must remain first in my research efforts. I also know that CRT will become an integral part of my teaching, inquiry, and scholar-activist efforts. CRT has, in fact, given me the framework and energy with which to re-engage my NCSS and CUFA colleagues in honest and sustained dialogue concerning the impact of race in our society, our schools, and our profession. Without this dialogue, social studies as a leading architect of social justice through emancipatory, liberatory, critical, and transformative pedagogy will remain an unfulfilled expectation of excellence.

> The struggle is about whether education is for social transformation or system maintenance. Through self-affirming resistance these teachers are choosing education for personal and social emancipation for their students. (King, 1991)

REFERENCES

Baber, C.R. (1993). An inclusionary pedagogy for ethnic minority adolescents. *Transescence, 21*(2), 5–14.

Baber, C.R. (1995). Leaders of color as catalysts for community building in a multicultural society. *Theory and Research in Social Education, 23*(4), 342–354.

Baber, C.R. (1997, Fall). 1994 CUFA resolution on proposition 187: Actualizing our moral imperative as social educators. *CUFA News*, 1.

Baber, C.R. (2000). Multicultural education. In A.E. Kazdin (Ed.), *Encyclopedia of Psychology* (pp. 0944–1-0944–14). New York: American Psychological Association and Oxford University Press.

Banks, J.A. (1991). Multicultural education: Its effects on students' racial and gender role attitudes. In J.P. Shaver (Ed.), *Handbook of research on social studies teaching and learning* (pp. 459–469). New York: Macmillan.

Banks, J.A. (1999). *An introduction to multicultural education* (2nd ed.). Boston: Allyn & Bacon.

Banks, J.A., & Banks, C.A.M. (2001). *Multicultural education: Issues and perspectives* (4th ed.). New York: Wiley.

Beal, F. (1970). Double jeopardy: To be black and female. In T. Cade (Ed.), *The Black woman* (pp. 90–100). New York: New American Library.

Bell, D. (1992). *Faces at the bottom of the well: The permanence of racism.* New York: Basic Books.

Bennett, C.I. (1999). *Comprehensive multicultural education: Theory and practice* (4th ed.). Boston: Allyn & Bacon.

Cooper, J.E. (1997). *"I want to be like me": An Ethnographic study of factors affecting ethnic identity development in contemporary African American adolescents.* Unpublished doctoral dissertation, University of North Carolina, Greensboro.

Cornbleth, C., & Waugh, D. (1995). *The great speckled bird: Multicultural politics and education policymaking.* New York: St. Martin's Press.

Crenshaw, K. (1988). Race, reform, and retrenchment: Transformation and legitimation in antidiscrimination law. *Harvard Law Review, 101*(7), 1331–1387.

Crichlow, W., Goodwin, S., Shakes, G., & Swartz, E. (1990). Multicultural ways of knowing: Implications for practice. *Journal of Education, 172*(2), 101–117.

Davidman, L., & Davidman, P.T. (2001). *Teaching with a multicultural perspective: A practical* guide (3rd ed.). New York: Longman.

Delgado, R. (Ed.). (1995). *Critical race theory: The cutting edge.* Philadelphia: Temple University.

Dinkelman, T. (2001, November). *Dewey, democracy, and social studies—when will we ever learn?* Paper presented at the meeting of the National Council for the Social Studies, Washington, D.C.

Federal Glass Ceiling Commission. (1995). *Good for business: Making full use of the nation's human capital.* Washington, DC: U.S. Department of Labor.

Gay, G. (1991). Culturally diverse students and social studies. In J.P. Shaver (Ed.), *Handbook of research on social studies teaching and learning* (pp. 144–156). New York: Macmillan.

Gay, G. (1994). *At the essence of learning: Multicultural education.* West Lafayette, IN: Kappa Delta Pi.

Giddings, P. (1984). *When and where I enter: The impact of Black women on race and sex in America.* Toronto: Bantam.

Gollnick, D.M. & Chinn, P.C. (2002). *Multicultural education in a pluralistic society* (6th ed.). Upper Saddle River, NJ: Merrill Prentice-Hall.

Greene, M. (1993). The passions of pluralism: Multiculturalism and the expanding community. *Educational Researcher, 22*(1), 13–18.

Jones, J. (1985). *Labor of love, labor of sorrow: Black women, work, and the family from slavery to the present.* New York: Basic Books.

King, D.K. (1988, Autumn). Multiple jeopardy, multiple consciousness: The context of a Black feminist ideology. *Signs, 14*, 42–72.

King, J.E. (1991). Unfinished business: Black students alienation and Black teachers' emancipation. In M. Foster (Ed.), *Readings on equal education: Volume 11. Qualitative investigations into schools and schooling* (pp. 245–271). New York: AMS Press.

Ladner, J. (1972). *Tomorrow's tomorrow: The Black woman.* New York: Doubleday.

Ladson-Billings, G. (1995). Toward a theory of culturally relevant pedagogy. *American Educational Research Journal, 32*(3), 465–91.

Ladson-Billings, G. (1999). Just what is critical race theory, and what's it doing in a nice field like education? In L. Parker, D. Deyhle, & S. Villenas (Eds.), *Race is. . . race isn't: Critical race theory and qualitative studies in education* (pp. 31–52). Boulder, CO: Westview.

Ladson-Billings, G., & Henry, A. (1990). Blurring the borders: Voices of African liberatory pedagogy in the United States and Canada. *Journal of Education, 172*(2), 72–87.

Ladson-Billings, G., & Tate, W.F. (1995). Toward a critical race theory of education. *Teachers College Record, 97*(1), 47–68.

Marshall, P., & Bennett, C.T. (1994). Social studies that is multicultural: Toward enhancing teaching about diversity. In A. Lockledge, R. Smith, & C.R. Baber (Eds.), *Teaching about diversity* (pp. 18–24). Graham, NC: North Carolina Council for the Social Studies.

McCarthy, C. (1993). After the canon: Knowledge and ideological representation in the multicultural discourse on curriculum reform. In C. McCarthy & W. Crichlow (Eds.), *Race identity and representation in education* (pp. 289–305). New York: Routledge.

Morrison, T. (1971, August 22). What the Black woman thinks about women's lib. *New York Times Magazine*, 14–15,63–64, 66.

National Council for the Social Studies Task Force on Ethnic Studies Curriculum Guidelines. (1992). Curriculum guidelines for multicultural education. *Social Education, 56*(5), 274–294.

National Council for the Social Studies Task Force on Standards for Teaching and Learning in the Social Studies. (1993). A vision of powerful teaching and learning in the social studies: Building social understanding and civic efficacy. *Social Education, 57*(5), 213–223.

National Council for the Social Studies Task Force on Standards for Teaching and Learning in the Social Studies. (1994). *Expectations of excellence: Curriculum standards for social studies.* Washington, DC: NCSS.

Nelson, J.L. (1991). Communities, local to national, as influences on social studies education. In J.P. Shaver (Ed.), *Handbook of research on social studies teaching and learning* (pp. 332–341). New York: Macmillan.

Nieto, S. (2000). *Affirming diversity: The sociopolitical context of multicultural education* (3rd ed.). New York: Longman.

Passe, J. (1997, Spring). More on CUFA's resolution to boycott the NCSS California meeting. *CUFA News*, 4.

Sanchez-Huchs, J.V. (1997). Jeopardy not bonus status for African American women in the work force: Why does the myth of advantage persist? *American Journal of Community Psychology, 25*(5), 565–580.

Sokoloff, N.J. (1992). *Black women and white women in the professions.* New York: Routledge.

Torres, C.A. (1998). Democracy, education, and multiculturalism: Dilemmas of citizenship in a global world. *Comparative Education Review, 42*(4), 421–447.

Woodson, C.G. (1969). *Mis-education of the Negro.* Washington, DC: Associated Publishers [Original work published in 1933].

part II

THE POLICIES

CHAPTER 5

THE PERSISTENT DERACIALIZATION OF THE AGENDA FOR DEMOCRATIC CITIZENSHIP EDUCATION

Twenty Years of Rhetoric and Unreality in Social Studies Position Statements

Patricia L. Marshall

ABSTRACT

This chapter examines NCSS policy over the twenty-year period since issuance of the National Commission on Excellence in Education report *A Nation at Risk*. Central concepts from critical race theory are used to illuminate ways NCSS has employed obfuscating diversity phrasing in its position statements and thereby deracialized the organization's agenda for democratic citizenship education. The author concludes by urging NCSS to abandon its race-aversion stance in order to promote a vibrant agenda for citizenship education that is in sync with the racialized realities of life in the United States.

Critical Race Theory Perspectives on the Social Studies, pages 71–97

INTRODUCTION

We are amazed but not amused
by all the things you say that you'll do.
Though much concerned but not involved
with decisions that are made by you.
But we are sick and tired of hearing your song,
tellin' how you are gonna change right from wrong
'Cause if you really want to hear our views,
you haven't done nothin'.
                                                    —S. Wonder

The *raison d'être* of social studies in U.S. schools is citizenship education for life in our representative democracy (National Council for the Social Studies, 1994; Shaver, 1996). Nevertheless, despite a long-standing identification with and embracement of this laudable goal, the National Council for the Social Studies (NCSS) has maintained a curious disengagement from the one aspect of U.S. citizenship that at once is its most enduring and its most disquieting. This is to say, since the formation of the republic the very notion of citizenship has been inextricably linked to the unrealities surrounding the reality that is race in America[1]. So conflicting is the actuality of race that it has been described thusly, "[r]ace is neither an essence nor an illusion, but rather an ongoing, contradictory, self-reinforcing, plastic process subject to the macro forces of social and political struggle and the micro effects of daily decision" (Haney López, 2000a, p. 165). Since the time of the Founding Fathers, politicians, jurists, and scholars alike have debated the nature of U.S. citizenship and the manners in which race (and by extension racism) has dictated to whom its fullest privileges will be extended (Haney López, 2000b; Harris, 1993; Omi & Winant, 1994; Wilkins, 2001). Still, this multifaceted and often contentious debate largely has gone unremarked in the policies of the NCSS as represented by its official position statements. Put differently, NCSS has persistently promoted a deracialized agenda for citizenship education that is both monotonous and impotent. A question that looms large is *what is the nature of the issues that have absorbed the attention of NCSS, and thereby permitted the organization to avoid substantive engagement with race and racism?* In this chapter I respond to this question by using concepts from critical race theory to analyze NCSS position statements produced over the 20-year period since issuance of the education reform proposal *A Nation at Risk*. I conclude with suggestions for next steps NCSS leadership can take to speak directly to the persistent reality of race and racism on the agenda for democratic citizenship education in our culturally diverse society.

EDUCATIONAL REFORM, COLOR-CODING, AND THE NCSS MISSED OPPORTUNITY

Schools have long been sites for reform measures initiated by entities within as well as beyond the education establishment. Many of these would-be reforms (e.g., voucher plans, increased graduation requirements) highlight issues that are significant to many; yet if implemented, would promote the genuine interests of a few (Berliner & Biddle, 1995). Under such circumstances, advances that ostensibly would be directed at lower status groups would be realized only to the extent that they also promote (or at least, do not conflict with) the interests of higher status groups. Pioneering critical race theorist and legal scholar Derrick A. Bell coined the phrase "interest convergence" to describe this phenomenon (Bell, 1995). It captures succinctly the essence of the inherently inequitable interaction between empowered and oppressed groups in the United States as experienced across all spheres of life including the social, economic, political, legal, and educational.

The reality of interest convergence makes it not at all surprising that within the educational sphere, the most radical reform proposals have claimed to champion unassailable yet imprecise goals such as "preparing students for effective citizenship in our democratic society." Indeed, one of the more brazen acknowledgments of this goal for an education reform proposal came in April 1983 when the National Commission on Excellence in Education[2] issued its open letter to the American people in the report *A Nation at Risk: The Imperative for Educational Reform*. Therein the Commission judged the quality of education in the United States (i.e., substance of student learning, curriculum content, and teaching quality) to be so abysmal that the economic, military, and political well-being of the nation itself was in jeopardy. Moreover, it described how the exceedingly poor condition of the teaching-learning process is rendering American high school students woefully unprepared for the role of citizen in our technologically advanced democratic society. Comparisons in educational achievement between U.S. students and those in other industrialized nations are cited in the report with *non-Americans* being characterized as "determined, well-educated, and strongly motivated competitors" (National Commission on Excellence in Education, 1983, p. 2). The report concludes with special messages to parents and to students that outline the responsibilities each must assume in order to make a personal commitment to high quality education.

To be sure, *A Nation at Risk* received accolades for its back-to-basics focus as well as its aim to *re-institute* standards of excellence in schools.[3] It also received high praise for its undergirding twin themes of patriotism and citizenship education. An especially intriguing statement in the report came in the form of a recommendation to increase graduation requirements such that all high school students would complete "3 years of social studies." Describing the educational outcomes for this particular recommendation, the Commission explained,

> The teaching of social studies ... should be designed to enable students to fix their places and possibilities within the larger social and cultural structure; to understand the broad sweep of ideas that shape and animate our economic, political, and social environment; and to grasp the difference between free and repressive societies. An understanding of each of these areas is requisite to the informed exercise of *citizenship* [italics added] in a free society. (p. 20)

Furthermore, the Commission acknowledged the work of professional organizations and offered the following statement of support for efforts undertaken to promote high quality education.

> We encourage the continuation of efforts by groups such as the American Chemical Society, the American Association for the Advancement of Science, the Modern Language Association, and the National Councils of Teachers of English and Teachers of Mathematics, to revise, update, improve, and make available new and more diverse curricular materials. We applaud such efforts, where consortia of educators and scientific, industrial, and scholarly societies cooperate to improve the school curriculum. (p. 21)

The *National Council for the Social Studies* is conspicuously absent from the list of professional education organizations receiving commendation from the Commission. This omission seems especially egregious in light of the report's patriotism and citizenship education emphases.

Partisanship and Color-Coding.   Although *A Nation at Risk* was applauded by some, to a great extent it represented little more than a politically-inspired education manifesto. The Commission had used xenophobia and citizenship education as thinly-veiled justifications to de-emphasize and eventually discontinue much needed compensatory education programs that had been instituted in prior years for African Americans and other students from low status groups. This trashing of the barely ripened educational fruits of civil rights legislation was coupled with a campaign to introduce what amounted to an elitist agenda to the nation's public schools. And that agenda was cloaked in alarmist patriotic hyperbole. If fully implemented, the Commission's recommendations clearly would have served the interests of the upper economic segments of the population. But according to the Commission, *A Nation at Risk* represented a nonpartisan analysis of and perspective on the overall quality of high school education. The report was bereft of ideas for how education would be improved for the hoards of failing and underachieving students of color in the nation's schools. Yet, its recommendations to increase high school graduation requirements and add rigor to curriculum content were purportedly directed at *all* students (not just upper economic Americans) and thereby, beneficial to the entire nation. This claim of neutrality and inclusiveness was offered by the Commission even as the nation witnessed a "rising tide" of social and political conservatism.

For example, a prominent feature of the 1980s era was the emergence of a bevy of jingoistic slogans that held enormous appeal for certain segments of the population. Emerging as they did in the age of *Rambo*[4], 1980s-era slogans such as "America, love it or leave it;" "born in the U.S.A."[5] and "a bushel of wheat for a barrel of oil" promoted the attitude that the U.S. government would be justified in undertaking whatever actions it deemed necessary to secure and protect the rights and privileges of American citizenry. For many, these actions necessarily included solidifying the nation's economic, political, and military dominance on a global scale; whereas for others it meant reconfiguring the domestic sociopolitical landscape. Therefore, accompanying these supposedly patriotic slogans was a pronounced retreat from the 1960s civil rights focus. The nation was being primed for what some of its citizens perceived to be a *necessary* re-emergence of the traditional race-dictates-rights climate. And in that climate racial group status determines how fully one enjoys both the rights and privileges that accompany citizenship including high quality education. Scholars report that many of the policies and legal statutes that emerged during the 1980s were explicitly aimed at reversing those instituted during the comparatively liberal era of the 1960s (Bell, 1995/2000; Crenshaw, 1995; Marable, 2000).

Although patriotic slogans were a prominent feature of the 1980s era, the retreat from civil rights legislation (which in many cases had successfully championed basic citizenship rights for America's lowest status groups) was buttressed by widespread use of racial code words that also gained popularity. Among the most frequently used code words were: *quotas, set-asides, color-blindness, Affirmative Action, reverse discrimination,* and *welfare queen.* When employed by prominent politicians, spin meisters, and media commentators code words were nothing short of magical in their ability to facilitate racial bonding and nostalgic longing for a bygone era among social and political conservatives. More important, code words were enormously valuable as psychological scaffolding for users' claims of racial innocence and victimhood in regard to what was perceived as the "repercussions" of civil rights legislation aimed at righting historical inequities in such fields as education. In fact, codeword usage in the public sphere had already provided inestimable support for the massive change in educational policy that resulted from the Supreme Court decision years prior in the case of *Regents of the University of California v. Bakke*[6] (Ross, 1990/2000). Thus, the Commission's claims of political neutrality and inclusiveness notwithstanding, the volatile combination of a Rambo-esque sociopolitical climate and the proliferation of racial code words provided an indisputably powerful backdrop for critics to question the intentions of the Commission as well as the sincerity of its recommendations. This is especially so in light of the fact that *A Nation at Risk* omitted any mention of the nature of inequity in the nation's public schools. Similarly, it failed to address the continuing impact of race and racism on the extension of full rights and privileges of citizenship to *all* Americans.

It can almost go without saying that the 1980s-era presented an opportune time for professional education organizations to commission their own policies and position statements on race and racism in U.S. society in general, and the schooling process in particular. Indeed, NCSS might have issued such a statement if for no other reason than to respond to the Commission's silence on the topic as well as its appropriation of the citizenship education agenda. Yet a review of position statements issued during the 1980s and since reveals that NCSS has remained mute on the issues of race, racism, and the continuing deleterious impact of both on education, and ultimately citizenship. All the same, NCSS did mention the report in a 1983 position statement, *Essential Characteristics of a Citizenship Education Program*. Therein it characterized the Commission's insinuation that citizenship education should become a new focus of social studies curricula as "recent rhetoric."

A Missed Opportunity to Append the Open Letter.   *A Nation at Risk* is one of the most (if not *the* most) significant, albeit flawed, analyses of the state of U.S. pre-collegiate education to emerge in the last half of the 20th century. This is especially apparent when the substance of the report is viewed from the vantage point of social studies. On the one hand, the Commission's recommendations for the content areas of English, Mathematics, and even Computer Science can be seen as representing its effort to draw attention to the expanding knowledge base for high school curricula. Yet the close association it insisted upon forging between high quality education and patriotism should have been interpreted as a compelling, if awkward, opportunity for social studies educators[7] to append the Commission's open letter to the nation.

Although clearly not its intention, the Commission inadvertently had extended an invitation to social studies educators to engage in a national assessment of the state of the agenda for democratic citizenship education. For their part, social studies educators should have introduced critical insights to the assessment by spotlighting the tripartite national pathology and exposing its impact on the nation's schools. This tripartite national pathology, made glaringly apparent in the 1980s sociopolitical climate, consisted of a racist past, intermittent efforts to deracialize the present, and a quest for globalization in an age of increasing global interdependence. In other words, *A Nation at Risk* can be understood as having laid bare the urgency for social studies educators to pose a number of critical questions about the preparation of youths for the role of citizen in the 1980s and beyond. And in light of the economic and sociopolitical shifts in the larger society of that era, foremost among these questions should have been, "what form [is] racism tak[ing] in ... education and how are these forms [being] used to maintain the subordination of Students of Color?" (Solórzano, 1997, p. 8). It can even be suggested that the Commission itself made explicit the impending outlook for a nation that neglects this complex though necessary exploration of the state of its schools vis-à-vis the education of its most vulnerable future citizens. Thus, the report presented an unusual opportunity for social studies educators to proffer leadership to the education profession and perhaps, the nation as a whole.

Clearly, *A Nation at Risk* was an incomplete open letter to the American people in that the Commission failed to examine the most intractable problems that have long diminished the quality of education in the nation's schools. Foremost among these problems are racism and poverty and the unequal opportunities and outcomes they engender. The simple fact is historically, these problems have rendered citizenship education little more than meaningless rhetoric and unreality for many youths from low-status cultural groups including African Americans, Native Americans, and many segments of the Latino/a population. Poor White Americans too have been fatalities even though many have been content to stave off an imagined racial enemy while relishing skin color privileges and related property rights (Bell, 1995/2000; Harris, 1993). The mere presence of racial "others" continues to leave many poor Whites oblivious to the fact that the schooling they receive renders them ill-equipped to exploit fully the rights and privileges of American citizenship (Pinar, 1993; Weis, 1990; Weis & Fine, 1996).

It is conceivable that if NCSS had acted by "appending" the Commission's open letter, its contributions could have represented important professional, ethical, and moral direction for social studies educators whose responsibility it is to bring meaning to citizenship education. But NCSS did not append the letter; instead, it issued a collection of documents that focused on what might be termed obfuscating particulars. This reluctance made NCSS a duplicitous partner with the Commission in perpetuating the silences surrounding racism and its deleterious impact on the democratic citizenship education agenda. In the next sections I examine the nature of the particulars that have absorbed the attention of NCSS as revealed in its position statements issued in the twenty years since *A Nation at Risk*.

A GLIMPSE AT NCSS VIEWPOINTS ON THE ISSUES

Scholars are wont to look to policies and/or position statements to acquire understanding of and appreciation for the basic tenets or tendencies of their professional organizations. Not only do such statements provide background information on the organization's formation, but they provide insights into matters the organization supports and defends as well as the reasons for its continued existence. Although the terms *policy statement* and *position statement* often are used interchangeably, for the purposes of this discussion they are differentiated on the basis of what, in my experience, has represented their scope and function. Typically an organization's policy statements are densely written declarations intended to outline the broad-based principles upon which the organization was established and under which it currently operates. Conversely, position statements focus on specific matters of significance to the organization, and they may or may not be dictated by the larger legal, sociopolitical, and/or economic contexts in which the organization exists and functions. As such, position statements tend to present an unequivocal articulation of the organization's official stand on a particular issue, concern, or even event. The aim of a position statement is to present the stand or viewpoint of the leadership of an organization (if not the collective voice of its membership) therefore, its language should be patent rather than obfuscating. Indeed, many scholars look to position statements for insight on the nature of the action an organization will undertake in the event that its official stand on a particular matter is infringed upon or violated outright. Thus, the official stand an organization assumes and defends in a given position statement may touch upon any or all of several dimensions including the ethical, legal, sociopolitical, moral, and even epistemological.

The Council Takes Positions.   Since 1983 the Board of Directors of the NCSS has approved and made available to the membership some nineteen documents representing the organization's official stand or position (see Table 5.1)[8] on a myriad of topics. Among these are microcomputer courseware, religion, testing and evaluation, ability grouping, service-learning, and commercial news in the classroom. Some of the documents include the phrase "position statement" in the title or introductory description (e.g., Position Statement on Interdisciplinary Learning, Pre-K-Grade 4; Service-Learning: An Essential Component of Citizenship Education; Creating Effective Citizens; NCSS Guidelines and Principles for Student Government); whereas others do not (e.g., Social Studies Microcomputer Courseware Evaluation; Study About Religions in the Social Studies Curriculum, Curriculum Guidelines for Multicultural Education). Also, the documents were prepared by different groups within the NCSS organizational structure including *standing committees* (e.g., Citizenship Committee; Select

Citizenship Subcommittee; Elementary/Early Childhood Education Committee; Religion in Schools Committee; Curriculum Committee); *task forces*
(e.g., Task Force on Ethnic Studies; Task Force on Standards for Teaching
and Learning in the Social Studies; Task Force on Character Education in
the Social Studies; Task Force on Revitalizing Citizenship Education) ad
hoc committees (e.g., Committee on Computer Courseware Evaluation
Guidelines; Committee on Ability Grouping); and the *NCSS administration*
itself (e.g., Policy on Commercial News Programs in the Classroom; Columbian Quincentenary; Testing and Evaluation). Thus, over the last twenty
years preparation of position statements for NCSS has been undertaken by
an array of entities within its membership.[9] Even so, there is a glaring omission in the statements in relation to the democratic citizenship education
agenda.

**Table 5.1.   National Council for the Social Studies Policy
and Position Statements 1983-2002**

1983	• Social Studies Microcomputer Courseware Evaluation • Essential Characteristics of A Citizenship Education Program
1984	• Social Studies for Young Children • Study About Religions in the Social Studies Curriculum
1989	• Teaching About Science, Technology, and Society in Social Studies: Education for Citizenship in the 21st Century • Citizenship Education of New Americans
1990	• Policy on Commercial Needs News Programs in the Classroom • Revised Code of Ethics for the Social Studies Profession*
1991	• The Columbian Quincentenary: An Educational Opportunity • Testing and Evaluation of Social Studies Students • Curriculum Guidelines for Multicultural Education*
1992	• Ability Grouping in Social Studies • A Vision of Powerful Teaching and Learning in the Social Studies: Building Social Understanding and Civic Efficacy
1994	• Position Statement on Interdisciplinary Learning, Pre-K-Grade 4
1996	• Fostering Civic Virtue: Character Education in the Social Studies
1999	• NCSS Principles for Corporate Involvement in the Schools
2000	• NCSS Guidelines and Principles for Student Government • Service-Learning: An Essential Component of Citizenship Education
2001	• Creating Effective Citizens

*These position/policy statements were originally issued prior to the 1983 issuance of *A
Nation At Risk* and were revised subsequent to that time.

Specifically, in the twenty years since *A Nation at Risk* was presented to the American people, NCSS has issued no position statement focusing on or alluding to either race or racism as a specific topic of impact or significance in citizenship education. In fact, of the nineteen position statements that have been issued, (five of which include *citizen* or *citizenship* in the titles) twelve do not even mention the word *race* or its variations and related concepts such as raced, racial, racism, racialism, racialized and so on. Not only has NCSS not issued a position statement on the topic of race in relation to its citizenship education agenda, but the organization has not issued a statement on the impact of race and racism on *any* aspect of the social studies. Such an omission is highly problematic in light of the centrality of race in American life. Not surprisingly, however, the Task Force on Ethnic Studies which formulated the *Curriculum Guidelines for Multicultural Education* (first issued in 1976 and later revised in 1991), recognized this problem by acknowledging the omission in its own work. The Task Force offered the following explanation:

> We rarely used the term race in the first edition, perhaps because of our vain hope that silence would facilitate racism's disappearance. The ugly racial incidents that have occurred in our society ... since the guidelines were first published have eroded our hope that racism would dry up like a raisin in the sun. Racism is cyclic, and is alive and well today.... (p. 2)

Despite its *mea culpa*, the Ethnic Studies Task Force's revised version of the guidelines still does not constitute a position statement on the impact of race and racism on social studies education. For example, the second version does not explore the anatomy of racism and its conscious and unconscious dimensions. Solóranzo (1997) in discussing the implications of critical race theory for teacher education advised "[n]ot only do we need to discuss the racial macroaggressions such as public or overt racial stereotypes, attitudes, and behaviors, but we also need to listen [to], understand, and analyze racial microaggressions..." (p. 11). While macroaggressions by their very nature constitute conscious and thereby deliberate racist abuses, microaggressions manifest on the unconscious or subconscious level. Pierce, Carew, Pierce-Gonzalez and Willis (as cited in Solórzano, 1998) defined racist microaggressions as:

> the chief vehicle for proracist behaviors.... These are subtle, stunning, often automatic, and non-verbal exchanges which are 'putdowns' of blacks by offenders. The offensive mechanisms used against blacks are often innocuous. The cumulative weight of their never-ending burden is the major ingredient in black-white interactions. (p. 124)

Similarly, Davis (1989/2000) explained microaggressions as "...acts of disregard that stem from unconscious attitudes of white superiority and constitute a verification of black inferiority" (p. 149). Version two of the *Curriculum Guidelines for Multicultural Education* says nothing about the nature of racist microaggression students as well as teachers of color continue to encounter in schools and that diminish the experience for all. Neither do the Guidelines touch upon the implications macro- and microaggressions present for the integrity of the democratic citizenship education agenda. To its credit the Task Force does discuss the importance of continuous staff development and cultural diversity among school staff; yet no discussion is included on the myriad ways that racism manifests in schools or the often unconscious manners that school personnel, curriculum, policy, and community structures are complicit in perpetuating the devalued status of children and youth of color and the depleted quality of the education they receive.

Long-standing Silence on Issues of Import.   At this point it should be noted that while this discussion focuses on the silence in NCSS surrounding the issues of race and racism on the citizenship education agenda, social studies scholars have acknowledged the reticence of the organization to deal with issues (writ large) of widespread import and significance. For instance, Nelson and Fernekes (1996) highlighted the sheer caginess exhibited by NCSS in regard to the connections between its citizenship education agenda and the 1960s civil rights movement. They reported,

> NCSS ... largely ignored the civil rights movement and in the process demonstrated indifference toward a social crises of immense significance, one that challenged the very basis of democratic institutions and posed difficult questions for educators who daily had to confront the gap between stated ideals and social experience. (p. 98)

Garcia and Buendia (1996) pointed to the "...general characteristics of the membership—their topical background, academic training, and place of employment..." (p. 60) as a possible explanation for organizational silence on issues of significance to minority populations. In other words, the dis-ease NCSS presents when it comes to taking a stand on issues that subvert and pervert the democratic citizenship education agenda may well be attributed to the sociopolitical leanings of the people who comprise the organization. In sum, these discussions reveal that the long-standing disinclination within NCSS to address "matters of great moment" (Davis, 1996, p. iii) has been recognized and explanations for this unfortunate state of affairs have been proffered.

Still, the persistent *deracialization* of the agenda for citizenship education represents a different sort of reluctance within the organization to deal with issues of import. Furthermore, a rather disturbing irony within NCSS is that in the midst of its disengagement with race and racism, the organization has maintained a mantra-like recognition of the multiethnic and multi-cultural character of contemporary society, schools, and the students therein. With only a few exceptions, each of the organizational position statements listed in Table 5.1 includes "diversity phrasing" in the form of insertions related to the contributions of diverse groups, tolerance and respect for diversity, or some similar sentiment. In other words, the ubiquitous attention given to the amorphous issue that is "diversity," however inadvertently, may well be functioning to deracialize the citizenship education agenda.

The diversity phrasing inserted in NCSS position statements and the organizational sensitivity it is meant to convey are not dissimilar to that which in recent years has been common across any number of private organizations and public sphere entities. As such, it seems an analytic framework that takes into account the broad rather particularistic sociopolitical context in which such diversity phrasing is generated would be most useful in understanding how it serves to obfuscate the more critical issues of race and racism. Specifically, examining the nature of issues that have prevented NCSS from putting forth a dynamic agenda for citizenship education might be best understood by examining manners in which this same type of race-aversion manifests in parallel venues. A number of scholars have proposed that comparisons with the area of legal scholarship known as *critical race theory* can provide important insights into some of the more complicated issues facing contemporary educators (Lynn, 1999; Solóranzo, 1997, 1998; Tate, 1997). This is because critical race theory offers a perceptual lens through which to understand how, despite the endemic position of racism in the national identity, there is widespread aversion to engaging critically with its deleterious impact on various life spheres. Among other explanations for this phenomenon, critical race theorists hold that race and racism are often cloaked, ignored, and recast through various conscious and unconscious means.

WHY RACE DOESN'T SEEM TO MATTER IN THE CITIZENSHIP EDUCATION AGENDA

If there is any certainty about contemporary life in the United States, it is that race still matters (West, 1993). And because race still matters, racism is still alive and well. As part of an exploration of the prominence of race and racism in the American psyche, one scholar noted,

Americans share a common historical and cultural heritage in which racism has played and still plays a dominant role. Because of this shared experience, we also inevitably share many ideas, attitudes, and beliefs that attach significance to an individual's race and induce negative feelings and opinions about nonwhites. (Lawrence, 1995, p. 237)

Although the phrase itself (*race matters*) can seem almost trite due to the sheer frequency with which it is invoked, the work of scholars across various academic disciplines and professional fields attests to how the state of being raced in America affects all aspects of people's lives. Psychologists, for example, have demonstrated that the centrality of race results in Americans developing personal and group identities based on perceptions of a common heritage and set of experiences between ourselves and those with whom we share racial classification (Carter, 1997; Cross, 1994; Flores-Gonzales, 1999; Helms, 1993; Thompson & Carter, 1997). They have also examined the inhibiting impact of racial stereotyping on academic performance (Steele & Aronson, 1995). Sociologists and historians have described the dominance of race in the formation of the nation (Omi & Winant, 1994; Wilkins, 2001) and at critical periods in its history (Roediger, 1991). Legal professionals have established an entire scholarly focus (critical race theory) that among other things, illuminates how institutional racism grounded in white supremacy and nonwhite inferiority is reinforced and perpetuated at all levels of U.S. jurisprudence (Crenshaw, Gotanda, Peller, & Thomas, 1995; Delgado & Stefancic, 2000). And medical professionals have acknowledged that although race has little biological basis (Witzig, 1996), it influences the quality of health care patients receive (Bell & Hudson, 2001; De Lew & Weinick, 2000). Yet even though teacher education professionals have explored the impact of race on the teaching-learning process (Irvine, 1991; Ladson-Billings, 1994; Marshall, 2002), NCSS has been persistent in promoting a deracialized agenda for its work that suggests race does not matter. In other words, the organization is oblivious to the impact of race and racism on social studies education. Or is it?

The prominence of race in our society as well as persistent allusions to diversity and multiculturalism in NCSS position statements since *A Nation at Risk* makes it unlikely that obliviousness explains the long-standing organizational reluctance to address implications race and racism present for the work of social studies educators. Rather, it is the complex interplay of phenomena across various dimensions including social, psychological, economic, political, moral, ethical, and epistemological that can best explain this situation. Moreover, the silencing effect of race-aversion is not unique to social studies educators, but has been identified in other professional collectives (e.g., the legal profession) that have potential to challenge and resist the group dominance, privilege, perceptions of superiority, and innocence that are hinged on racial whiteness. It should be reiterated at this juncture, however, that the work of social studies educators focuses on citizenship education; and citizenship education is based on the highest ideals of U.S. society. For these reasons, the inertia within NCSS to formulate position statements that speak directly to the deleterious impact of race and racism on the citizenship education agenda is not only intolerable, but irresponsible.

There are a host of concepts from critical race theory that could be utilized to explain the race-aversion within NCSS. For the purposes of this discussion, however, the three that will be drawn upon are *color-blindness*, *process defect*, and *conscious intent*. Coupled with the impact of diversity phrasing, the following discussion will offer insights into possible roles these phenomena have played in the development of NCSS position statements and the persistent deracialization of the democratic citizenship education agenda.

Color-Blindness and Education for Citizenship. The concept of *color-blindness* is a very powerful one by which the reality of race and the impact of racism have been ignored, dismissed, and even recast into non-racial matters. In effect it holds that traits that speak to the content of one's character (rather than the illusive notion of race) should represent the basis of the analytic framework in explorations of individuals' rights and privileges in relation to public sphere entities such as government, law, and education. More important, color-blindness holds that except where individuals make it so, there is no particular specialness about race in the nation's social, political, or historical memory that suggests it (race) should be separated or singled out from other human traits in relation to *contemporary* matters. Put differently, racism is no more burdensome, urgent, or damaging than any other "ism" resulting from the ignorance, prejudice, and discrimination directed at one individual by another individual.

Legal scholars report that adherents to the notion of color-blindness exhibit uncritical acceptance of the Constitutional principle that "equal protection of the law" is extended to all Americans (Gotanda, 1995, p. 263). From the color-blind perceptual lens, claims of widespread racism are usually dismissed with "[t]he charge ... [itself] seen as egregious defamation ... carry[ing] an aura of irresponsibility" (Davis, 1989/2000, p. 141). Because race is considered an anachronism, introducing it into public sphere discourse is perceived by color-blindness adherents as irrelevant, contentious, and divisive (Crenshaw, et al., 1995; Peller, 1995). On the other hand, color-blindness appeals to those who would acknowledge the existence of prejudice and discrimination, yet discard race as an analytic framework in explorations of these phenomena. This preference to discard race represents a rejection of the essentialist[10] notion of "race as biology" and acceptance of race as a sociopolitical construct (Crenshaw, et al.,

1995). It also is intended to convey transcendence of the very notion of race. There is evidence to suggest that the principle of color-blindness in its various manifestations has operated as a sub-textual undercurrent in the development of NCSS position statements. And this adherence, whether resulting from the deliberate intentions of the NCSS leadership or mere happenstance, has served to make a direct, in-depth, exclusive focus on race and racism appears superfluous if not redundant. This is especially evident from the manner in which position statements have been conspicuously interspersed with diversity phrasing.

For instance, the 1983 statement *Social Studies Microcomputer Courseware Evaluation* includes insertions to highlight the importance of helping students "understand and appreciate cultural diversity throughout the world" (p. 1). Correspondingly, NCSS takes a stand on appropriate evaluation of microcomputer courseware by imploring social studies educators to ask "Does the course avoid bias and/or stereotyping with regard to gender, ethnicity, racial background, religious application, or cultural group?..." (p. 2). A follow-up point addresses "pervasive and enduring issues" by encouraging evaluators to ask "does the courseware focus on problems and/or issues that are socially significant?" (p. 2). From a critical race perspective, however, this latter point provokes the question, isn't *racism* a socially significant issue? Racism is clearly a socially significant issue, yet one is left to wonder how NCSS proposes evaluators respond to racism when it presents in the context of microcomputer software. Moreover, this position statement invites speculation about the actions (individual and collective) NCSS proposes should be undertaken in response to the perpetuation of racism through instructional software. No insights are offered. Rather, because this position statement examines microcomputer software evaluation from a color-blind perspective buttressed by diversity phrasing, questions about racism have no relevance. Indeed, they represent little more than irritating non-sequiturs.

Use of diversity phrasing to obfuscate race is also evident in the 1983 position statement *Essential Characteristics of a Citizenship Education Program.* There NCSS notes that one goal is to "provide opportunities for students to learn about and appreciate multicultural contributions to our civic heritage" (p. 2); whereas in its 1984 position statement, *Social Studies for Young Children,* it reports that children are expected to "acquire knowledge and understanding of the multiplicity of cultures within the society and the world and to recognize the contributions of each and to explore their value systems" (p. 2). Neither position statement mentions the word race, and from a color-blind perspective there is little reason either should. The color-blind perspective is manifest in the NCSS viewpoint despite the fact that research reveals young children develop perceptions about racial "others" at an early age (Banks, 1993). More disturbingly, this viewpoint prevails despite the fact that more than 200 years of American history has consistently demonstrated that race has always had a place in the discussion of "essential characteristics" of U.S. citizenship.

The 1984 position statement, *Study About Religions in the Social Studies Curriculum* not only ignores race by infusing diversity phrasing, but it also neglects to mention that religious adherence has been at the core of many conflicts between groups historically. The obligatory diversity phrasing is inserted as follows: "[k]nowledge of religion is not only a characteristic of an educated person but is absolutely necessary for understanding and living in a world of diversity" (p. 1). Additional diversity phrasing includes "study about religions should emphasize the necessity and importance of tolerance, respect, and mutual understanding in a nation and world of diversity" (p. 3). NCSS offers no insights on its position regarding how religion has been utilized to promote and sustain racist policy in the larger society. But again, drawing on the color-blind perspective the subject itself is clearly irrelevant. Nevertheless, in light of this example of race-aversion in relation to the study about religion in social studies, Malcolm X's oft-quoted adage warrants mentioning—"the most segregated hour in American life is high noon on Sunday" (Thorsen & Miles, 1989).

According to critical race theorists, part of the appeal of color-blindness is that it supports the viewpoint that race can be transcended thereby making allusions to it is pointless. Peller (1995) referred to this viewpoint as an "integrationist orientation" whereas Gotanda (1995) described it as "assimilationist" color-blindness. The outcome of both orientations is deracialization of phenomena by delegitimizing and devaluing the impact of race in "...the customs, beliefs, and intellectual and artistic traditions ... as well as institutions ... [of a non-white racial group]" (Gotanda, 1995, p. 269). Another tool in the arsenal of color-blind adherents, however, is the devaluation of race by presenting it as simply one among many other "equivalent ... forms of prejudice and discrimination based on irrational stereotype" (Peller, 1995, p. 130).

Evidence of the "equivalent forms" of prejudice color-blindness orientation is apparent in the 1990 *Revised Code of Ethics for the Social Studies Profession*. There, race is equated with other diversity forms in the following phrasing: "Social studies professionals should respect the dignity and integrity of every student regardless of color, race, creed, sex, sexual orientation, ethnic background, handicap condition, or socioeconomic level, and should help each student to achieve effective citizenship" (p. 2). While it is obvious that every student should be respected, the major problem with the equivalent forms or all-inclusive diversity phrasing in social studies position statements is that it ignores the unique and historically uninterrupted status of race as a "permanent and unbridgeable" (Fredrickson, 2002, p. 9) marker of difference in the United States. Hence, this particular form of diversity phrasing suggests that NCSS equates the continuing realties of racism with the discomfort one may encounter for holding say, unpopular beliefs. In short, the equivalent forms color-blindness orientation renders irrelevant the disproportionately onerous impact of racism in schools and the larger society.

The 1991 position statement *Testing and Evaluation of Social Studies Students* uses the color-blindness orientation to promote an illogical end. On the one hand, the statement urges teachers to acknowledge differences, yet on the other it urges teachers to de-emphasize the significance of race and culture. For example, it notes "Social studies educators in our pluralistic society must see that their teaching and curriculum materials are fair to all people, regardless of their ethnic backgrounds, beliefs, genders, or handicaps" (p. 3). But it also indicates that "...all assessment materials, whether produced by publishers or by teachers, are *blind* [emphasis added] to learner characteristics, such as culture and gender" (p. 3). In this instance of contradictory diversity phrasing, NCSS dismisses the significance of race as an aspect of culture while it urges fairness to all in teaching and curricular materials. By urging teachers to be "blind" to culture NCSS nullifies the issue of fairness since race (and other aspects of culture) does impinge on testing and evaluation.

The color-blindness orientation in its various manifestations has contributed to the deracialization of the agenda for democratic citizenship education. In many circumstances the deleterious impact of race has been ignored outright under the guise that NCSS has risen above race. This is to say, although race continues to be a significant aspect of U.S. life and remains a disturbingly prevalent element in the schooling process, NCSS has dealt with race by not dealing with race. And the most disturbing irony is that the organization has "not dealt with race" through its ubiquitous reliance on diversity phrasing.

A Defective Process in Agenda Formulation. A complimentary factor to the color-blindness orientation, and that to varying degrees, undoubtedly has contributed to the deracialization of the NCSS agenda for citizenship education, is the phenomenon of process defect. Lawrence (1995) described how this phenomenon manifests.

> ... [T]he ... decision maker may be unaware that she has devalued the cost of a chosen path, because a group with which she does not identify will bear that cost. Indeed, because of her lack of empathy with the group, she may have never even thought of the cost at all. (p. 243)

The development of the 1996 position statement, *Fostering Civic Virtue: Character Education in the Social Studies,* is a case that illustrates the deracializing impact of process defect.

I served as a member of the Task Force on Character Education (TFCE) that developed the *Fostering Civic Virtue* position statement. At the time we were engaged in this important undertaking I held the firm impression that the TFCE carried out its charge with a seriousness of purpose and commitment to the formulation of a high quality organizational statement. Moreover, I believed then (as I do now) that based on the guidelines given and the charge assigned, the TFCE formulated a position statement that spoke to a matter of great import to social studies professionals. Nevertheless, as I reflect on concerns that emerged for me in conjunction with my role on the task force, I recognize that the composition of the TFCE itself (i.e., the process by which this was determined) may have all but assured that the statement it produced would be devoid of any exploration of race and racism in the very conceputalization of something called civic virtue.

Soon after being asked to serve on the TFCE, I inquired about its composition (i.e., the names of the other members) to determine if anyone I already knew was also serving. Upon learning the names, I realized that I had not previously made the acquaintance of any of the other members, had known of one casually, and had attended an NCSS presentation of another several years prior. I also discovered that the TFCE was composed equally along gender lines in that there were three men and three women; two of the men served as co-chairs for the group. Also, I learned that I was the only person of color on the TFCE. Although not major, this latter revelation did present some cause for concern. This is because, similar to many of my colleagues of color around the United States, one significant reality in other aspects of my professional life is that I have been the only person of color in my academic department, in various committees on which I have served at the university, and in the context of other professional responsibilities. Also like many of my colleagues of color, in situations where I have been "the only," I have had the all too familiar experience of presenting a viewpoint that differs substantively from that being endorsed by the numeric/racial majority. Likewise, I have experienced the disaffirming experience of offering ideas on a topic of discussion only to have them ignored or devalued outright. I have protested when my just rejected ideas (or modified versions thereof), have been repeated by a white colleague and then accepted as useful by the group. And I have engaged in the personally affirming resistance technique of resigning to silence in order to rest from the battle and replenish my energies for another day. Because these experiences were well known to me at the time, and since I knew nothing of the orientations toward race, racism, and multicultural education of the members of the TFCE, I had hoped another person of color would be asked to serve. In order to enhance this possibility, I made a number of inquiries.

There were several NCSS members (persons of color) from whom I could have selected, but I had in mind to recommend an African American male to serve on the TFCE because I knew personally of his potentially beneficial contributions to the work group. He was a longtime member of NCSS and was very active in the work of the organization at the time. Although his presence would have offset the gender balance of the work group, the relative racial equity that would have been introduced by his membership would have been critically important for the document that ultimately would be produced. Thus, I inquired about the possibility of another person of color being invited to membership on the TFCE. After a brief exchange of communiqués that included an allusion to impropriety in my prolonging the topic of the work group's composition, an inquiry was made as to whether I was offering to be replaced on the TFCE. I have no way of knowing whether it was so intended, but I was stunned by the bold suggestion of this follow-up query. This was because the question itself had made glaringly apparent (albeit perhaps unbeknownst to the person by whom it was posed), that nothing in the committee assignment protocol of NCSS suggested it would be problematic to limit the representation of people of color on the TFCE to one person. I was not, of course, proposing that I be replaced on the TFCE and communicated as much. Yet, the fact that an offer was made to replace me with another person of color made disturbingly obvious the substance of the concept of diverse representation within the organization's membership.

The composition of the TFCE and the response to my effort to diversify its racial balance represented aspects of process defect within the NCSS. In particular, the decision to retain the gross cultural imbalance resulted in the dilution of the input that could have been offered if the membership had been made more racially diverse. Lest I be misunderstood, it is not my intention here to indict my fellow task force members or any particular individual involved in this process. We all endorsed the final draft of the document. Rather, it is my goal to spotlight the defectiveness in the process of committee selection and the deracializing impact that resulted. I did then, as I do now, recognize that the position statement we drafted never even mentioned the words race or racism. Indeed, one statement that I was concerned about during the development of the document was "Today we have plenty of *pluribus* in the United States, but little *unum*" (p. 2). While on the face of it the statement is certainly correct, little in the document invites social studies educators to grapple critically with the notion of unum that has been put forth historically and in contemporary times and the infusion of race and racism therein. In other words, whose notion of unum does the NCSS encourage social studies educators to pursue and defend? Nor, for that matter, was there any attention devoted to exploration of the degree to which pluribus manifests in the full extension of citizenship rights and privileges. Why has race historically been perceived as a factor that diminishes (rather than enhances) the realities of pluribus?

The point here is not to examine the *degree* to which the composition of the TFCE itself silenced dialogue that might have emerged (and been included in the position statement) on the role of race and racism in prevailing notions of civic virtue. Rather it is to expose how the composition of this or any task force, committee, subcommittee, or ad hoc group can directly (and perhaps even deliberately) diminish the likelihood of exploration of the topics of race and racism. This can occur if for no other reason than because the issues themselves simply do not register as significant to the members of the group. The solitary persons of color in such work groups "bear the cost" of this dismissal of race; while the leadership of NCSS bears the process defect responsibility. The fact that I was asked directly whether I was looking to be replaced on the TFCE may suggest that on some level process defect represented an intentional and deliberate dismissal of the impact of race on the citizenship education agenda and the work of the NCSS. I am not prepared to make a definitive assertion on this point in either direction. Instead, I offer that legal scholars propose process defect itself is a form of unconscious racism. That being the case, I guess ultimately "... [i]t matters not that the decisionmaker's motive may lie outside her awareness" (Lawrence, 1995, p. 243).

CONCLUSION: DERACIALIZATION BY CHANCE OR ON PURPOSE?

The late writer and social critic James Baldwin in a 1960s television interview commented, "I don't know what most white people in this country feel, but I can only [conclude] what they feel from the state of their institutions" (Thorsen & Miles, 1989). He went on to outline briefly the disturbing incongruities between the celebrated ideals of American society and the lived realities of her Black citizens. And then concluding his remarks Baldwin noted sardonically, "you want me to make ... [a leap] of faith, risking myself ... [and] my children on some idealism which you assure me exists in America [but] which I have never seen." As I reflect on the contradictions between the touted *raison d'être* of the NCSS and the nature of its position statements issued over the last 20 years, Baldwin's words resonate loudly. The persistent deracialization of the citizenship education agenda when contrasted with the focus of NCSS position statements makes evident that social studies professionals have long been expected to have faith in the organization's leadership as it navigates around the familiar yet intractable obstacles of race and racism. Additionally, the NCSS asks social studies professionals to ignore the reality that it has consistently taken a stand on these issues by simply not taking a stand. Even when the focus of its position statements have screamed for analysis of the impact of race and racism such as in the *Policy on Commercial News Programs in the Classroom* (1990) and *Principles for Corporate Involvement in Schools* (1999), NCSS has simply refused to broach these topics. Neither of these position statements even mentions the word race or racism. Most importantly, however, the organization has invited professionals to accept diversity phrasing as a worthy consolation for its "non-stand" stance. The consistency and sheer determination with which race and racism have been circumvented in position statements causes one to speculate whether this has been the result of happenstance or deliberate effort. Put differently, would it be possible to demonstrate the conscious intent of NCSS leadership to engage in persistent deracialization of the citizenship education agenda?

Critical race theorists have examined the numerous and complex challenges surrounding efforts to eliminate racial injustice in the society at large. They have also examined how the principle of conscious intent as interpreted by the courts has served to make eliminating racial injustice a near impossibility. In short, *conscious intent* holds that in order for the courts to issue remedial orders in claims of racial discrimination, plaintiffs must demonstrate that acts of racism were committed with the deliberate objective to violate the Constitutional rights of the victim. In other words, while the actual violence of racism (physical, psychological and otherwise) done to its victims are recognized, the courts have tended to empathize with and view as more worthy of protection the possible "innocence" (absence of intent) among the perpetrators of racism. This looking glass orientation results in the courts imposing heightened scrutiny in cases where requests for damages resulting from racial discrimination are made. Typically, the heightened scrutiny requirement results in damages going unrewarded and the acts unpunished because most contemporary racist do not act in a blatant fashion. Instead, contemporary racism is often muffled and disguised in such a manner than it can readily be interpreted by those for whom it is *not* intended as something other than what it is. Responding to this reality, legal scholar Charles R. Lawrence (1995) proposed use of an analytic framework he termed the "cultural meaning test." Describing its primary features he notes,

> the test would evaluate ... conduct to see if it conveys a symbolic message to which the culture attaches racial significance.... . If [it is] determined by a preponderance of the evidenced that a significant portion of the population thinks of the ... action in racial terms, then it would presume that socially shared, unconscious racial attitudes made evident by the action's meaning had influenced the decisionmakers. (p. 247)

In some respects, the principle of conscious intent is disturbing because the burden of proving racist intentionality is extremely difficult in light of the unconscious manifestations and dimensions of racism (Lawrence, 19995). Yet when juxtaposed with the NCSS context the enormous appeal of examining conscious intent comes from its ability to raise the specter of doubt and concern about the mechanisms (deliberate or chance) that have contributed to the persistent race-aversion in the organization as evidenced in its position statements. Although the idea of examining the reasons for persistent race-aversion in NCSS provokes interest, and the persistent deracialization of the citizenship education agenda raises disturbing concerns about intentionality, the notion of putting "evidence to the test" sparks intriguing questions. For example, what might be the nature of the additional evidence that would be brought forth to assess intentionality? Which constituencies from among the NCSS membership should comprise the "population" that judges the nature of the evidence? It is likely that if the issue of conscious intent were raised in any serious manner, various dimensions of the inner sanctum of the organization would have to be examined. And no doubt, in its own defense, the leadership would point to its pervasive references to diversity and multiculturalism as evidence that the intent of NCSS has been to racialize (rather than deracialize) its agenda. Such is the circular nature of the non-stand stance.

But conscious intent notwithstanding, it is for certain the NCSS will need to engage in efforts to root out its entrenched race-aversion if it is ever to emerge as a vital and relevant professional organization for the 21st century. The extent to which it fails to do so will undoubtedly be dictated by the extent to which it continues to make a mockery of its purported goal as evidenced by the staleness of its organization rhetoric and its ubiquitous diversity phrasing in official documents. A simple yet critical next step for the organization is to begin the retreat from its race-aversive stance by commissioning a statement (or series of statements) on the impact of race and racism on the American educational enterprise in general, and the social studies in particular. In so doing, the organization will have to take a long look inward. Among the sub-topical issues that it should explore are: (1) mechanisms (both historical and contemporary) within the leadership structure of the NCSS that obfuscate and thereby perpetuate the organization's race aversive orientation; (2) strategies by which social studies professionals can begin working individually and collectively to expose and eliminate racist practices and policies within the various domains of the organization and profession; (3) outlets for professional and community-based coalition building between and among social studies educators and anti-racist activists; and (4) techniques for engaging in analysis and critique of political and economic dimensions of racism and its continuing impact on the full extension of rights and privileges of citizenship to all Americans. The agenda for citizenship education can never be deracialized and at the same time, be democratic, dynamic, and in step with the actuality of life in these United States. This is to say, the leap of faith will simply never happen. The sooner NCSS leaders accept this reality, the sooner they can begin doing their part to dismantle the dehumanizing unrealities racism imposes on us all.

NOTES

1. The term "America" is used in this chapter in reference to the geopolitical entity that is the United States of America; whereas "American" refers to its inhabitants (legal citizen status notwithstanding) as well as their celebrated multi-cultural identities. I acknowledge that unqualified use of the term "America" literally represents two great landmasses (North America and South America) and thereby, encompasses a diverse collection of "Americas" as it were. Moreover, I appreciate the hegemonic significance of terminology appropriation as is exemplified when "American" is utilized uncritically to refer exclusively to United States denizens, or to spotlight any one of its many cultural groups as representative of the whole. Nonetheless, I have employed these terms as writerly expedients intended to draw upon common usage and hopefully, to facilitate comprehension.

2. The introduction to the report provides background information on the origins of the Commission and the nature of the task it was assigned to undertake. It notes, "Secretary of Education T. H. Bell [a Reagan administration appointee] created the National Commission on Excellence in Education on August 26, 1981, directing it to examine the quality of education in the United States and to make a report to the Nation and to him within 18 months of its first meeting."

3. In recent years, William Bennett, former Secretary of Education and Drug Czar, has reported that the nation remains at risk because previous reform proposals "underestimated ... the resilience of the status quo and the strength of the interests wedded to it." See Bennett (1998).

4. The 1980s popular culture icon "Rambo" (portrayed by actor Sylvester Stallone) was introduced to the American public in the 1981 movie *First Blood*. The story focuses on Rambo who, having survived the horrors of war in Vietnam, returns home to the Pacific Northwest only to discover he must draw upon his well-honed commando skills to rid an otherwise peaceful environment of injustices. The patriotic albeit "kick-ass" persona that is Rambo was enormously popular among movie-going audiences. Moreover, the box-office success of the first film inspired movie sequels. *Rambo: First Blood Part II* opened nationwide in 1985 followed by *Rambo III* in 1988. In the sequel films Rambo moves beyond the U.S. borders to tackle injustice in Vietnam and Afghanistan.

5. Rock music recording artist Bruce Springsteen introduced his album "Born In the U.S.A." in 1984 with a mega-hit single by the same name. The lyrics of that song and others on the album exposed the various manners in which blue-collar Americans were suffering under the economic and political structures of the 1980s era. Even so, his catchy refrain, "born in the U.S.A.," was

appropriated by partisan political strategists and used as a patriotic slogan. In the end, Springsteen's powerful musical message depicting the socioeconomic discontent of America's working people was effectively muffled.

6. In brief, this 1978 decision struck down as unconstitutional a policy implemented at the University of California Berkeley medical school that allotted a fraction of the openings for entering students to those applicants from racial groups that historically had been critically under-represented in the medical profession including African Americans, Latinos/as, and Native Americans.

7. For the purpose of this discussion, the collective professional entity designated as "social studies educators" is embodied in the leadership of the National Council for the Social Studies (NCSS). The leadership of the NCSS is defined as the Board of Directors.

8. The position statements used for this chapter were accessed through the NCSS organizational website at http://www.ncss.org under the link "Standards and Position Statements."

9. No doubt it is possible to identify the exact composition of each group (e.g., names of members) that composed each position statement; however, this information was not always included in the documents.

10. The essentialist notion of race holds that human groups can be differentiated from each other on the basis of something called race. Critical to the essentialist conceptualization of race is the notion that differences between and among human groups derive from each group's basic or "essential" features or traits. Among the traits that have been included as racial group variables are skin and eye color, nose shape, hair texture, cranial structure, mental capacity, temperament, and even body odor. According to essentialism, individuals within a given race are born with a collection of traits that are accepted as common to and unique among members of that particular racial group and thereby substantively different from traits found among the members of other "racial" groups. Because one is born with a particular set of traits, the notion of race represents the "essence" as it were of the difference between human groups.

REFERENCES

Banks, J.A. (1993). Multicultural education for young children: Racial and ethnic attitudes and their modification. In B. Spodek (Ed.), *Handbook of research on the education of young children* (pp. 236–250). New York: Macmillan.

Bell, D.A., Jr. (1995). Brown v. board of education and the interest convergence dilemma. In K. Crenshaw, N. Gotanda, G. Peller, & K. Thomas (Eds.), *Critical race theory: The key writings that formed the movement* (pp. 20–29). New York: The New Press.

Bell, D.A., Jr. (1995/2000). After we're gone: Prudent speculations on America in a post-racial epoch. In R. Delgado & J. Stefancic (Eds.) *Critical race theory: The cutting edge* (2nd ed., pp. 2–8). Philadelphia, PA: Temple University Press.

Bell, P.D., & Hudson, S. (2001). Equity in the diagnosis of chest pain: Race and gender. *American Journal of Health Behavior, 25*(1), 60–71.

Berliner, D.C., & Biddle, B.J. (1995). *The manufactured crises.* Reading, MA: Addison-Wesley Publishing Co.

Carter, R.T. (1997). Is white a race? Expressions of white racial identity. In M. Fine, L. Weiss, L.C. Powell, & L. Mun Wond (Eds.), *Off white: Readings on race, power, and society* (pp. 198–209). New York: Routledge.

Crenshaw, K.W. (1995). Race, reform, and retrenchment: Transformation and legitimation in antidiscrimination law. In K. Crenshaw, N. Gotanda, G. Peller, & K. Thomas (Eds.), *Critical race theory: The key writings that formed the movement* (pp. 103–122). New York: The New Press.

Crenshaw, K., Gotanda, N., Peller, G., & Thomas, K. (Eds.). (1995). *Critical race theory: The key writings that formed the movement.* New York: The New Press.

Cross, W.E., Jr. (1994). Nigrescence theory: Historical and explanatory notes. *Journal of Vocational Behavior, 44,* 119–123.

Davis, O.L. Jr. (1996). Toward celebration and continuance: An invitation to reflection. In O.L. Davis, Jr. (Ed.). *NCSS in retrospect: Bulletin 92* (pp. i-iii). Washington, DC: National Council for the Social Studies.

Davis, P.C. (1989/2000). Law as microaggression. In R. Delgado & J. Stefancic (Eds.), *Critical race theory: The cutting edge* (2nd ed., pp. 141–151). Philadelphia, PA: Temple University Press.

De Lew, N., & Weinick, R.M. (2000). An overview: Eliminating racial, ethnic, and ses disparities in health care. *Health Care Financing Review, 21*(4), 1–7.

Delgado, R., & Stefancic, J. (Eds.). (2000). *Critical race theory: The cutting edge* (2nd ed.). Philadelphia, PA: Temple University Press.

Flores-Gonzalez, N. (1999). The racialization of Latinos: The meaning of Latino identity for the second generation. *Latino Studies Journal, 10*(3), 3–31.

Fredrickson, G.M. (2002). *Racism.* Princeton, NJ: Princeton University Press.

Garcia, J., & Buendia, E. (1996). NCSS and ethnic/cultural diversity. In O.L. Davis, Jr. (Ed.), *NCSS in retrospect: Bulletin 92* (pp. 55–65). Washington, DC: National Council for the Social Studies.

Gotanda, N. (1995). A critique of "our constitution is color-blind." In K. Crenshaw, N. Gotanda, G. Peller, & K. Thomas (Eds.), *Critical race theory: The key writings that formed the movement* (pp. 257–275). New York: The New Press.

Haney López, I. F. (2000a). The social construction of race. In R. Delgado & J. Stefancic (Eds.), *Critical race theory: The cutting edge* (2nd ed., pp. 163–175). Philadelphia, PA: Temple University Press.

Haney López, I. F. (2000b). White by law. In R. Delgado & J. Stefancic (Eds.), *Critical race theory: The cutting edge* (2nd ed., pp. 448–454). Philadelphia, PA: Temple University Press.

Harris, C. (1993). Whiteness as property. *Harvard Law Review, 106*(8), 1709–1791.

Helms, J.E. (Ed.) (1993). *Black and white racial identity: Theory, research, and practice.* Westport, CT: Praeger.

Irvine, J.J. (1991). *Black students and school failure.* New York: Praeger.

Ladson-Billings, G. (1994). *The dreamkeepers: Successful teachers of African American children.* San Francisco: Jossey-Bass.

Lawrence, C.R., III. (1995). The id, the ego, and equal protection: Reckoning with unconscious racism. In K. Crenshaw, N. Gotanda, G. Peller, & K. Thomas

(Eds.), *Critical race theory: The key writings that formed the movement* (pp. 235–257). New York: The New Press.

Lynn, M. (1999). Toward a critical race pedagogy: A research note. *Urban Education, 33*(5), 606–626.

Marable, M. (2000). Beyond racial identity politics: Towards a liberation theory for multicultural democracy. In R. Delgado & J. Stefancic (Eds.), *Critical race theory: The cutting edge* (2nd ed., pp. 448–454). Philadelphia, PA: Temple University Press.

Marshall, P.L. (2002). *Cultural diversity in our schools.* Belmont, CA: Wadsworth.

National Commission on Excellence in Education. (1983). *A nation at risk: The imperative for educational reform.* Washington, DC: U.S. Department of Education.

National Council for the Social Studies. (1994). *Curriculum standards for social studies: Expectations of Excellence.* Bulletin 89. Washington, DC: Author.

Nelson, J.L., & Fernekes, W.R. (1996). NCSS and social crises. In O.L. Davis, Jr. (Ed.), *NCSS in retrospect: Bulletin 92* (pp. 89–101). Washington, DC: National Council for the Social Studies.

Omi, M., & Winant, H. (1994). *Racial formation in the United States* (2nd ed.). New York: Routledge.

Peller, G. (1995). Race-consciousness. In K. Crenshaw, N. Gotanda, G. Peller, & K. Thomas (Eds.), *Critical race theory: The key writings that formed the movement* (pp. 127–158). New York: The New Press.

Pinar, W.F. (1993). Notes on understanding curriculum as a racial text. In C. McCarthy & W. Crichlow (Eds.), *Race, identity, and representation in education* (pp. 61–70). New York: Routledge.

Roediger, D.R. (1991). *The wages of whiteness: Race and the making of the American working class.* New York: Verso.

Ross, T. (1990/2000). Innocence and affirmative action. In R. Delgado & J. Stefancic (Eds.), *Critical race theory: The cutting edge* (2nd ed., pp. 635–647). Philadelphia, PA: Temple University Press.

Shaver, J.P. (1996). NCSS and citizenship education. In O.L. Davis, Jr. (Ed.), *NCSS in retrospect, Bulletin 92. (35–44), Washington, DC: National Council for the Social Studies.*

Solórzano, D.G. (1998). Critical race theory, race and gender microaggressions, and the experience of Chicana and Chicano scholars. *Qualitative Studies in Education, 11*(1), 121–136.

Solórzano, D.G. (1997). Images and words that wound: Critical race theory, racial stereotyping, and teacher education. *Teacher Education Quarterly, 24*(3), 5–19.

Steele, C.M., & Aronson, J. (1995). Stereotype threat and the intellectual test performance of African Americans. *Journal of Personality and Social Psychology, 69*(5), 797–811.

Tate, W.F., IV. (1997). Critical race theory and education: History, theory, and implications. In M.W. Apple (Ed.). *Review of research in education* (pp.195–247). Washington, DC: American Educational Research Association.

Thompson, C.E., & Carter, R.T. (Eds.). (1997). *Racial identity theory.* Mahwah, NJ: Lawrence Erlbaum Associates.

Thorsen, K., & Miles, W. (producers); Thorsen, K. (director). (1989). *James Baldwin: The price of the ticket.* [Film]. (Nobody Knows Production, Maysles Films, Inc. & WNET New York).

Weis, L. (1990). *Working class without work.* New York: Routledge.

Weiss, L., & Fine, M. (1996). Narrating the 1980s and 1990s: Voices of poor and working class white and African American men. *Anthropology & Education Quarterly, 27*(4), 493–516.

West, C. (1993). *Race matters.* Boston: Beacon Press.

Wilkins, R. (2001). *Jefferson's pillow: The founding fathers and the dilemma of Black patriotism.* Boston: Beacon Press.

Witzig, R. (1996). The medicalization of race: Scientific legitimization of a flawed social construct. *Annals of Internal Medicine, 125*(8), 675–679.

CHAPTER 6

A LOOK AT RACE IN THE NATIONAL STANDARDS FOR THE SOCIAL STUDIES

Another Bad Check

André J. Branch

ABSTRACT

The author reviews the genesis and development of the NCSS Curriculum Standards as policy regarding race in the social studies. After a brief review of the four standards which lend themselves easily to teaching about race and racism in the social studies, the writer finds that they represent a "bad check." Although the Standards promise attention to race and racism in the social studies, evidence suggests that students are not learning very much about race and racism in their social studies classes. Critical Race Theory reveals five possible reasons for the near silence on race and racism in the social studies: fear of race, the colorblind perspective, a race-less consciousness, the interest-convergence principle, and high stakes testing.

Critical Race Theory Perspectives on the Social Studies, pages 99–120
Copyright © 2003 by Information Age Publishing
All rights of reproduction in any form reserved.

INTRODUCTION

In the 1970s Critical Race Theory emerged as a tool for explaining racial reform in the United States and understanding the law (Ladson-Billings, 1999). More recently educational scholars have employed Critical Race Theory to re-evaluate and critique policies and practices in education, as well as educational reform movements (Ladson-Billings, 1999; Ladson-Billings & Tate, 1995; Tate, 1997; Tate, Ladson-Billings, & Grant, 1993). Tate (1997) has suggested that Critical Race Theory could be used to evaluate policy shifts in education, such as the shift from fiscal equality to high standards for all.

With the publication of *A Nation at Risk* and *America 2000* by the United States Department of Education, the United States saw a new focus on accountability and standards in education. Accompanying these new foci were heated debates by the public and academics (Ochoa-Becker, 2001; Tate, 1997) that continues in the new millennium (Amrein & Berliner, 2002). Beginning with the National Council for Teachers of Mathematics, professional organizations for the subject matter areas have created national standards documents that are to guide instruction in their respective subject matter areas. This creation of Standards did not escape the National Council for the Social Studies (NCSS). In 1994, the NCSS published *Expectations of excellence: Curriculum standards for social studies*. In this chapter, I will not take up Tate's (1997) challenge in toto, but will use Critical Race Theory to investigate the Standards in one subject matter area—social studies—and specifically as regards race in the social studies. I will not examine the shift from fiscal equality, but will evaluate the result, the creation of national Standards, in one subject matter area. Specifically, I will review the genesis of the NCSS national standards as social studies policy regarding race and social studies and review the warrant therein for teaching about race and racism in the social studies. I will explain how these policy statements represent a "bad check," and suggest from a Critical Race Theory perspective possible reasons for this "bad check" or silence about race in the social studies.

THE GENESIS OF THE NCSS NATIONAL STANDARDS AND WARRANT FOR TEACHING ABOUT RACE AND RACISM IN THE SOCIAL STUDIES

Genesis of the NCSS National Standards

Two documents served as co-catalysts for the national standards movement: *A Nation at Risk* and *America 2000* (Adler, 1994). Following the release of these pivotal documents, and the production of national standards in mathematics by the National Council for Teachers of Mathematics, the National Council for the Social Studies felt pressured to join this fray (Adler, 2001). Adler, a former president of the National Council for the Social Studies, acknowledges that "taking up the question of standards was controversial and polarizing" (Adler, 2001, p. 315). Adler cites unnamed "others" who would have stolen the voice of the NCSS on the standards issue if the NCSS Board of Directors had not approved the creation of curriculum standards (Adler, 2001).

In the creation of national standards for the social studies, the NCSS Board wanted a document that would be "useful, meaningful, and representative of the diverse individuals within NCSS" (Adler, 2001, p. 315). The NCSS Task Force on Standards describes the intention of the standards this way: "To provide an integrated social science, behavioral science, and humanities approach for achieving academic and civic competence" (NCSS Task Force on Standards, 1994, p. 365). To accomplish this work, the NCSS assembled a majority of elementary, middle, and high school teachers, joined by university professors, and local, state, and district supervisors (Adler, 2001; NCSS Task Force on Standards, 1994). After three revisions, national critique, and consensus, the final document was approved for implementation as guidelines suggesting what students should know after instruction, and criteria for decisions about what should be taught (Adler, 2001). Comprising ten strands or themes, each theme has a curricular statement and performance indicator for each of three grade levels: early grades, middle grades, and high school (NCSS, 1994). Each of the standards has an accompanying vignette demonstrating how the standard could be implemented, as well as an example of an assessment task (NCSS, 1994). Created by consensus, and with the benefit of nationwide critique, at least four of the ten standards provide a warrant for teaching about race in the social studies.

Warrant for Teaching about Race and Racism

A clear warrant for teaching about race and racism in Social Studies is provided in the National Standards developed by the National Council for the Social Studies. Culture is the first theme in the framework for the social studies standards. According to the Eighty-ninth Bulletin, published by the National Council for the Social Studies, "In a democratic and multicultural society, students need to understand multiple perspectives that derive from different cultural vantage points. This understanding will allow them to relate to people in our nation and throughout the world" (National Council for the Social Studies, 1994, p. 21). The public reaction to recent major national events reminds us that responses to and interpretations of these events frequently differ along racial lines. Consider that the public responses to the outcome of the 2000 Presidential election differed along racial lines. Fifty percent of African Americans say Bush "stole the election," as compared to 14% of Whites who say the election was stolen (Simmons, 2000). When asked to describe their reaction to the fact that George W. Bush had been declared the winner of the presidency, 68% of African Americans said they felt cheated (Simmons, 2000). Only 28% of Whites said they felt cheated (Simmons, 2000). Whereas only 7% of African Americans say George Bush won the presidency "fair and square," 54% of Whites say the election was won fair and square (Simmons, 2000). Other examples of differing public opinion along racial lines include the responses to the O.J. Simpson verdict, the Rodney King beating, the verdict in the Simi Valley Rodney King trial, the verdict in the wrongful death case of Vincent Chin in Detroit, and the Supreme Court decision in the case of Bakke almost three decades ago. Even the perspectives regarding the prevalence and persistence of racism in the United States society and its institutions are markedly different along racial lines (Saad, 2001; Saad & Newport, 2001; Wise, 2001).

An understanding of our differing racial perspectives as North American citizens is critical to our living and working together peacefully in the United States and building a democratic society. Individuals from different racial groups are not likely to be singular in their thinking, decision-making processes, and execution of their academic and/or job-related responsibilities. Even values such as "freedom" and "justice," held in common by most citizens of the United States may be perceived and interpreted differently by United States citizens from different racial groups and within those groups. Knowing the ways in which we differ will assist us in becoming unified nationally. Different racial groups are likely to have different meanings for democratic values such as justice, human dignity, and equality. Understanding these different perspectives helps citizens know which groups and goals in their society they can support and how best to offer support. Understanding multiple racial perspectives has long-term political implications, and translates into skills for citizenship and democratic thinking (Banks, 1994).

Theme four in the social studies framework is Individual Development and Identity. Implementation of this theme allows teachers to help students investigate their culture and racial influences on their culture toward the development of their personal and racial identity. Write the authors of the 89th Bulletin, "Central to this development are the exploration, identification, and analysis of how individuals relate to others" (National Council for the Social Studies, 1994, p. 24). Race relations have long been a subject of research and debate in the academic arena particularly and in United States society generally (Myrdal, 1944). It is reasonable then that policy documents in the social studies provide students with an opportunity to learn about the influence of race on individual identity.

Relating authentically and successfully to those who are racially different necessarily presupposes a reasonable degree of understanding and comfort with oneself racially. When students are comfortable with themselves racially, they can interact confidently with those who are racially different. When students are intimidated racially and feel racially inferior, they lack the ability to think clearly and excel academically (Chard-Yaron & Kingsbury, 1996; Rogers, 1961; Steele & Aronson, 1995). When students are comfortable with whom they are racially, they are eager to interact with those who are racially different and to hear their differing points of view. Students who are uncomfortable with themselves racially feel threatened by individuals who are racially different. Likely results of a failure to understand oneself racially could include personal insecurity in a race conscious society, a lack of motivation to succeed academically and professionally, and thus contribute less to the larger society, poor and personally dangerous decision-making, and a lack of ability to see the good beyond race unity.

Theme five in the social studies framework, Individuals, Groups, and Institutions, is intended to move students beyond consideration of their individual identity to an understanding of their various group memberships—including racial group memberships. Carter and Goodwin (1994) are certain that the struggle for racial identity is not simply a matter of physical characteristics, but an ongoing process of self and group assessment and negotiation with those in and outside of one's racial group. Helms (1990) understands this dynamic as not simply referring to one's race category but to a "sense of group or collective identity based on one's *perception* that he or she shares a common racial heritage with a particular racial group" (p. 3). The curriculum standards for the social studies even offer support for addressing racial conflict in the nation's schools. "Young children," say the standards, "should be assisted in recognizing the tensions that occur when the goals, values, and principles of two or more institutions or groups conflict..." (National Council for the Social Studies, 1994). Certainly the ongoing conflict between racial groups in our society is worthy of recognition and investigation.

The sixth theme, Power, Authority, and Governance, also provides opportunity for students to view issues of race and racism as they intersect with power, authority, and governance in a substantive way. The NCSS Task Force on Standards (1994) write, "Through study of the dynamic relationships between individual rights and responsibilities, the needs of social groups, and concepts of a just society, learners become more effective problem-solvers and decision-makers when addressing the persistent issues and social problems encountered in public life" (p. 367).

THE IMPORTANCE OF TEACHING ABOUT RACE
IN THE SOCIAL STUDIES

Teachers should address race in their social studies classes because doing so may help prepare students for living in a racially diverse world without fear and suspicion of people who are racially different. In a country and world that are increasingly culturally and racially diverse, children need not grow up fearful and suspicious of people who are racially and culturally different from themselves. Some children take racism to school and others encounter racism while there (Katz & Zalk, 1978). Teaching children about race and racism is one strategy for developing in them more demo-cratic racial values (Banks & Banks, 1997). Teaching children about race and racism prepares them for the racial discrimination that they will inevi-tably face in school and in the larger society in the United States.

Children will benefit from an understanding of racism as a destructive impediment to their healthy racial identity development. If students are not taught about race and assisted in their racial identity clarification, they are likely to be racially and culturally homeless. I have come to describe as "racial and/or cultural homelessness" the phenomenon of the cultural and racial alienation experienced by some of my university students. When con-fronted with the task of making presentations related to culture, race, or ethnicity, some students have difficulty, insisting instead that they, "don't have culture," or "don't do the race thing." Some declare, "I'm just a per-son," or "I'm Heinz 57," or "I'm just a ... (and they insert some state desig-nation such as "New Yorker," "Californian," or "Washingtonian"). Some offer the well worn and most degrading response, "I'm just a mutt." Racial and ethnic identity researchers would say these floundering individuals, lack a sense of belonging racially and ethnically (Gonzales & Cauce, 1995; Helms, 1994; Phinney, 1996). They lack racial security because they have not had or have not taken opportunities to clarify their racial and ethnic identity (Lawrence & Tatum, 1997a). These racially and ethnically home-less souls will have no shelter from the destructive power of racism because they do not see themselves as racial beings have not learned appropriate responses to racism.

THE BAD CHECK AND EXPLANATIONS FOR THE BAD
CHECK FROM A CRITICAL RACE THEORY PERSPECTIVE

The Bad Check

In spite of the importance of teaching about race in the social studies, and the clear warrant in the Curriculum Standards for Social Studies for students to learn about race and racism, the testimony and evidence from students who have come through the public school system in the United States is that race and racism was not a part of their curricula. Gay and Howard (2000) have identified a "resistance to dealing directly with race and racism" (p. 3) as one of the troubling attitudes held by teachers and teacher education students. These researchers examined their teacher education students' fears of dealing with race and racism. Their students reported that they had, "never lived near or had any close contact with Native, African, or Latino Americans" (Gay & Howard, 2000, p. 3).

Ladson-Billings (1997) reports that her White student teachers did not understand "the dynamics of racism and how it contributed to unequal access to power and opportunities" (p. 15). I have observed a similar phenomenon in my own work as a teacher educator. In the past three years, I have taught twenty sections of Introduction to Multicultural Education, a prerequisite to admission to our teacher education program. For two consecutive class sessions in this course, which meets over a fifteen-week period, students are required to read prejudice reduction literature, and discuss strategies for reducing prejudice and racism in students. During these two sessions, and at other times during the course, students consistently report that their K–12 social studies teachers did not address race or racism in their classes or lesson designs.

Lawrence and Tatum (1997a) conducted a study of eighty-four suburban White teachers in the Boston area. These researchers report here and elsewhere (Lawrence & Tatum 1997b) that teachers have limited experience with race, racism, and people of color. They remark that race is, "A taboo topic that Whites are socialized to avoid" (Lawrence & Tatum, 1997a, p. 163). Educators in many schools have outlawed the word "race" altogether (Carter, 2000; Grant & Zozakiewicz, 1995; Schofield, 1997). The negative responses about race from my students, as well as reports about the silence on race from the writings of researchers in different parts of the country suggest that national policy standards have made no difference in the teaching of race in the social studies. It is reasonable to conclude, then, that the experience of these teacher education students in the North West, South West, Midwestern, and North Eastern United States provide clues about the extent to which race and racism are ignored in K–12 schools across the country in spite of guidelines to the contrary in the curriculum standards.

Four of the ten curriculum themes or standards that have been generated by the National Council for the Social Studies are "Culture," "Individual Development and Identity," "Individuals, Groups, and Institutions," and "Power, Authority, and Governance" (National Council for the Social Studies, 1994). Although each of these four standards provides warrant for social studies teachers to address race and racial issues in their classes, teachers appear not to have taken advantage of this opportunity (Anand Marri, this volume). In general, public school students do not appear to be learning about race as an aspect of their culture (Carter, 2000). Interviews with teachers suggest that the majority of them are not teaching students that racial identity development is a critical process and part of the human condition (Branch, 1999; Gay, 1985). It is reasonable that teachers who have not examined their racial identity development have not taught students that racism is an impediment to their healthy racial identity development (Lawrence & Tatum, 1997A). Although race is salient in American society (Ladson-Billings & Tate, 1995), a lack of teaching about race in the public schools would suggest that students do not learn that racial group membership significantly influences all other social group interactions. According to curriculum theme six, students are to study "the historical development of structures of power" (Banks & Banks, 1999). Given the continuing lack of understanding about power dynamics in the United States society (Fine, Powell, Weis, & Wong, 1997), it is reasonable to conclude that students are either not learning or not retaining their lessons about how race has and continues to influence who has and who wields power in the United States.

The clear connection between race and the social studies, and the silence of race discourse in Social Studies classrooms is reminiscent of the "bad check" Martin Luther King (1963) said the United States government wrote to African Americans in depriving them of civil rights. Like the civil rights bad check, which King said had been returned to African Americans marked "insufficient funds," the Social Studies curriculum does not deliver to public school students what its policy documents promise.

Although some would argue that the NCSS Curriculum Standards are written in the language of mandates (Ochoa-Becker (2001), they are not mandates, but guidelines (Adler, 2001). They are guidelines however, created by a broad audience, the majority of whom were classroom teachers (Adler, 2001; NCSS Task Force on Standards, 1994; Ochoa-Becker, 2001). It is reasonable, then, to expect students would be better prepared by teachers to respond to issues of race and racism. In the next section I ask Why from a critical race perspective might teachers not be teaching more about race and racism.

Explanations for the Bad Check from a Critical Race Theory Perspective

Explaining broken promises in the law, or providing explanations for why the law fails to deliver to people of color in equal measure what it succeeds in delivering to Whites has been one of the roles of Critical Race theorists and Critical Legal Scholars before them (Tate, 1997). In this section, I will identify and explain some of the important elements of Critical Race Theory (CRT) to investigate plausible explanations for the apparent silence on race and racism in the social studies. For a more detailed explication of Critical Race Theory, readers should see Ladson-Billings and Tate (1995) and Tate (1997).

One of the elements of CRT that is used to critique inequity in the law and society is story telling or narrative (Ladson-Billings, 1999). Just as "the voice of the individual can provide insight into the political, structural, and representational dimensions of the legal system," (Tate, 1997), I believe the experience of the individual can provide insight regarding silence about race in the social studies. Throughout this section, I will reference this individual's story about race in the United States.

Virginia's Story

A not so long time ago there was a little Black girl named Virginia Jackson. Virginia was a curious little girl and often had questions for her parents. One of her questions was about the differences in skin color. She asked her mother why people had different colored skin. Her mother told her that, "skin color doesn't matter, Whites and Blacks are the same under the skin." Virginia's mother also said, "God loves us all the same." When Virginia started school in a large city in the United States, she heard from her teachers that they were color-blind and treated all their students the same. She heard this until she graduated from the twelfth grade. But she noticed that all of her school books only had pictures of White children in them. Although she never saw Black children in any of the books at school, she was comforted in knowing that, "God loved us all the same." Virginia believed there really was no difference between Blacks and Whites because none of her teachers ever said anything about race. Because she could see people of different colors, she secretly wondered how people, especially her teachers, who were the smartest people in the world to her, could not see skin color. She especially did not understand how people could miss her color (she was dark-skinned), but she remained convinced that they either did not see her color, or that it just made no difference to them that she was Black. She felt shame whenever she caught herself pondering skin color differences, as if they actually mattered.

Because she trusted her teachers and believed they would have taught her about race if it was important, she was surprised in high school when she realized people did see that she was Black, and treated her differently because of it. In college, she felt cheated and betrayed by her former teachers because she knew her experiences were different because she was Black.

The societal slaps she had received in high school and college with regard to race were repeated as she began to work and attend graduate school in the United States. Even in her daily activities at the bank, grocery store, cleaners, DMV, etc. it was clear—everybody knew she was Black and treated her accordingly. These metaphorical slaps hurt. She wondered why the people she trusted had not taught her about race and prepared her for life in the real world.

Everywhere she turns, it seems she hears people claiming they are color-blind. Supervisors at work brag about their color-blind hiring practices; politicians insist their motivations are color-blind; educators still talk about being color-blind; university admissions personnel are beginning to talk about using color-blind admissions policies; the police use a color-blind defense for their actions. She winces when she hears people say, "this has nothing to do with race." All this talk of color blindness infuriates her because she knows all these liars see color. Why won't people who constantly plead color blindness just admit they see color, she wonders? What do they gain by denying race? What will they lose by admitting to recognizing race? She is no longer ashamed about her musing about racial differences. She believes it is possible to see racial differences and treat people with dignity and respect. In fact, she has come to believe that the first step toward disrespecting people is dismissing their race.

Fear of Race

Although there may be many more reasons for the "bad check" or the silence of race and racism in the teaching of social studies, five will be considered here. First, there is evidence of fear of the very topics of race and racism among many public school teachers (Branch, in press; Cochran-Smith, 1995; Neuharth-Pritchett, Reiff, & Pearson, 2001; Paley, 1989). Students in my class, "Introduction to Multicultural Education," a prerequisite class for all individuals entering our credential program, express their discomfort with discussing race and race-related issues in our class. "Why," many ask, "must we talk about race and racism so much?" Many of the questioners remember the negative experiences they have had with race and ethnicity and they would rather forget these uncomfortable feelings. In the United States of America, where we are in racial crisis, it is likely that these students have experienced deep emotional hurts as regards race and do not want to be reminded of these hurts. Some of these students fear and resent the suggestion, indicative in the required nature of this class, that they might need the class to help them unearth and resolve some unresolved prejudices. It is common practice in the United States to teach children that "it is not polite to stare at people who are racially different." Learning early to not see race, and avoid verbal references to race, it is a common occurrence to see parents shield their children's eyes, or turn their heads away from seeing their first Black person, or first large group of Black people (Thompson, 1998).

In *White Teacher,* Vivian Paley (1989) discusses her own development as a teacher in this area of talking about differences:

> In the beginning it was more comfortable to pretend the black child was white. Having perceived this, I then saw it was my inclination to avoid talking about other differences as well. Stuttering, obesity, shyness, divorced parents—the list was long.... As I watched and reacted to black children, I came to see a common need in every child. Anything a child feels is different about himself which cannot be referred to spontaneously, casually, naturally, and uncritically by the teacher can become a cause for anxiety and an obstacle to learning. (p. xv)

Karen Evans, a white third grade teacher, visits my "Introduction to Multicultural Education" class each semester to demonstrate for my students some of the multicultural education lessons she designs and teaches in her third grade class. She regularly shocks my college students when she tells them that her third graders want to talk about race and ethnicity, while it is her colleagues and other adults who have concerns about her teaching lessons and doing projects that call attention to race in the school setting. Evans' third graders take their cues from her; she is comfortable discussing these concepts and related issues, so her students do not know they should be uncomfortable. This is reasonable because adults are more likely than third graders to have painful memories related to issues of race and ethnicity. It's the adults who remember the awkwardness, confusion, and sadness associated with race-related experiences. They do not want to feel this pain, so they avoid any discussion of race and any distinctions related to race—within or without the curriculum. Because some teachers are confused about what racism is and what it means to be a racist, they may also fear being racially offensive and/or appearing to be racist. Simply calling attention to one's race or another's racial category is not necessarily an example of racism. Similarly, recognizing racial differences is not racist. Because racism, like race, is a social construct, there are many different definitions of racism. A simple, yet effective traditional definition of racism is useful here: "Racism is a set of ideas used to legitimate or rationalize the inferior status of a group" (Healey, 1998). What this definition should include, but does not, is that the "inferior status" is an ascribed inferior status. Making a distinction between "traditional racism," which he says is characterized by adherence to stereotypes, Healey has summarized the work of a number of scholars to define what he has called, "modern racism" (1998, p. 123). Healey believes that modern racists have negative feelings about people of color, but do not attribute the inferiority of people of color to genetics. Modern racists, accordingly, do not believe that discrimination exists in the United States; they believe that any lingering inequality is caused by people of color; and they say, "demands for preferential treatment or affirmative action for minorities are unfair and unjustified" (Healey, 1998, p. 124). Consistent with this thinking is a "blame the victim" mentality and a placing of "responsibility for change and improvements on the minority groups, not on the larger society" (Healey, 1998, p. 124).

Teachers are confused about or fear discussion of race, or they lack confidence concerning their own thoughts about individuals or groups who are racially different. They resist calling attention to race—even when it would be appropriate to do so. Recently, I conducted a workshop for teachers representing various subject matter content areas. One of the challenges to identifying the race of authors came from a European American female. She said, "I don't like the idea of telling students when the authors in the curriculum are minorities. I include minority authors in my curriculum because they provide examples of good writing, not because they are minorities." This response represents a widespread pernicious resistance to the recognition and celebration of racial and ethnic differences particularly, as well as a resistance to multicultural education generally. To avoid identification of the race and ethnicity of authors of color is to sabotage one of the purposes for their inclusion in the curriculum. Authors of color are included in the curriculum and their race and ethnicity are highlighted in order to facilitate the academic achievement of students of color by ensuring that they see themselves in the curriculum. Authors of color are also included to disrupt White students' beliefs about who is accomplished or intelligent. The race and ethnicity of writers often provide important clues to the writer's perspective—a perspective that might be shared by students in one's class.

Fear of race may also be manifested in what is considered by some to be a racist practice—deciding for others what their views and feelings on race should be. When teachers, school principals, and other policy makers, because of their own views and fears about race, decide that race is insignificant and that students will not discuss race or deal with race-related issues, they are making judgements and inappropriate decisions best left to individuals. To teach children that race is irrelevant is likely to endanger the very lives of African American students, and other students of color who must live with the reality of the difference that race makes in their lives every day. When teachers affirm that race is irrelevant either by audible words or by their silence about race, they reveal their perhaps unwitting racist assumption that all people are alike. They also reveal their lack of understanding of the differences that children of color bring to the teaching/learning enterprise every day. Teachers, principals, and other policymakers will facilitate students' academic achievement when they notice, value and appreciate students differences—including their racial differences—and use the culture reflected in these differences to teach subject matter content. Educators who refuse to see racial differences may believe erroneously that they are choosing equity. They would rather be color-blind.

The Color-blind Perspective

Fear of addressing race is likely to lead to adopting the color-blind perspective, a second reason teachers may not teach about race and racism in the social studies. The color-blind perspective, widely held and evident in legal scholarship (Tate, 1997) as well as educational scholarship (Schofield, 1997), is a weak attempt to ignore the influence of race in society. Using the color-blind perspective, individuals deny that they see the color or race of others; they deny that race has any bearing in any of their decision-making. Rather than avoid or deny race, Critical Race Theorists *focus* on race (Tate, 1997) as one of the most salient sociocultural factors in United States society. Critical Race Theorists (CRTs) understand Virginia's early confusion encountering people who said they did not see color: CRTs and Virginia know that the color-blind must see color in order to deny it. Aleinikoff (1991) as cited in Tate (1997) asserts, "To be truly color blind in this way . . . requires color consciousness; one must notice race in order to tell oneself not to trigger the usual mental processes that take race into account" (p. 203).

Perhaps these teachers who espouse color blindness have been so well socialized into color blindness that they, too, feel shame when they catch themselves seeing color. Perhaps they want to be equitable toward all children, and do not understand how they can be equitable without being color-blind. But, as Crenshaw (1988, cited in Tate, 1997) informs, "A belief in color blindness and equal process is illogical in a society in which specific groups have been treated different historically and in which the outcomes of this differential treatment continue into the present" (p. 229). It is indeed ironic that teachers would insist on being color-blind in the places we call "schools," where social inequities are practiced daily (Ladson-Billings, 1994).

The color-blind perspective, for all its faults, is much in vogue, as Virginia's story reveals, and can have devastating results for children. Consistent with Paley's (1989) conclusion about pretending that all children are White, Ladson-Billings (1997) has written that ignoring race is "a dangerous game of ignoring reality" (p. 15). Schofield (1997) identifies an additional negative consequence of the color-blind perspective: the assumption that individuals and groups whose accomplishments and contributions are worthy of academic study are White. Schofield (1997) and her colleagues studied peer relations between Blacks and Whites at a middle school in which the administrators had outlawed all references to race or ethnicity by all school personnel and students. Whether in the execution of lesson plans, the resolution of conflicts between students, or casual conversations in the halls, offices, or cafeterias, no mention of race was to be made in spite of the awkwardness that this sometime created (Schofield, 1997).

In her summary of the consequences of this perspective in public schools, Schofield (1997) writes,

> The colorblind perspective and its corollaries not only made it more likely that individual faculty members would ignore the challenge of presenting students with materials which related in motivating ways to their own experience, but actually led to a constriction of the education provided to students. (p. 266)

In her conclusion, Schofield (1997) cites a teacher at the school she studied who specifically did not mention the race of individuals on a list of great Americans whom students could choose for further study. The list included one African American. Of the decision not to mention race in a context in which the color-blind principle influenced all aspects of the school environment, Schofield (1997) writes:

> In the best of all worlds, there would be no need to make such mention, because children would have no preconceptions that famous people are generally White. However, in a school where one White child was surprised to learn from a member of our research team that Martin Luther King was Black, not White, it would seen reasonable to argue that highlighting the accomplishments of Black Americans and making sure that students do not assume famous figures are White is a reasonable practice. (p. 266)

While many teachers choose not to see color, others are unable to see the perspectives of people of color because of a different consciousness.

A Race-less Consciousness

Another important element of CRT is its recognition that the consciousness of people of color is markedly different from Whites because of our ongoing experience of racism (Tate, 1997). Delgado (1988) is cited by Tate (1997) arguing that, "White people rarely see acts of blatant or subtle racism, while minority people experience them all the time" (p. 219). This difference in consciousness may also help to explain why some teachers do not address race and racism in their social studies classrooms. Since Whites are not targets in the systematic oppression called racism, it is reasonable that they would not understand the importance of making sure children of color and White children understood the devastating effects of racism. A consciousness that does not include race could explain how teaching about power and authority, two subjects in theme six of the standards, would not include such issues as the maintenance of power by the White majority in both government and education in the United States from its birth (Spring, 1994).

It is reasonable that individuals without a sense of their own racial identity and racial consciousness would not recognize that racial identity is an integral part of Individual Development and Identity, Standard four in the NCSS curriculum standards. In 1994, The NCSS Task Force on Standards wrote concerning personal identity, "Central to this development are the exploration, identification, and analysis of how individuals relate to others" (p. 366). It is most likely that relating to others racially would be important and central to the conversation to those who are racially conscious; and this reality would not be so to those for whom racial consciousness is not a reality. If race is not salient in the consciousness of White people, it makes sense that teaching about race would not be important to White teachers. It is critical that these teachers who may not be conscious of race learn to be conscious of race. White teachers make up 86% of the teaching force in United States Schools (Gay & Howard, 2000) and most of their students are students of color (Branch, 2001). Given these demographic data, it seems that having teachers become race conscious would be in the interest of students of color in the public school system. Critical Race Theorists have suggested that the convergence of White interests and those of People of Color is the most likely and successful scenario in any effort to realize gains for African Americans and other People of Color.

Interest-Convergence Principle

Tate (1997) has defined the interest-convergence principle succinctly, "The interest-convergence principle is built on political history as legal precedent and emphasizes that significant progress for African Americans is achieved only when the goals of Blacks are consistent with the needs of Whites" (p. 214). Tate (1997) cites the landmark cases of *Brown* and *Bakke*, as well as Derrick Bell's commentary on these cases, to demonstrate historically that African American societal goals are achieved only when they are consistent with Whites' interests and do not disrupt Whites "superior social status" (p. 215).

With this historical, legal understanding, it is reasonable to ask the question, Is it in the interests of the mostly White, female, social studies teaching force to teach their students, who are primarily of color, about race and racism in their social studies classes? Explaining theme four, Individual Development and Identity, The NCSS Task Force on Standards declared that examining "various forms of human behavior enhances understanding of the relationships among social norms and emerging personal identities" (NCSS Task Force on Standards, 1994, p. 366). Perhaps classroom teachers do not see it in their best interests to investigate the social norms that produce identities of domination in Whites (Horsman, 1981) and identities of inferiority in People of Color (Spring, 1997).

Recognizing and investigating the tensions that exist between groups is one of the stated goals of theme five, Individuals, Groups, and Institutions (NCSS Task Force on Standards, 1994). The Task Force writes, "Young children should be assisted in recognizing the tensions that occur when the goals, values, and principles of two or more institutions or groups conflict..." (NCSS Task Force on Standards, 1994, p. 366). Perhaps the Whites who do not teach about race and racism in social studies do not see a benefit to themselves (read pedagogical value) in investigating present and historical tensions that exist between Whites and People of Color. It is possible that teachers' needs for comfort may trump student needs. Researchers in teacher education remind us that "students are uncomfortable discussing race when teacher educators explicitly try to prepare them to teach in racially diverse schools" (Neuharth-Pritchett et al., 2001, p. 257). Perhaps this discomfort does not flee with the attaining of the teaching certificate.

Explaining how theme five, Individuals, Groups, and Institutions, applies to high school students, the NCSS Task Force on Standards wrote, "High School students must understand the paradigms and traditions that undergird social and political institutions" (p. 367). A paradigm of imputed inferiority undergirded the social institutions of slavery, segregation, and Jim Crow. The same paradigm undergirded programs such at Head Start, Title I (Ladson-Billings, 1999), and deficit models of education that support other programs like them that are embraced today. Cultural deprivation paradigms have been promulgated by authors such as Benjamin Bloom (Banks, 1995), whose work continues to influence teacher education programs in the United States. It is not likely that teachers will see it in their interest to interrogate these paradigms that likely influenced their teacher education program, and in turn their own pedagogy. What some educators have determined is that high stakes testing, as a necessary part of the focus on high standards and accountability, is in their best interest.

High Stakes Testing

Some policymakers have determined that high stakes testing, not teaching, is the way to bring about increased academic achievement (Spielvogel & Magee, 2001). In at least one school district that is gaining national attention in Southern California, emphasis on testing has resulted in not only the absence of teaching race in the social studies, but in some "focus schools," the absence of a social studies curriculum altogether. Students in this Southern California school district must take the SAT-9 examination. Schools whose students perform poorly on this standardized measure are labeled "focus schools." Teachers at these schools are required to teach literacy for a three-hour block in the morning of each school day. At some schools, after lunch, teachers have the option of teaching mathematics, science, or social studies. Student teachers enrolled in my graduate courses expressed frustration that at their schools the option of teaching social studies was not offered. Some teachers in California believe omitting social studies in the early grades is especially detrimental because, in their view, all learning in the upper grades is based on social studies and science (Amrein & Berliner, 2002).

Annually the results of the SAT-9 are published in the daily newspaper, and annually the schools whose students have performed poorly and are subsequently labeled "focus" are those in which the majority of students are of color. Depriving these students of the opportunity to learn social studies in order to focus on standardized testing has had mixed results (Spielvogel & Magee, 2001). Standardized test scores in the previous two years have increased in this Southern California school district. The increases, however, have been in those schools where White students are in the majority. In fact, the "focus schools," those with the lowest scores, have consistently been those schools in which students of color are the majority (Spielvogel, 2001). In their study of 18 states that use high stakes testing, Amrein and Berliner (2002) caution those who invest in high stakes testing to consider Heisenberg's Uncertainty Principle. They state the principle, "The more important that any quantitative social indicator becomes in decision-making, the more likely it will be to distort and corrupt the social process it is intended to monitor" (Amrein & Berliner, 2002, p. 7), and comment as follows:

> When applied to a high-stakes testing environment, this principle warns us that attaching serious personal and educational consequences to performance on tests for schools, administrators, teachers, and students, may have distorting and corrupting effects. The distortions and corruptions that accompany high-stakes tests make inferences about the meanings of the scores on those tests uncertain. If there is uncertainty about the meaning of a test score the test may not be valid. Unaware of this ominous warning, supporter of high-stakes testing, particularly politicians, have caused high-stakes testing to proliferate. (p. 7)

A focus on standardized test scores as the sole measure of academic achievement will continue to have negative results for a majority of students of color because of the bias inherent in standardized tests (Moss & Schutz, 1999, 2001). That standardized tests are not normed on students of color and that the content of test items does not reflect the knowledge base or cultural background of students of color are but two areas of bias inherent in standardized tests (Cole & Moss, 1989). Other forms of bias include the nature of test items (Popham, 1998), the timed nature of the tests (Amrein & Berliner, 2002), restricted areas of assessment (Popham, 1998), and the cognitive style of learning called for (Vasquez, 1992). Popham (1998) has written that, "In many instances as much as 50–65% of what's tested is not even taught in schools—or even supposed to be taught" (p. 424). Test scores should indicate a broad range of knowledge and demonstrate a transfer of learning in areas such as reading, writing, and science (Amrein & Berliner, 2002). Test scores in California and the other 17 states studied by Amrein and Berliner (2002) rose on specific tests (the SAT-9 in California), not in domain scores that cover a broad range of knowledge. According to Amrein and Berliner (2002), there is no evidence that high stakes testing policies "result in transfer to the broader domains of knowledge and skill for which high-stakes test scores *must* (authors' emphasis) be indicators" (p. 68). Concluding that high stakes testing as a policy initiative is a failure, Amrein and Berliner (2002) warn:

> If failure in attaining the goals for which the policy was created results in disproportionate negative affects on the life chances of America's poor and minority students, as it appears to do, then a high-stakes testing policy is more than a benign error in political judgment. It is an error in policy that results in structural and institutional mechanisms that discriminate against all of America's poor and many of America's minority students. (p. 68)

This focus on high stakes testing to the deprivation of social studies content will have devastating results measured in the lack of knowledge, skills, and decision-making ability in each of the ten themes in the national standards for the social studies. Not the least of what students will lack is valuable and necessary instruction in race, racism, and race-relations.

MAKING THE CHECK GOOD

Teaching students about race in social studies will not take place in isolation. We should not forget that social studies lessons are taught in classrooms, which are a part of schools, which find their place in school districts, in cities, in some representative's political district, in one of the fifty states of our nation. In all of these contexts, there are constituents whose needs and voices should not be ignored if policies regarding the teaching of race in social studies classrooms are to be successful.

Those responsible for implementing the standards should consider seriously their own thoughts and feelings about Virginia Jackson's story and the five reasons offered here for the near absence of teaching about race in the social studies. Fear of race could be preventing one from teaching more about these important concepts. The color-blind perspective, though widespread, is detrimental and teachers should rethink behavior motivated by this principle. Teachers who show evidence of a race-less consciousness should seek help for cultivating a race-consciousness. All teachers should re-evaluate interests they may have which obviate the teaching of race and racism. Excellent teaching, not testing, will increase academic achievement for all students. Rather than preparing better tests, teachers and administrators would do well to spend more time and energy developing successful culturally relevant strategies for instruction.

REFERENCES

Adler, S. (1994). Standards in the social studies. *Social Studies and the Young Learner,* *6*(3), 17–19,22.

Adler, S. (2001). The NCSS curriculum standards. *Social Education, 65*(5), 315–318.

Aleinikoff, A.T. (1991). A case for race-consciousness. *Columbia law Review, 91,* 1060–1123.

Amrein, A.L., & Berliner, D.C. (2002, March 28). High-stakes testing, uncertainty, and student learning. *Education Policy Analysis Archives, 10,* 18. Retrieved 21 February 2003 from http://epaa.asu.edu/epaa/v10n18/.

Banks, J.A. (1994). *Multiethnic education: Theory and practice* (3rd ed.). Boston: Allyn and Bacon.

Banks, J.A., & Banks, C.A.M. (1997). *Multicultural education: Issues and perspectives* (3rd ed.). Boston: Allyn and Bacon.

Banks, J.A., & Banks, C.A.M. (1999). *Teaching strategies for the social studies: Decision-making and citizen action* (5th ed.). New York: Longman.

Branch, A.J. (1999). *Teachers conceptions of their role in the facilitation of students ethnic identitiy development.* Unpublished doctoral dissertation. University of Washington.

Branch, A.J. (2001). Increasing the numbers of Teachers of color in K–12 public schools. *The Educational Forum, 41,* 254–261.

Branch, A.J. (In Press). Practicing multicultural education: Answering recurring questions about what it is and what it is not. In M.C. Brown & R.R. Land (Eds.), *The politics of curricular change: Race, hegemony, and power in education.* New York: Peter Lang Publishing.

Carter, R. (2000). Reimagining race in education: A new paradigm from psychology. *Teachers College Record, 102*(5), 864–897.

Carter, R.T., & Goodwin, A.L. (1994). Racial identity and education. In L. Darling-Hammond (Ed.), *Review of research in education* (Vol. 20, pp. 291–336). Washington, DC: American Educational Research Association.

Chard-Yaron, S., & Kingsbury, J. (1996). Ethnic/Racial identity development: Considerations for program planning and educational practice. In C.A. Grant (Ed.), *Proceedings of the 1996 National Association for Multicultural Education* (pp. 35–45).

Cochran-Smith, M. (1995). Uncertain allies: Understanding the boundaries of race and teaching. *Harvard Educational Review, 65*(4), 541–570.

Cole, N., & Moss, P. A. (1989). Bias in test use. In R.A. Linn (Ed.), *Educational measurement* (3rd ed.). New York: Macmillan.

Elmore, R., & Sykes, G. (1992). Curriculum policy. In P.W. Jackson (Ed.), *Handbook of research on curriculum* (pp. 185–215). New York: Macmillan.

Fine, M., Powell, L.C., Weis, L., & Wong, L.M. (1997). *Off white: Readings on race, power, and society.* New York: Routledge.

Gay, G. (1985). Implications of selected models of ethnic identity development for educators. *Journal of Negro Education, 54*(1), 43–55.

Gay, G., & Howard, T.C. (2000). Multicultural teacher education for the 21st century. *The Teacher Educator, 36*(1), 1–16.

Gonzales, N.A., & Cauce, A.M. (1995). Ethnic identity and multicultural competence: Dilemmas and challenges for minority youth. In W.D. Hawley & A.W. Jackson (Eds.), *Toward a common destiny: Improving race and ethnic relations in America* (pp. 131–161). San Francisco: Jossey-Bass.

Grant, C.A., & Zozakiewicz, C.A. (1995). Student teachers, cooperating teachers and supervisors: Interrupting the multicultural silences of student teaching. In J.M. Larkin & C.E. Sleeter (Eds.), *Developing multicultural teacher education curricula* (pp. 259–273). Albany: SUNY Press.

Healey, J.F. (1998). *Race, ethnicity, gender, and class: The sociology of group conflict and change* (2nd ed.). Thousand Oaks, CA: Pine Forge Press.

Helms, J.E. (1990). *Black and white racial identity: Theory, research, and practice.* New York: Greenwood Press.

Helms, J.E. (1994). The conceptualization of racial identity and other "racial" constructs. In E.J. Trickett, R.J. Watts, & D. Birman (Eds.), *Human diversity: Perspectives on people in context* (pp. 285–311). San Francisco: Jossey-Bass.

Horsman, R. (1981). *Race and manifest destiny.* Cambridge: Harvard University Press.

Katz, P.A., & Zalk, S.R. (1978). Modification of children_s racial attitudes. *Developmental Psychology, 14*(5), 447–461.

King, M.L. (1963). "I Have A Dream." Speech delivered at the March on Washington, on the steps at the Lincoln Memorial in Washington, DC.

Ladson-Billings, G. (1995). Toward a theory of culturally relevant pedagogy. *American Educational Research Journal, 32*, 465–491.

Ladson-Billings, G. (1997). I don't see color, I just see children: Dealing with stereotyping and prejudice in young children. In M.E. Haas, & M.A. Laughlin (Eds.), *Meeting the standards: Social studies readings for K–6 educators* (pp. 15–18). Washington, DC: National Council for the Social Studies.

Ladson-Billings, G. (1999). Preparing teachers for diverse student populations: A critical race theory perspective. In A. Iran-Nejad & P.D. Pearson (Eds.), *Review of research in education* (Vol. 24, pp. 211–247). Washington, DC: American Educational Research Association.

Ladson-Billings, G., & Tate, W.F. (1995). Toward a critical race theory of education. *Teachers College Record, 97*(1), 47–68.

Lawrence, S., & Tatum, B.D. (1997a). Teachers in transition: The impact of antiracist professional development on classroom practice. *Teachers College Record, 99*(1), 162–178.

Lawrence, S., & Tatum, B.D. (1997b). White educators as allies: Moving from awareness to action. In M. Fine, L. Weiss, L. Powell, & M. Wong (Eds.), *Off white: Readings on race, power, and society* (pp. 333–342). New York: Routledge.

Moss, P.A., & Schutz, A. (2001). Educational standards assessment and the search for consensus. *American Educational Research Journal*, 38, 37–70.

Moss, P.A., & Schutz, A. (1999). Risking frankness in Educational assessment. *Phi Delta Kappan*, 80, 680–687.

Myrdal, G., with the assistance of Sterner, R., & Rose, A. (1944). *An American dilemma: The negro problem and modern democracy*. New York: Harper & Row.

National Council for the Social Studies. (1994). *Expectations of excellence: Curriculum standards for social studies*. Washington, DC: National Council for the Social Studies.

NCSS Task Force On Standards. (1994). Ten thematic strands in social studies. *Social Education*, 58(6), 365–368.

Neuharth-Pritchett, S., Reiff, J.C., & Pearson, C.A. (2001). Through the eyes of pre-service teachers: Implications for the multicultural journey from teacher education. *Journal of Research in Childhood Education*, 15(2), 256–269.

Ochoa-Becker, A.S. (2001). A critique of the ncss curriculum standards. *Social Education*, 65(3), 165–168.

Paley, V.G. (1989). *White teacher*. Cambridge, MA: Harvard University Press.

Phinney, J.S. (1996). When we talk about American ethnic groups, what do we mean? *American Psychologist*, 51(9), 918–927.

Popham, W.J. (2000). *Modern education*. Boston: Allyn & Bacon.

Porter, A. (1989). External standards and good teaching: The pros and cons of telling teachers what to do. *Educational Evaluation and Policy Analysis*, 11, 343–356.

Rogers, C. (1961). *On becoming a person*. Boston: Houghton Mifflin.

Saad, L. (2001, June). Blacks less satisfied than hispanics with their quality of life. *The Gallup Poll Monthly*, 429, 47–51.

Saad, L., & Newport, F. (2001, July). Blacks and whites differ about treatment of Blacks in America Today. *The Gallup Poll Monthly*, 430, 58–63.

Schofield, J.W. (1997). Causes and consequences of the colorblind perspective. In J.A. Banks & C.A.M. Banks (Eds.), *Multicultural education: Issues and perspectives* (3rd ed., pp. 251–271). Boston: Allyn and Bacon.

Schwille, J., Porter, A., Belli, G., Floden, R., Freeman, D., Knappen, L., Kuhs, T., & Schmidt, W. (1986). Teachers as policy brokers in the context of elementary school mathematics. In L. Shulman & G. Sykes (Eds.), *The handbook of teaching and policy* (pp. 370–391). New York: Longmans.

Simmons, W.W. (2000, July-December). Black Americans feel "cheated" by election 2000. *The Gallup Poll Monthly*, 423, 24–30.

Smylie, M.A. (1994). Redesigning teachers' work: Connection to the classroom. *Review of Research in Education*, 20, 129–177.

Spielvogel, J. (2001, August 16). Scores on writing exam "sobering," here and statewide. *The San Diego Union-Tribune*, pp. B1, B8–9.

Spielvogel, J., & Magee, M. (2001, August 16). County students merely hold their own on basic skills test. *The San Diego Union-Tribune*, pp. B1, B8–9.

Spring, J. (1994). *Deculturalization and the struggle for equality: A brief history of the education of dominated cultures in the United States*. New York: McGraw-Hill.

Steele, C.M., & Aronson, J. (1995). Stereotype threat and the intellectual test performance of African Americans. *Journal of personality and Social Psychology, 69*(5), 797–812.

Talbert, J.E., & McLaughlin, M.W. (1993). Understanding teaching in context. In D.K. Cohen, M.W. McLaughlin, & J.E. Talbert (Eds.), *Teaching for understanding: issues for policy and practice* (pp. 167–206). San Francisco: Jossey-Bass.

Tate, W.F. (1997). Critical race theory and education: History, theory, and implications. In M.W. Apple (Ed.), *Review of research in education* (Vol. 22, pp. 195–247). Washington, DC: American Educational Research Association.

Tate, W.F., Ladson-Billings, G., & Grant, C. (1993). The Brown decision revisited: Mathematizing social problems. *Educational Policy, 7,* 255–275.

Thompson, A. (1998). Not the color purple: Black feminist lessons for educational caring. *Harvard Educational Review, 68*(4), 522–554.

U.S. Department of Education. (1992). *America 2000.* Washington, DC: U.S. Department of Education.

U.S. Department of Education (1983). *A nation at risk: the imperative for educational reform: a report to the nation and the secretary of education, United States Department of Education.* Washington, DC: The Commission On Excellence in Education.

Vasquez, J. (1992). Cognitive style and academic attainment. In J. Lynch, C. Modgill, & S. Modgill (Eds.), *Cultural diversity and the schools, Vol. III, Equity or excellence? Education and cultural reproduction* (pp. 163–179). London: Falmer Press.

Wise, T. (2001). See no evil: Perception and reality in black and white. *The Washington Informer, 38,* 36, 12.

part III

THE CURRICULUM

CHAPTER 7

DERACIALIZATION IN SOCIAL STUDIES TEACHER EDUCATION TEXTBOOKS

Geneva Gay

ABSTRACT

The results of a review of ten social studies teacher education textbooks are presented in this chapter. The books selected for review are authored by leading scholars and were published between 1994 and 2001. They were examined to determine if race and racism were dealt with explicitly, at high levels of significance, depth and comprehensiveness of analysis, within the mainstream narrative text, and if techniques were presented for how prospective teachers can deal with these issues in their K–12 classrooms. The results were consistently negative across all of the books reviewed. All of them either avoid race and racism entirely, or treat these issues superficially and sporadically. The author suggests that these shortcomings in professional instruction materials place prospective teachers in peril by not providing them with adequate knowledge and skills about how to engage with race and to combat racism.

Critical Race Theory Perspectives on the Social Studies, pages 123–147
Copyright © 2003 by Information Age Publishing

INTRODUCTION

There is a long history of content analysis research on social studies textbooks to determine how they treat the life experiences, contributions, sociopolitical issues, and living conditions of groups of color in the United States, as well as relationships between racial minorities and mainstream European Americans. This tradition goes back to the 1880s, and has focused on textbooks for students in elementary, middle, and high schools. Data produced by these studies reveal that blatant racism toward and stereotypical portrayals of African, Latino, Native, and Asian Americans have diminished significantly over time. Technical elements of social studies education, such as the inclusion of original documents, more accurate maps, a wider range of resource materials, and variety in instructional strategies also have improved. However, these texts still are not as good as they need to be in their treatment of racial issues, ethnic and cultural diversity, or anything else that is potentially controversial and contentious. They continue to be rather bland and dull; do not discuss topics with much action, coherency, or depth of detail; ignore new compelling events and individuals; and are much more descriptive than critical or analytical (Beck & McKeown, 1991; Gordy & Pritchard, 1995; Loewen, 1995; Zarrillo, 2000).

Consequently, many students find social studies textbooks boring, especially U.S. history. Loewen (1995) attributes this boredom to the fact that:

> The stories that history textbooks tell are predictable; every problem has already been solved or is about to be solved. Textbooks exclude conflict or real suspense. They leave out anything that might reflect badly upon our national character. When they try drama they achieve only melodrama, because readers know that everything will turn out fine in the end.... Most authors of history textbooks don't even try for melodrama. Instead, they write in a tone that if heard aloud might be described as "mumbling lecturer." No wonder students lose interest. (p. 2)

Textbooks also "almost never use the present to illuminate the past ... [or] the past to illuminate the present. They portray the past as a simple-minded morality play. "Be a good citizen" is the message that textbooks extract from the past. "You have a proud heritage. Be all that you can be. After all, look what the United States has accomplished" (Loewen 1995, p. 3). These promotions of unquestionable patriotism distort historical realities. They do not provide ample opportunities for students to analyze the validity of the U.S. claims to unblemished greatness, how the nation's accomplishments came to be, who is served best by them, and the problematic consequences of its historical legacies. As Loewen (1995) explains,

While there is nothing wrong with optimism, it can become something of a burden for students of color, children from working-class parents, girls who notice a dearth of female historical figures, or members of any group that has not achieved socioeconomic success. The optimistic approach prevents any understanding of failure other than blaming the victim. No wonder children of color are alienated. Even for male children from affluent white families, bland optimism gets pretty boring after eight hundred pages. (p. 3)

IMPORTANCE OF TEXTBOOKS

Despite these limitations textbooks continue to monopolize social studies instructional materials. They account for 70 to 95% of the content presented in K–12 classroom instruction (Altbach, Kelly, Petrie, & Weis, 1991; Davis, Ponder, Burlbaw, Garza-Lubeck, & Moss, 1986; Finkelstein, Nielsen, & Switzer, 1993; Goldstein, 1978; Wade, 1993). History textbooks are within the higher end of this range (Loewen, 1995).

Many teachers do not extend or replace the analyses of issues presented in textbooks with other sources. This is so for a host of reasons, including time limitations; the persuasive power of professional socialization and tradition; lack of appropriate preparatory, learning experiences; and the fact that many teachers do not have a depth of countervailing knowledge about topics included in and excluded from social studies textbooks. Several researchers (Crabtree & O'Shea, 1991; Engle 1986; Loewen, 1995; Nelson & Stanley, 1985) report that many teachers do not know much history, and are intimidated by controversy and uncertainty. Nor do they know how to handle these topics in their instruction. And, too many students, at every level of the educational enterprise, continue to assume that if something is in the textbooks it must be true, and if it's not included it must not be very important. On this point Loewen (1995, p. 5) explains that, "Because textbooks employ such a godlike tone, it never occurs to most students to question them." The "rhetoric of certainty" (p. 281) that characterizes the narrative of most social studies textbooks makes it difficult for teachers to "introduce either controversy or uncertainty into the classroom without deviating from the usual standards of discourse" (p. 218). These situations are extremely problematic for teaching challenging topics that are routinely excluded from or treated superficially in textbooks, such as racism and other forms of oppression, race relations, social injustices, human rights, ethnic and cultural diversity, and sociopolitical activism.

Textbooks are as prominent in teacher education as they are in K–12 classrooms. This may indeed be the place where dependence of teachers on textbooks for instructional content is firmly entrenched. What they have experienced as students is reinforced in their professional preparation. Even in learning situations for prospective teachers where textbooks are supplemented with other sources of information, such as journal articles, book chapters, and personal or practical experiences, authors tend not to speak fundamentally different in them from how they write in their textbooks. As instructors they may not provide resources, perspectives, and learning experiences that are radically different from what is included in their own and their colleagues' authored materials. The adage that teachers teach as they were taught holds true as much for the selection of instructional materials as for methodology. Thus, teachers who have learned through reliance of textbooks, in turn, perpetuate this reliance in teaching their own students.

An additional complicating factor about the dominance of textbooks in classroom instruction is their incontestability. Teachers are not taught, nor do they encourage their students, to critically examine what is presented in textbooks, and what is excluded. Kincheloe (2001) refers to this approach to teaching in methods classes as "nonconceptual" (p. 19), and describes it as:

> consistently marked by an absence of analytical questions about and critical examination of the nature of the social studies curriculum. Questions concerning the origins of practices, the implicit assumptions underlying certain language used in the discipline, the connections between social studies teaching and larger socio-political issues, and the general purposes of social studies methods classes in a democratic society [are] almost always ignored. (p. 19)

Loewen (1995) attributes this kind of uncritical acceptance of what is taught in textbooks to the socialization function of education, which "tells people what to think and how to act and requires them to conform ... [and] simply to accept the rightness of our society" (p. 301). While his comments are directed specifically to teaching historical distortions to high school students they also are applicable to the education of social studies teachers.

To what extent do textbooks for pre-service social studies teachers reflect or deviate from these claims, and the trends found in social studies materials for K–12 students? How do social studies textbooks written for use in teacher education programs deal with race, racism, and the life experiences of racial groups within the United States? What messages do these resources model for teaching about race and racism? These are the issues of emphasis in this discussion. They are of utmost importance because of their centrality to the mission of social studies education; their prominence in U.S. history, culture, and life; and the impact that professional preparation has on the subsequent performance of teaching in classrooms. Race and racism are definitive, persistent, and pervasive features of

U.S. history and life. Loewen (1995) makes several observations that support this viewpoint. Among them are:

- "Perhaps the most pervasive theme in our history is the domination of black America by white America. Race is the sharpest and deepest division in American life" (p. 131)
- "Slavery's twin legacies to the present are the social and economic inferiority it conferred upon blacks and the cultural racism it instilled in whites. Both continue to haunt our society" (p. 136).
- "In omitting racism or treating it so poorly, history textbooks shirk a critical responsibility. . . ." (p. 138).
- "Educators justify teaching history because it gives us perspective on the present. If there is one issue in the present to which authors should relate the history they tell, the issue is racism" (p. 163).

Race and racism are deeply intertwined with students developing skills (such as moral courage and political activism for social justice and transformation) for democratic citizenship. One way to assess whether social studies teachers are prepared to deal effectively with these challenges in their classroom instruction is to determine how they are addressed in their professional preparation. Social studies methods textbooks for pre-service teachers is a valuable source of information in this assessment.

SEARCHING FOR ANSWERS

I began the search for answers to the questions of interest in this discussion by checking ERIC documents and the library collections at my university (which is a tier one research institution) for research and scholarship on social studies education textbooks. None was revealed. The next step was to search web sites looking for the same information. The third task was to identify methods textbooks for review.

Ten social studies methods textbooks were chosen for this analysis. All of them are synoptic texts, written by well established and highly reputable scholars in the field, and intended for use in pre-service teacher education and /or graduate studies programs. Synoptic texts present overviews of state-of-the -field portrayals of the theoretical developments, principles, and practices in a given area of study (Schubert, 1986). This type of textbook was selected as the unit of analysis because they allow authors to deal with issues in greater depth, in a variety of ways, and over the span of different dimensions of a field of study. They are more broadly focused, cohesive, and comprehensive than book chapters or journal articles, which tend to be issues-specific. Authors may not address a particular issue in a given article or book chapter because it was beyond the boundaries of the overall project, or because of limited space allocations. For example, an author may not include issues about world peace in an article or book chapter on racial discrimination in U.S. employment practices because they are not relevant to the assigned task. Conversely, a synoptic textbook may rightly include both topics without any incompatibility issues. The subsequent discussion presents the results of the textbook reviews, and suggests some ways their treatment of race and racism can be improved.

Of the ten books selected for review (see Appendix A for the complete list) four are targeted specifically for teaching in elementary schools (Chapin & Messick, 1996; Ellis, 1995; Parker, 2001; Zarrillo, 2000). Presumably, they can be used for college students enrolled in pre-service teacher education as well as graduate degree programs. One of the books (Garcia & Michaelis, 2001) is intended for preparing pre-service social studies teachers for grades K–8. Two of the textbooks reviewed (Laughlin & Hartoonian, 1995; Singer, 1997) are directed toward secondary teaching, with one claiming "secondary schools" as its focus and the other emphasizing "middle and high schools." The other two books (Banks & Banks, 1999; Kincheloe, 2001) do not specify any given school level of teaching. One of these fits the conventions of a methods textbook, but the other one does not. The last one is much more critical and analytical than a typical "how to do" book for teaching social studies to K–12 students. As such, it is more appropriate for graduate student seminars. This book, entitled *Getting Beyond the Facts* (Kincheloe, 2001) declares a postmodernist and knowledge construction ideology. It is described on the cover as "focusing on the importance of knowledge production and interpretation" (n.p.). The author "calls for the education of social studies teachers as researchers who can critique and reconstruct curriculum as they expose the covert, ideological functions of contemporary educational reforms and top-down standards-driven social studies subject matter" (n.p.).

All of the books reviewed were published between 1994 and 2001. However, only four of the ten are first editions. Of the others, one each is the second, fourth, fifth, sixth, eleventh, and twelfth edition. All of these editions claim, in some form or another, that their content has been revised to reflect the most recent research and development in social studies education, and pressing issues in the United States and the world. The specific publication dates for selecting books for review were not established in advance, but a conscious decision was made to examine the most recently published books possible. The decision was based on the assumption that more recently published textbooks would include discussions of race-related issues and racism. Research on textbooks has provided evidence that instructional materials designed for K–12 students published as recently as the early 1990s continue to avoid controversial issues related to ethnic. racial, and cultural diversity. Textbooks for teacher education students may follow similar trends.

Therefore, older books would not produce a wealth of information on the topics of interest in this review. Stated differently, I hoped recent social studies education textbooks would have features similar to those embedded in Zarrillo's (2000) declaration that "diversity is a theme which unifies social studies teaching and learning," and "we must acknowledge it in our students, present it as our curriculum, and build upon it as a civic value" (p. iv). If this statement were taken seriously in teacher preparation programs, then the controversies, challenges, invitations, and enrichments embedded in racial, ethnic, and cultural diversity for building national community and citizenship would be examined openly and thoroughly.

Once the books were selected, a list of criteria were identified for use in analyzing their content to determine if deracialization were evident, and if so, how is it manifested and to what extent. For purposes of this discussion "deracialization" is defined as de-emphasizing, distorting, excluding, or avoiding elements of race and racism in the presentation of individuals, the analysis of critical events, and the exploration of sociopolitical issues in educational programs and practices. The first level of analysis was guided by the criterion of *inclusion or visibility*—that is, whether race, racism, and other race-related issues are present overtly in the content of the textbooks. For example, do social studies methods textbooks routinely specify the racial identity of individuals named in their content, and is racism examined explicitly as a political, moral, ethical, economic, and social justice challenge to principles of democracy and human rights.

The inclusion analyses were to be complemented with higher order evaluative criteria to determine the *quality* of the treatment given to race-related issues and racism. The criteria used for this purpose were selected from prior content analysis research on social studies textbooks for K–12 students. They included *significance, comprehensiveness, balance, concreteness, depth, realism,* and *integration* (Davis et al., 1986; Henry, 1970; Kane, 1970; Michigan State Department of Education, 1972; www.american.education/ sadker/curriculum bias.htm). These criteria helped to determine if the information presented about race and racism is important and meaningful; offer specific descriptive, analytical, and critical details; provide multiple perspectives (positive, negative, insider/outsider; transformative possibilities and consequences); and is incorporated into or marginalized from the mainstream narrative text. They seemed appropriate for two reasons. First, no content analysis research on social studies teacher education textbooks has been conducted to produce its own criteria. Second, the criteria used to analyze K–12 textbooks have been "tested" and validated over time. Since there should be some parallelism between what teacher education students learn about how to teach social studies and what K–12 students are to be taught, the criteria for analysis should apply, with minor modifications, to both sets of instructional materials.

I used several different strategies to try to locate actual substantive content within the textbooks that might deal with race and racism. I began by reading the Preface to see what were the authors' philosophical orientations and the focal parameters of the books. Next, I scanned the tables of content and the indexes looking for organizational cues pertinent to my issues of interest. If any existed, I went to those sections of the books and read them, looking first to find out what was included and then to determine its quality. These efforts were followed with looking for other words, phrases, and names of highly recognizable individuals and events that are racially-specific and associated with experiences of and/or resistance to racism. For example, the names of ethnic categories of color, such as African, Latino, Native, and Asian Americans, as well as specific groups within these clusters (i.e., Mexican Americans, Vietnamese Americans, Yakimas, etc.). Searching for discussions of racism through high profile contemporary individuals from different ethnic groups who were victims of or resistors to racism (such as Morris Dees, Marian Wright Edleman, Randall Robinson) produced no results. I then turned to well-known historical luminaries such as Caesar Chavez, Martin Luther King, Jr., Mary McLeod Bethune, Chief Seattle, Rosa Parks, Sitting Bull, Fannie Lou Hammer, and Frederick Douglass.

I also tried to track how the books on my review list dealt with race and racism through critical events and major organizations, such as the interment of Japanese Americans; the enslavement of African Americans; the placement of Native Americans on reservations; *Brown vs. Board of Education* and school desegregation; racial disparities in employment, criminal justice, and educational achievement; the 1960s and 1970s Civil Rights Movements and voter registration campaigns; ethnic demographics and population trends; La Raza; the NAACP; the KKK and Aryan Nation; the United Farmer Workers Union; and the Children's Defense Fund. Finally, I scanned the entire content of the books, and did close reading of the sections that showed any indications of having information about anything even remotely related to race and racism. Here I focused on the narrative text as well as other kinds of content such as visual illustrations, sample lesson plans, suggested readings, and extending learning activities.

SIMILARITIES AND DIFFERENCES AMONG TEXTBOOKS

At first look the social studies education textbooks I reviewed seem to be quite different. They certainly vary in length, with the shortest having 307 pages and longest having 818. Eight of them fall within the 372–502 range.

Books designated for secondary social studies teaching, and the ones that do not specify a school level focus tend to be longer than those for elementary education. Some purport to be basic guides to social studies instruction and educating for effective, enlighten, and actively engaged citizenship, while others declare a focus on translating theoretical principles into practical applications, and teaching social studies knowledge, skills, and curriculum transformation. On closer scrutiny, however, these are minor differences. With the exception of one, these books are much more alike than they are different, and this commonality is to the detriment of the inclusion of race and racism.

The organizational structures and content emphases of these books are strikingly similar, and may be a deterrent to overt discussions of race and racism. They exemplify the common "technical view of social studies teaching" described by Kincheloe (2001, p. 19). It is promoted by methods textbooks examining, "in varying degrees of sophistication" (p. 19) lesson planning, behavioral objectives, evaluation, social studies materials, current events, and instructional strategies. The topics in the books I reviewed varied somewhat from this list, but not significantly. Behavioral objectives have been replaced in some of the texts by references to standards of the National Council for the Social Studies, the disciplines (history, geography, economics, etc.), and state departments of education. The "technical components" or "fundamentals" of social studies teaching common to these books parallel those identified by Kincheloe, and add others on the conceptual foundations of the social studies. Frequently discussed instructional techniques such as cooperative learning, inquiry, critical thinking and decision-making, values analysis, simulations, and concept mastery; reading in the social studies; democratic citizenship; contemporary issues like global education, multicultural education, environmental education, and gender equity; teaching through social science disciplinary perspectives (e.g., history, geography, political science, economics, sociology, anthropology); technology; and instructional resources such as personal experiences, primary sources, major documents, and oral histories. Even through Kincheloe's (2001) *Getting Beyond the Facts* represents a significant departure from this pattern, it does not abandoned it entirely. One section of his book is still devoted to "the foundations of the social studies," and another one to "the disciplines and the social studies."

The persistence of this organizational structure seems to be more of an obstacle than an invitation to the inclusion of teaching prospective teachers about race and racism, and how to deal with these issues in their own classroom instruction. The question is, where would they fit. The theoretical answer is, "everywhere." But the authors of these textbooks do not seem to think so. Some of them make concessions by inserting a chapter or section on multicultural education, cultural diversity, and ethnic groups. For example, Chapin and Messick (1999) devote a chapter to "cultural learning." Ellis (1998) presents a two-page "multicultural perspective" on citizenship through a personal interview with a colleague, who is a "recognized authority on multicultural education" (p. 292), and a lesson prompt about Zuni culture for teaching values analysis. Martorella (1994) provides a two-page lesson plan outline that focuses on the concepts of culture and diversity as they relate to Navajos. It appears in a chapter entitled, "Preparing Children to Live in a Global and Culturally Diverse World" (pp. 247–274), along with discussions of multicultural education and social consciousness. Much of Parker's (2001) second chapter on "Knowing the Children We Teach" provide guidelines for teaching in ethnically, culturally, and linguistically diverse classrooms, and understanding changing demographics related to race, ethnicity, culture, gender, language, special needs, and multiple intelligence. Race and racism are not openly discussed in any of these topics.

LOCATING RACE AND RACISM

The results of the substantive review of social studies teacher education textbooks are shocking and bewildering. There is very little about race and racism in these textbooks. While social studies textbooks for K–12 students are often described as "sanitized" when it comes to racism and other potentially troubling race-conscious issues the books in this review went even further. They are virtually bleached! The most distinguished features of their treatment of these issues are avoidance and invisibility. They practice an extreme form of deracialization by excluding race related issues, events, and experiences almost entirely. This is particularly troubling since so much of what social studies education is supposed to be about have direct implications and opportunities for analyzing racial challenges, resisting racism, and developing the knowledge and skills needed as citizens of a race-conscious society and world.

Evidence to support these conclusions derives from the application of the inclusion, significance, concreteness, and comprehensiveness criteria to the indexes and narrative content of the textbooks. My findings are similar to Loewen's (1995). Of the twelve books for high school students that he analyzed "racism, racial prejudice, or any term beginning with race" (p. 137) were included in the indexes of only five. In my review of ten social studies teacher education three of them (Garcia & Michaelis, 2001; Ellis, 1995; Singer, 1997) have single references to race and/or racism in their indexes. One (Parker 2001) has a single page index for race, and 10 page references for racism. Another (Kincheloe, 2001) has 20 page references distributed across race, class, and gender; racial biases, prejudice, justice, hatred, fear, violence, and racism. Searches for other topics in the indexes that might evoke discussions of racism and race—such as the names of specific ethnic groups, sociopolitical incidents like riots and hate crimes, and civil rights activism—produced very few references.

On rare occasion there is an index mention of an ethnic group, but often not more than one within any textbook; they have a very restricted range of information; and virtually none are centered in discussions of race and racism. For example, Ellis (1995) includes one index entry for Native Americans, and Hopis, but no other ethnic groups of color. Three page references are given for African Americans by Singer (1997), but no other group. Kincheloe (1997) includes index references for all four categories of ethnic groups of color—African, Asian, Latino, and Native Americans. All of these except Latinos are included in Zarrillo's (2000) index as well, but are limited to a four-page discussion of cultural diversity. The index to Parker's (2001) book also identifies African, Asian, and Native Americans, and a single listing for Hispanics, but they often address students (i.e., Native American students, etc.) rather than the histories, lives , cultures, contributions, and conditions of these groups. Even those textbooks that have a few index references to groups of color limit them to the categorical names and do not identify specific constituent groups. For instance, Chinese Americans, Japanese Americans, Puerto Ricans, and immigrants from different African and Caribbean nations are not mentioned in the indexes.

While the results from checking the indexes of the textbooks in this review are very disturbing, they are viewed cautiously because they may not be very dependable. All the items included in the narrative content of texts are not always indexed. For example, Parker (2001) and Zarrillo (2000) make reference to a wide range of different ethnic groups throughout most of the narrative content of their textbooks, even though they are not identified in the indexes. Furthermore, the appearance of something in the index is no indication of the quality of its treatment in the narrative text. One illustration of this occurs in Parker's textbook. The index reference for race and one of those for racism deal with definitions, all of which are rather genteel and nonthreatening. Racism is defined as negative social values associated with the physical characteristics of groups of color (p. 41). This definition is more closely akin to prejudice than racism. The content on two of the pages cited in the index is about gender (not racial) discrimination in classroom interactions, and two others simply mention the phrase, "racial stereotyping." The extent of yet another citation is the single statement that "racism and sexism, like language and body image, are learned from these social environments" (Parker, p. 134).

Loewen (1995) and Kincheloe (2001) provide explanations that may account, at least in part, for the blatant absence of discussions of race and racism in textbooks for social studies teacher preparation. Loewen points out that social studies education routinely ignores controversial issues, or anything that might reflect negatively on the United States, and emphasizes optimism and progressivism in portrayals of U.S. history and life. For textbooks to explicitly acknowledge and thoroughly analyze race and racism would conflict with these value orientations and academic conventions. Kincheloe's analyses of social studies methods textbooks indicates that most present a "nonconceptual, technical view of social studies teaching" (p. 19), and there is a strong similarity of content across different authors that concentrates on the mechanics of teaching. These technical mechanics are taught in a decontextualized manner and divorced from substantive content about certain issues and experiences in U.S. society, particularly those dealing with race and racism.

Although Kincheloe makes a persuasive general argument about the importance of social studies teachers being critical researchers, and connecting what is taught with what is lived he, too, avoids dealing explicitly with highly controversial issues. He explains that "Who we are is always influenced by the location in the web of reality from which life is experienced and understood"; that "Depending on such infinite possibilities of places to stand in the web, many of us see the world in very different ways"; that "Whatever our viewpoint, it is limited by what we have experienced, and the information about the world we have encountered"; and that "power wielders play a profound role in filtering the way all of us come to see and make sense of the world, ourselves, and our relationships to it" (pp. 52–53). These points are well taken, but Kincheloe does not provide specific and detailed racially-specific examples to illustrate the meaning of these conceptual ideas. There are many racial situations and events throughout U.S. history, and across a wide variety of disciplinary arenas, that attest graphically to the verity of experience, location, perspective, positionality, and knowledge manipulation on conceptions of reality. Among them are racially motivated oppressive practices, and the long-range economic, political, cultural, psychological, and educational consequences of disparities in power, privilege, and marginality among diverse ethnic and racial groups in contemporary society. Yet, these are repeatedly ignored in social studies teacher education textbooks.

INSIDE THE SUBSTANTIVE CONTENT

Looking at the actual content of the texts indicates that the situation is not much better than examining the indexes with respect to the treatment of race and racism. These issues are mentioned more frequently than the indexes would suggest, but the quality of their treatment is incredibly poor.

In fact, none of the 10 textbooks comes close to providing an adequate discussion of these topics. In most instances, race and racism receive only passing reference without any detailed explanations, critical analyses, or transformative instructional possibilities. If these words were deleted from the content of the texts that do include them, nothing of value would be lost. There are several ways in which the textbooks reviewed for this discussion practice deracialization within their substantive content. These are treating race and racism as insignificant topics, making them invisible, avoiding them, excluding contemporary references, not naming individuals and events, and limiting issues related to race and racism to restricted aspects of the text. Each of these is explained in greater detail.

Insignificance

For Kincheloe (2001), who has the greatest number of index references to race and racism in his text, "race" is merely part of a general phrase embedded in other statements. Illustrative of this pattern are the following notations he makes within a single page of narration:

- "The economic divisions of class serve to structure the way race and gender manifest themselves."
- "...connections between race, class, and gender exists, [but] we never know how to predict the effects of the interactions.
- "racial and gender hostilities ... can subvert class solidarity."
- "As these race, class, and gender forces interact, sometimes in complementary and sometimes in contradictory ways,..."
- "Race, class, and gender dynamics combine to create a larger playing field with more options for some and a smaller, more limited field for others."
- "As it integrates and connects the study of race, class, and gender to the nature of consciousness construction, knowledge production, and modes of expression, a critical democratic social studies embraces a social vision that moves beyond the particular concerns of specific social groups" (p. 138).

These statements sound rather ritualistic, sloganistic, and tokenistic—as if the author were being "politically correct" in mentioning the words "race, class, and gender," but does not give the issues any rigorous scholarly treatment. A similar "passing reference" is exhibited toward racism. It is evident in Kincheloe's (2001) discussion of "multidisciplinarity, connectedness, and knowledge production" (pp. 54–56). He argues that "Racism can't be understood as simply a sociological issue, but as a historical, cultural, psychological, psychoanalytic, economic, and political dynamic.

Racism, and other issues like it, can only be understood as an integrated whole" (pp. 54–55). The textbooks included in this review do not follow this advice. Their treatment of race and racism is consistent with criticisms against social studies textbooks for K–12 students on their inadequate explanations and analyses of complex topics and events (Beck & McKeown, 1991).

None of the textbooks reviewed discusses *race and racism as significant topics in their own right which deserve independent and thorough examination.* When mentioned at all they are embedded in other topics, simply identified as issues that need to be studied, or included as part of sample lessons collected by the textbook authors. Nowhere in these books will prospective teachers find any substantial information about what race and racism mean; how they function in shaping the life and experiences of individuals, groups, and societies; why they should be central themes in social studies education; or the explicit identification of racially motivated attitudes, values, and behaviors. Nor will they find any carefully constructed instructions on how to teach these issues to K–12 students.

Singer's (1997) textbook is a little better than most of the others. In one instance, he describes why a Brooklyn, New York middle school teacher realized that "building a transformative classroom community meant he had to deal with the impact of racism in the lives of his African-American, Caribbean, and Latino/a students" (p. 76). The presentation is an interesting story but it is more about the teacher in question than teaching techniques for understanding and resisting racism. The explanation is too sketchy for readers to extrapolate strategies for potential use in their own classroom instruction, and they receive no assistance from the author in how to do this. At other times Singer does provide rich details on sample lesson plans and instructional strategies. One instance of this occurs in the classroom activities suggested in a section on organizing "a controversy-centered, thematic curriculum," that emphasizes the idea of resistance to oppression as a human right (pp. 242 –248). These activities include different approaches to teaching this topic, but, curiously, racism is never mentioned. Race appears only once, and not within the context of the main discussion. At the end of the section, the author asks reflectively of readers, "Would the race or ethnicity of your students influence your approach to these questions and activities? Why or why not?" This is an important question, but it still skates around the more critical point of social studies methods textbooks dealing explicitly and deeply with race and racism.

Occasionally, Banks and Banks (1999) offer small glimpses of hope that some worthwhile content about racial issues will be treated seriously. But, most of the time this hope does not reach full realization. In addition to the typical narrative content, their textbook includes three other recurring substantive features— profiles, inquiry strategies, and features. The profiles present highly accomplished individuals in the different social sciences, such as historians, sociologists, economists, political scientists, and anthropologists. Of the 10 people profiled across several chapters three are people of color—a Japanese American male historian, an African American female historian, and an African American male sociologist. While they are placed in the chapter that deals with their disciplinary expertise, they, too, serve more of a decorative and symbolic function than a substantive one because no direct linkage is made between these inserts and the rest of the text. The inquiry strategies and features are about events and situations that exemplify a social studies education concept, skill, or instructional strategy, and suggestions are provided for how teachers can use them with students. Several of these deal with racially-specific issues, such as the Montgomery Bus Boycott of the 1950s, Sojourner Truth's struggle against racial and gender discrimination, racism experienced by African Americans in college, the continuing importance of race in the United States, and the geography of Latinos.

Unfortunately, these positive features of the Banks and Banks text simultaneously represent an important way that deracialization is practiced in social studies methods textbooks. This is *imbalance* in the treatment of different groups of color. What little information is provided attends more to African Americans than other groups, followed in frequency by Native and Latino Americans. Asian Americans are virtually invisible in all of the textbooks included in this review, except for the infrequent reference to the internment and the historical immigration of Japanese and Chinese Americans. Other groups in the Asian American ethnic cluster who are recent arrivals to the United States, such as Hmongs, Vietnamese, and Cambodians, as well as immigrants from various Caribbean, African, and Spanish-speaking countries are never mentioned.

Avoidance

Deracialization also is transmitted *through understating and avoiding* addressing race and racism. Even the few racially-related situations that are included in the social studies methods textbooks do not address the harshest atrocities of racism. The presentations are devoid of the anguish, violation of human rights and dignity, and immorality wrought by racism. A case in point is Banks and Banks' (1999) treatment of Sojourner Truth's "Ain't I a Woman" speech presented at the Ohio Women's Rights Convention in 1851. It is presented as an "inquiry strategy" on developing hypotheses using primary sources. In addition to reading the passage and using it to test hypotheses about women's rights, the authors suggest that students "note how the rights of African American women and White women were alike and different" (p. 71). This task could be completed without the students ever mentioning racism.

Another example of understating race and racism is found in the discussion of multicultural education by Martorella (1994). He emphasizes its "gentler" and least controversial goals, such as acquiring information about diverse cultural groups, learning tolerance for diversity, improving cross-cultural interactions, cultural and gender perspective-taking, and identifying stereotypes, prejudices, and discrimination. No mention is made of combating racism, and transforming society to redistribute power and privilege among racial groups. This oversight may be defended by some on the basis that Martorella's text is designed for teaching elementary school children, and young students are not developmentally ready to grapple with such harsh realities. This is not a defensible justification for skirting race and racism in social studies education for any age. It is never too soon to begin to teach students skills for confronting and combating racism, and for understanding the role of race in our individual and collective lives. To argue the contrary is, in itself, an act of deracialization.

Laughlin and Hartoonian (1995) provide another illustration of how race and racism are avoided in social studies methods textbooks. They raise the question of bias in testing (p. 369). This is a very critical, persistent, and problematic issue, but their discussion of it is overly terse and superficial. It provides some very general statements without sufficient concrete explanations, references to specific racial groups, and suggestions for how social studies educators can grapple with bias and discrimination in testing. Among these are the comments that "minority group students and students from lower socioeconomic backgrounds usually score lower than middle-class students on most standardized tests ... , although the gap is lessening" (p. 369). Why aren't the "minority groups named," and the claim that the achievement gap is declining explained fully or problematized? Laughlin and Hartoonian continue with "experts, parents, and educators are more and more concerned about the effects of testing on minority students" (p. 369). It would have been helpful to know specifically who some of these people are and their particular concerns. Similarly, the suggestions that "To help students overcome test anxiety teachers should teach test-taking skills ... [and] simplify test-taking procedures and mechanics" (p. 362) is too vague to be of much instructional value. This advice is fine as far is it goes; it just doesn't go nearly far enough. The extent of the lack of depth and specificity in this discussion leaves the impression that the authors are engaging in "ritualistic representation." While they recognize the need to include test bias in their text, they aren't willing to give it the serious analysis the topic deserves, and that prospective teachers need to begin to comprehend its complexity, and to develop skills to deal with it in their classroom teaching.

A promising possibility exists in the proposal made by Ellis (1995) for children to act as "researchers by conducting investigations into racism and sexism" (pp. 196–199). Unfortunately, the promise is not realized because he fails to include significant manifestations of racism to be researched. The examples he provides are shifts in the racial composition of a particular school over a 10-year period of time, changing portrayal of minorities and race bias in textbooks, studies of minorities in television programs and commercials; and conducting experiments on the pre-posttest attitudes of students who watch a movie that deals with racial prejudices and the effects of guests who speak about racism. While all of these topics do touch lightly on racism, they don't deal with it in depth or at high levels of significance. They do not target racist actions that are life-altering at the institutional level, and operate in mainstream political, economic, social, and educational programs and practices.

Parker (2001) comes closest to breaking these patterns of avoiding race and racism. His text includes several examples that can provide pre-service teachers with knowledge, skills, and techniques for dealing with these issues in their classrooms. However, he tends to advise but does not model his proposals in his own narrative content, and the suggestions he offers do not have sufficient operational details. Among his guidelines for implementing multicultural curriculum is, "Teach directly about prejudice, racism, discrimination, and stereotyping," because "These are central social science concepts that children need to understand as social studies students and as citizens" (p. 36). By limiting their significance to "social science concepts" Parker takes away much of the veracity of these issues as determining influences in the lives of individuals, groups, and societies.

Other teaching suggestions include having students read stories about discrimination and prejudice from a U.S. Department of Justice web site that will prompt them to "decide how they might act in a similar circumstance," and to invite social scientists to the classroom who are members of racial or minority ethnic groups. These experiences are supposed to help "break stereotypes while teaching social studies content" (p. 37). Later on Parker reminds his readers that:

> even in relatively homogeneous classrooms, . . . teachers and students *still* will have to come to grips with racial, ethnic, and cultural diversity. This will be required particularly in social studies where the subject matter children encounter—the peoples and places, the races and regions, the customs and beliefs—can just as easily be interpreted through prejudiced and ethnocentric eyes as through curious and respectful eyes. (pp. 38–39)

Although he stops short of saying it, this statement by Parker comes much closer to making it explicit that racism is an important element in social studies education than the other textbook authors.

Excluding the Contemporary

A third recurring way that social studies education textbooks practice deracialization is by *excluding contemporary situations, events, and individuals.* An example of this is evident in Zarrillo's (2000) *Teaching Elementary Social Studies.* He makes a persuasive argument for separating the social studies assessment of English language learners from English literacy tasks. He then uses a historical situation to amplify his point, stating that "if one of our content objectives is that students will accurately describe the dwellings of four 15th-century Native American tribal groups, it doesn't matter if the description are written in English or Spanish. . . ." (p. 181). Surely there are many race-related issues and experiences in the lives of contemporary Native Americans that could have been used as illustrations. This author also deracializes all English learners who are not Spanish speakers. The exclusion of contemporary references to many different ethnic groups leaves the impression that race and racism are historical phenomena that have no present day currency or significance, and is limited to only a few groups of color. Keeping these issues frozen in time also has an anesthetizing effect; it makes them seem less pervasive, profound, and in urgent need of resolution.

In an earlier chapter on lesson planning (pp. 79–100) Zarrillo describes a comparative unit on Native Americans taught by a fifth grade teacher. The students studied the Mohawks, Seminoles, Oglala Sioux, Tlingits, and Navajos to compare their histories, cultures, and life styles, and to understand problems of stereotyping cultural groups based on limited knowledge. This unit description is used to illustrate various ideas about planning for instruction that are discussed throughout the remainder of the chapter. The problem with the unit is that it also has only an historical emphasis. The content focuses on the hunting practices of the different tribal groups in the past. No mention is made of their contemporary career and employment patterns.

Even if the textbooks were to provide compelling presentations of historical acts of racism, such as the genocidal practices imposed upon Native Americans by the encroachment of Europeans into their worlds, the experiences are still historical artifacts; their potential value is sometimes offset by the limitations of temporal distance and abstraction from the viewpoint of students. The further students are personally removed from the occurrence of events, the harder it is for them to get deeply and emotionally invested in issues they symbolize. At best, students are likely to view only the historical study of racial dilemmas as purely an academic exercise, and at worst, to dismiss them as "has beens" and "old news." Such underestimations invite the perpetuation of racism by making it appear as if it is not as widespread and destructive as it really is. They also leave students vulnerable and unprepared to be effective agents of change to overcome racism.

Unnamed Individuals and Events

It is amazing how infrequently social studies methods textbooks identify any individuals and events by name, least of all specify their racial identities, experiences, and concerns. Page after page of narration is presented about what the authors consider to be knowledge and skills essential to social studies instruction, but they are not personified. Even the most high profile racially-specific events in U.S. history (such as the Civil Rights Movements of the 1960s and 1970s, the Black Panther Party, the relocation of different groups of Native Americans, the Ku Klux Klan, the unionization of Mexican American migrant and farm laborers, the Internment of Japanese Americans) and exemplary individuals are not named. Often principles and concepts for teaching critical thinking, reading, conflict resolution, human rights, and various map skills are taught without placing them in any concrete human application contexts. Even the few times when individuals of color are included in the texts typically their racial and ethnic identities are not specified. The reader has to have this prior knowledge to know who these individuals are rather than acquiring it from reading the texts. Many prospective teachers do not have this knowledge.

Kincheloe (2001) deviates from these tendencies in two ways. First, he does name numerous and varied individuals throughout his text. But, more often than not their race and ethnicity are not specified. The exception occurs when the individuals discussed are from countries other than the United States. Their ethnicity is mentioned as part of their introductions, such as "the French historian Marc Bloch" (p. 629), "Iranain Premier Mohammed Mossedegh" (p. 631), "German social analyst Heinz Sünker" (p. 168), and "Paulo Freire, the great Brazilian educator" (p. 31). The problem is nationality and ethnicity are not analogous to race. These individuals could be members of any racial group. It is conceivable, for instance, that "the French historian Marc Bloch" could be of Senegalese, Chinese, Jamaican, or East Indian ancestry. Second, Kincheloe names some individuals of color (particularly African Americans) within the context of explaining an issue or event in a way that their race and ethnicity are assumed or identified by association. An example of this occurs on page 629 of *Getting Beyond the Facts* in a discussion of whether "disinterested" history is possible and for whom. Kincheloe observes that:

> Disinterested history is a luxury only dominant groups can afford When
> W.E.B. DuBois ... viewed the past, he saw a useful chronicle of methods

employed by his Black ancestors to fight slavery and oppression—methods, he believed, that could be put to use in present struggles against racial tyranny. The blueprints for the Black future ... must be based on problems, dreams, and frustrations.... . Echoing this theme, Maulana Karenga ... argued almost 40 years later that African American history is a reflection not only of what Black people have done but what they can do.

DuBois' racial identity is stated while Karanga's has to be assumed or inferred.

Zarrillo's (2000) *Teaching Elementary Social Studies* also occasionally specifies the racial identity of individuals named. Several specific African Americans and Native Americans are named in advising social studies teachers to present a wider spectrum of biographies about the Revolutionary War (p. 73). Yet, this effort falls short of the desirable because the racial visibility included is not extended equally to all groups of color. Latino and Asian Americans are racially identified less often, and the racial identity of European Americans is never given. This pattern exists across all of the social studies education textbooks reviewed.

There are two other manifestations of the non-naming phenomenon that is present in the textbooks. One is where the little ethnic and racial identifications that do occur are placed in the organization of the books. In most instances, this information is restricted to topics dealing with diversity, multicultural education, conflict and controversy, and current events. Overall, these issues consume a very small percentage of the entire texts—a single chapter or short sections within a chapter. This means that race-specific information is simply not present in the greater portion of these books where the most fundamental components of social studies education are addressed.

For example, eight of the ten books include discussions about the role of history, geography, economics, political science, sociology, and anthropology in social studies education. But, only one incorporates racially-related issues in these discussions. Banks and Banks (1999) have features about race matters in the chapter on sociology, African American women in the Montgomery Bus Boycott in the chapter on history, and the population and settlement trends of Latinos in their discussion of geography. Ellis (1995) presents long lists of concepts central to each of the social sciences discussed. Neither race nor racism appears on these lists. In addition to being highly marginalizing, this restrictive placement conveys a strong negative connotation that people of color and issues of importance to them can be divorced from the rest of the social studies education agenda, and they are always controversial. Typecasting racially-related issues and individuals, or making them one-dimensional is a very effective way to deracialize them, in that it denies the complexity, dynamism, and prevalence of race and racism in U.S. history, life, and culture.

Positive Presence of Race

The strongest counteracting features in the textbooks to their tendency to deracialize people of color and their experiences is the visual illustrations. All of the books except two (Chapin & Messick, 1999; Kincheloe, 2001) include photographs of people from different ethnic and racial backgrounds individually and in groups. Most of the images involve children in different learning situations. In fact, the children in the photographs are doing something that illustrates different learning strategies, such as reading maps, hypothesizing, collecting data, role-playing, and participating in dramatic reenactments. There also are good mixtures of different racial configurations. In some of the visual illustrations children of color are in the majority and others European Americans are in this position. And, racially diverse individuals and groups are shown in active engagements. In most instances, direct linkages are made between what is shown in the visual illustrations and what is going on in the narrative text. One notable example is a photograph of Mary McLeod Bethune with a group of African American girls at the school she founded in Banks and Banks (1999, p. 67). It appears in a section on teaching inquiry. The caption for the photograph identifies Bethune and explains how photographs such as the one presented can be used to conduct inquiry lessons.

Parker's (2001) textbook uses more photographs of racially mixed groups of children than the other authors. He begins each chapter with a photograph of a group of children engaged in some action that represents the theme idea, concept, or skill examined. For instance, Chapter 3 on "Citizenship Education and Democratic Values" opens with a photograph of children with raised hands, suggesting voting on an issue. Chapter 5, which deals with time lines, maps, globes, and graphics, begins with a photograph of a teacher working with an African American female student and a European American male student at a globe and wall map. The visual used to symbolize the integrated education theme of Chapter 13 is a group of students working together with two adults on a manual construction.

These are impressive (although limiting) efforts of how to weave racial diversity into routine social studies content and teaching—so much so that one is left to ponder, if racial representations are worth including in the illustrations of textbooks, why not in other content dimensions. The answer to this question may be equally apparent. Methods textbook authors seem to take the path of least resistance in dealing with racially-specific images and information by including them in aspects of the texts

that do not challenge conventional knowledge canons. The pictorial illustrations are mostly of children engaging with social studies content that is
almost totally devoid of racial information. Including visual images of
diverse children in textbooks is important, but it is not sufficient treatment
of race and racial issues in the social studies. Consequently, one of the
"strongest" racial inclusion components of social studies education textbooks included in this review is also one of their major weaknesses. That is,
images of racially diverse children are used to depict disciplinary ideas, but
their racial groups' contributions, histories, experiences, and concerns are
excluded almost entirely for the substantive content of the textbooks. Race
is once again marginalized, and racism is ignored.

MISSED OPPORTUNITIES

If it is indeed true that teachers teach as they were taught (Cuban, 1993),
and that textbooks are overwhelmingly the most commonly used source of
content in teaching then it is not surprising that Pre-K–12 social studies
classroom teachers give little attention to race and racism in their classroom instruction. They receive consistent and compelling messages and
models for doing this from the textbooks they use in their professional
preparation. Information about race, racism, and racially-identified issues,
individuals, experiences, and events included in these books is minimal in
both quantity and quality. It is fragmented, lacks specific details, and
depth, and is peripheral to the core of the narrative text. This absence of
substantial explanations and instructional strategies is puzzling since
strained racial relations and acts of racism continue to be prevalent in the
United States and world communities. When are prospective teachers supposed to learn about these challenges and how to teach the knowledge, values, and skills students need to deal with them, if not in their professional
education courses? And, if not in the social studies—the school subject
whose primary responsibility is teaching skills for community membership
and citizenship—then where?

The effects of the deracialization found in social studies methods textbooks may not be quite as extreme for secondary as for elementary prospective teachers. Pre-service middle and high school teachers come to
their methods classes with majors in one or more of the social sciences.
Thus, they may have acquired content knowledge about race, racism, and
the concerns, actions, experiences, perspectives, and contributions of different racial groups in these subject matter courses. Even if this speculation
is true, it should not excuse secondary methods textbooks from explicitly
examining pedagogical skills and implications related to race and racism.
Elementary teachers are in a more compromising situation. Most of them

have not taken any specialized courses in the social science disciplines beyond the general history, sociology, or political science undergraduate core requirements. They are dependent upon methods classes to teach them the content, as well as the techniques needed for social studies instruction.

The pedagogical efficacy of teachers is affected by their feelings of competence and confidence (Ashton & Webb, 1986; Pang & Sablan, 1995). Neither is likely to be very high if teachers have limited knowledge of the topics, concepts, skills, issues, and events they are expected to teach. Excluding race and racism from social studies methods textbooks places prospective teachers in an untenable position. They are expected to do something in their own classrooms that they have not been sufficiently prepared to do. Even more telling is the message this absence conveys. If something is not in the textbooks it must not be important enough to be taken seriously. By not dealing directly, substantively, and significantly with issues of race and racism methods textbook authors are sending this message strongly and clearly to their readers.

It is difficult to image the reasons authors of textbooks might provide for giving such little attention to race and racism in their constructions of social studies education. The oversight seems inexcusable given this subject's mission and the authors' advocacy for preparing students for democratic citizenship, critical thinking, problem solving, conflict resolution, socio-political activism, and to be change agents for social reconstruction. Underlying these goals is the need to bridge the gap between societal ideals and realities. One of these realities is the fact that race, racism, and related issues are some of the most persistent and definitive features of U.S. history, life, and culture. Therefore, they should be a significant part of all instructional materials used in social studies teacher preparation and classroom practice. Without their inclusion teachers and the discipline itself will not fully realize their potentials or promises.

Simply put, the missed opportunities of methods textbooks to demonstrate how to deal directly, seriously, and transformatively with race and racism means social studies education in both teacher preparation and K–12 classroom instruction is not nearly as good as it can and should be. Teaching to genuinely promote social justice, to eliminate racism and other forms of oppression, and to create a truly democratic society has to be anchored as much in confronting racially-specific conflicts, controversies, contributions, and concerns as in celebrating the stellar accomplishments of the ethnic, social, and cultural individuals and groups who comprise the United States.

REFERENCES

Altbach, P.G., Kelly, G.P., Petrie, H.G., & Weis, L. (Eds.). (1991). *Textbooks in American society: Politics, policy, and pedagogy.* Albany: State University of New York Press.

Apple, M., & Christian-Smith, L. (Eds.). (1991). *The politics of the textbook.* New York: Routledge.

Ashton, P.T., & Webb, R.B. (1986). *Making a difference: Teachers' sense of efficacy and student achievement.* New York: Longman.

Banks, J.A., & Banks, C.A.M. (with contributions by Clegg, A.A., Jr.). (1999). *Teaching strategies for the social studies: Decision-making and citizen action* (5th ed.). New York: Longman.

Beck, I.L., & McKeown, M.G. (1991). Substantive and methodological considerations for productive textbook analysis. In J.P. Shaver (Ed.), *Handbook of research on social studies teaching and learning* (pp. 496–512). New York: Macmillan.

Chapin, J.A., & Messick, R.G. (1996). *Elementary social studies: A practical guide* (3rd ed.). New York: Longman.

Crabtree, C., & O'Shea, D. (November 1991). Teachers' academic preparation in history. National Center for History in the Schools *Newsletter, 1*(3), 4, 10.

Cuban, L. (1993). *How teachers taught: Constancy and change in American classrooms, 1890–1990* (2nd ed.). New York: Teachers College Press.

Davis, O.L., Jr., Ponder, G., Burlbaw, L.M., Garza-Lubeck, M., & Moss A. (1986). *Looking at history: A review of major U.S. history textbooks.* Washington, DC: People for the American Way.

Ellis, A.K. (1995). *Teaching and learning elementary social studies* (5th ed.). Boston: Allyn and Bacon.

Engle, S. (1986). Late night thoughts about the new social studies. *Social Education, 50*(1), 20–22.

Finklestein, J.M., Nielsen, L.E., & Switzer, T. (1993). Primary elementary social studies instruction. *Social Education, 57*(1), 64–69.

Garcia, J., & Michaelis, J.U. (2001). *Social studies for children: A guide to basic instruction* (12th ed.). Boston: Allyn and Bacon.

Goldstein, P. (1978). *Changing the American schoolbook.* Lexington, MA: D.C. Heath.

Gordy, L.L., & Pritchard, A.M. (1995). Redirecting our voyage through history: A content analysis of social studies textbooks. *Urban Education, 30*(2), 195–218.

Henry, J. (1970). *Textbooks and the American Indian.* San Francisco: The Indian Historian Press.

Kane, M.B. (1970). *Minorities in textbooks: A study of their treatment in social studies texts.* Chicago: Quadrangle Books.

Kincheloe, J.L. (2001). *Getting beyond the facts: Teaching social studies/social sciences in the twenty-first century* (2nd ed.). New York: Peter Lang.

Laughlin, M.A., & Hartoonian, H.M. (1995). *Challenges of social studies instruction in middle and high schools: Developing enlightened citizens.* New York: Harcourt Brace.

Loewen, J.W. (1995). *Lies my teacher told me: Everything you American history textbook got wrong.* New York: New Press.

Martorella, P.H. (1994). *Social studies for elementary school children: Developing young citizens*. Englewood Cliffs, NJ: Merrill/Prentice-Hall.

Michigan State Department of Education. (1972, January). *Early elementary level social studies textbooks: A report in regards to their treatment of minorities*. Lansing: Michigan State Department of Education.

Nelson, J.L., & Stanley, W.B. (1985). Academic freedom: Fifty years standing still. *Social Education, 49*(8), 662–664, 666.

Pang, V.O, & Sablan, V. (1995, April). *Teacher efficacy: Do teachers believe they can be effective with African American students*. Paper presented at the annual meeting of the American Educational Research Association, San Francisco.

Parker, W.C. (2001). *Social studies in elementary education* (11th ed.). Upper Saddle River, NJ: Merrill/Prentice-Hall.

Sadker, David. *Some practical ideas for confronting curricular bias*. (Retrieved September, 2003). http://www.american.edu/sadker/curricularbias.htm

Schubert, W.H. (1986). *Curriculum: Perspective, paradigm, and possibility*. New York: Macmillan.

Singer, A.J. (1997). *Social studies foe secondary schools: Teaching to learn, learning to teach*. Mahwah, NJ: Lawrence Erlbaum.

Wade, R.C. (1993). Content analysis of social studies textbooks: A review of ten years of research. *Theory and Research in Social Education, 21*(3), 232–256.

Zarrillo, J.J. (2000). *Teaching elementary social studies: Principles and applications*. Upper Saddle River, NJ: Merrill/Prentice-Hall.

APPENDIX A

Textbooks Selected for Review

Banks, J.A., & Banks, C.A.M. (with contributions by Clegg, A.A., Jr.). (1999). *Teaching strategies for the social studies: Decision-making and citizen action* (5th ed.). New York: Longman.

Chapin, J.A., & Messick, R.G. (1996). *Elementary social studies: A practical guide* (3rd ed.). New York: Longman.

Ellis, A.K. (1995). *Teaching and learning elementary social studies* (5th ed.). Boston: Allyn and Bacon.

Garcia, J., & Michaelis, J.U. (2001). *Social studies for children: A guide to basic instruction* (12th ed.). Boston: Allyn and Bacon.

Kincheloe, J.L. (2001). *Getting beyond the facts: Teaching social studies/social sciences in the twenty-first century* (2nd ed.). New York: Peter Lang.

Laughlin, M.A., & Hartoonian, H.M. (1995). *Challenges of social studies instruction in middle and high schools: Developing enlightened citizens*. New York: Harcourt Brace.

Martorella, P.H. (1994) *Social studies for elementary school children: Developing young citizens*. Englewood Cliffs, NJ: Merrill/Prentice Hall.

Parker, W.C. (2001). *Social studies in elementary education* (11th ed.). Upper Saddle River, NJ: Merrill/Prentice-Hall.

Singer, A.J. (1997). *Social studies for secondary schools: Teaching to learn, learning to teach.* Mahwah, NJ: Lawrence Erlbaum.

Zarrillo, J.J. (2000). *Teaching elementary social studies: Principles and applications.* Upper Saddle River, NJ: Merrill/Prentice-Hall.

CHAPTER 8

UNEASY SIMILARITIES, UNEVEN PARALLELS

Race, Sexuality and Civil Rights Discourse

Lisa W. Loutzenheiser

ABSTRACT

Seeking to make sense of and interconnect the experiences of variously marginalized students, this chapter questions the normalizing desires of dominant culture with curriculums and pedagogies. While attempting to understand the complicated and incomplete picture that these subjectivities and identities offer, I explore the ways in which race, sexualities and their intersections are both silent and present within social studies curricula.

I argue that the very process of incorporating and utilizing frameworks of fluidity and intersectionality entails attending to the complicated and incomplete picture that subjectivities and identities offer and requires one to interrogate dialogue and empathy, thereby altering practice. This essay explores how these discussions have emerged within Critical Race Theory and within and among Latino/a Crit and Queer Crit. How might these explorations offer avenues for deconstructing race and sexualities in social studies pedagogies and curricula?

Critical Race Theory Perspectives on the Social Studies, pages 149–170
Copyright © 2003 by Information Age Publishing

149

INTRODUCTION

I come to this project as a teacher, a researcher and a theorist searching for ways to complicate, make sense of and interconnect the experiences of students who are both queer[1] and of color, of color, queer and women, disabled and queer, etc. I also seek alternatives ways to work with pre-service and master's level teachers that highlight identities as intersecting and fluid. These desires move me toward working the spaces between critical race and queer theories. The lack of language, or the ways we articulate and disrupt identities, exceeds discourse and send me to other theoretical openings that might rework what occurs in social studies classrooms from Kindergarten through teacher education. For the purposes of this chapter, I am most interested in secondary classrooms, teaching, and teacher education.

In part, desires of anti-oppressive and multicultural curricula and pedagogies in social studies classrooms are to encourage students (of whatever level) to *understand* other cultures. Most states and provinces incorporate these notions within official curriculum frameworks such as those in California, or Integrated Resource Packet (IRP), which are found in British Columbia. However, the meanings of *understanding* or *cultures* within the official curricula, as well as how schools ought to go about integrating these ideas, are open to debate. As utilized below, the notion of *difference* might offer a more productive organizing notion than the overly broad, and under defined *culture*.[2] Those who focus on gay, lesbian, bisexual, transgender and queer (GLBTQ) issues argue that discussions must happen in classrooms if change is to occur (Barnard, 1994; Evans, 2002; Gordon, 1994; Jennings, 1994, Massachusetts Governor's Commission on Gay and Lesbian Youth, 1993; Uribe & Harbeck, 1991). Different groups who focus primarily on ethnic and racial groups have made similar arguments. Schools are believed to be places where change can take place—commonsense language in schools and schools of education says that if started early enough, we can "catch" children, or even pre-service teachers. This seems to assume that students walk into social studies, teacher education or other classrooms as blank slates, or at the very least, slates that can be written over by force of instructor will. That is, if students can *be made to* understand difference then oppression (and I would argue if the logic follows, difference) will disappear.

Similarly, some argue that if equal protections are offered to all groups then everyone will be treated the same. This sameness would be fair and just. Civil rights discourse such as this, assumes a desire for assimilation (and therefore) sameness—discourses which Patricia Williams (1995) calls "color blind discourse." This chapter questions whether viewing everyone as the same is desirable. I am exploring ways that race, sexualities and their intersections are both silent and present within social studies curricula, how the discussions that have emerged within critical race theory (CRT or RaceCrit) and within and amongst its Lat(ino/a)Crit and QueerCrit cousins might offer avenues for (de)constructing race and sexualities in social studies curricula.

This will not be an argument that race and sexualities are the same, or that their trajectories run parallel. However, I am interested in interrogating what is meant by intersectionality and fluidity of identities.[3] What might be lost or gained by expanding how multiple identities are both silent and present within legal theories as way to read secondary social studies curricul? It is as if many of the conversations about critical race theory ignore those of color who are also gay, lesbian, bisexual or transgendered. Similarly, the queer theory and gay and lesbian legal studies (QueerCrit) movements largely overlook discrimination based upon race, gender or disability. What do queer theories have to learn from CRT and what does CRT have to learn from queer theories? How is this conversation productive in talking about race and sexualities in social studies teacher education courses and secondary classrooms in North America? What benefits might reading civil rights discourses and empathy pedagogies through critical race, post-structural queer theories bring to pedagogies in social studies classrooms?

WHAT CRT BRINGS TO THE CONVERSATION

An early tenet of CRT was Derrick Bell's (1995) principle of "interest convergence" which provides that "the interest of blacks in achieving racial equality will be accommodated only when it converges with the interests of Whites" (p. 21). He argues that interest convergence is always in play when issues of privilege, race and racism are being decided. Bell states:

> Whites may agree in the abstract that blacks are citizens and are entitled to constitutional protection against racial discrimination, but few are willing to recognize that racial segregation is much more than a series of quaint customs that can be remedied effectively without altering the status of whites. (p. 22)

Therefore, according to Bell, no action will be taken or remedies offered if they do not, in some way, feed the interests or bring little or no harm to the interests of the dominant groups. The *Brown v. Board of Education* decision was, according to Bell, just such an example.

Brown has been hailed as one of the most significant court cases to affect civil rights in the United States. The lawyers for *Brown* believed that the way to ensure that Blacks would receive equal educational opportunity was to force the removal of racial barriers in public school. Legal strategies for *Brown* were forged among notions that discrimination in the United States would change through the strength of the courts. While one cannot discount its impact, many argue that *Brown* has not been the overarching remedy for the lack of educational opportunity for African Americans, or increasing other students of color that many hoped it would be (Bell, 1995; Calabrese, 1986; Carter, 1995; Russo, Harris, & Sandidge, 1994; Williams, 1995). While the outcomes have not brought about equity or equal achievement, *Brown* and the hundreds of cases it spawned were successful in:

> introducing race into discussions of equal opportunity but also altered the substance of those discussions ... In stressing the impact of segregation on the life chances of black students, Brown began to shift the terms of the discourse .... (Kirp, 1982, p. 41)

Perhaps it is not so much that the discourse changed, but that within White dominated systems, African American experiences became more visible. However, as Robert L. Carter (1995) argues:

> dismal progress has been made in achieving the equal educational opportunity for black children supposedly "guaranteed" by *Brown* ... more black children are in all or virtually all black schools than in 1954. These schools ... are unequal ... in any measurement of educational equality—to predominantly white schools, and, with rare exceptions, lag in tests measuring achievement in reading, writing, and arithmetic. (p. 619)

The *Brown* case and other cases that looked to the courts to remedy racial discrimination continued the notion that civil rights could be legislated—that legislated change could act as a catalyst, and fundamental change in relation to racism should start in the schools. It institutionalized a reliance on the courts and a discourse of equal opportunity, and "civil rights," looking to the U.S. Constitution to alter the lived experiences of African Americans in school and elsewhere.

Yet, Williams (1995) argues that change advocated from a mask of sheep's clothing of stability (i.e., rights) can be effective, even as it destabilizes certain other establishment values (i.e., segregation). Accordingly,

> ... the battle is not deconstructing rights, in a world of no rights; nor of constructing statements of need, in a world of abundantly apparent need. Rather, the goal is to find a political mechanism that can confront the denial of need . (p. 89)

However, the failure of *Brown* and anti-discrimination legislation encouraged those who would become critical race scholars to question the status quo that many liberal (mostly White) legal scholars had supported through the types of legal scholarship they undertook and the ways they categorized the experiences of those in systemically dominated groups (Tate, 1997). Critical race theorists take as a project the forefronting of their own narratives and explicit questioning the systems of power upon which legal arguments depend.

What has been characterized as first wave critical race theory was created in opposition to the silences within White dominated Critical Legal Studies (Harris, 1994). Critical race theorists such as Bell (1992), Delgado (1995), and Matsuda (1993) argue (in part) that race and racism are central to North American culture; that the role of critical race theorists is to interrogate the dominant ideology from the perspective of the oppressed; and storytelling from the perspective of those systemically dominated is a form of "naming one's own" (Delgado, 1995). CRT explodes the notion of color blindness or race neutrality—ideas that remain very much in evidence in both teachers and students at all levels. Relying on the understanding that there are political underpinnings for racial emancipation, CRT scholars remind us that color blindness or race neutrality "repress and render irrelevant the ways race shapes social relationships" (Rothmayer, 1999, p. 2). This is particularly important to remember when few participants in highly racially charged environments such as many classrooms, openly discuss or deconstruct race or racism.

Delgado argues that racism is "normal, not aberrant in American society" and the role of CRT is to forge critical understandings of race and racism (cited in Ladson-Billings, 1999). Understanding the ways that the normalization and the silence which racism incorporates lead to what counts as knowledge and who is allowed to tell or use his/her story. It offers as "powerful means for destroying and changing mindsets" (Delgado cited in Tate, 1997, p. 219).

However, it is not as easy as stating that civil rights discourse is fatally flawed. In working with the complexity of what are civil rights arguments, Williams (1995) further states:

> to say that blacks never truly believed in rights is true; yet it is also true that blacks believed in them so much and so hard that we gave them life where there was none before ... constitutional foreground of "rights" was shaped by whites, parceled out to blacks in pieces ... Perhaps the predominance of that imbalance obscures the fact that the recursive insistence of those rights is also defined by black desire for them .... (p. 92)

Here, Williams points out the paradoxical nature of civil rights rhetoric. There is an essential belief and disbelief in the system. But the alternative—that is, the lack of fighting for or attaining what little has been won— is so noxious as to be untenable. Yet, what is lost in the assimilationist turn?

What is lost when the argument hinges on a notion that non-dominant groups, in this case African Americans, must rely on (and incorporate) the belief that they are more like Whites than different? Later, I will return to the notion of assimilation, difference and civil rights discourses.

However, rights rhetoric and struggles of African Americans within the courts had major impacts on other groups. Women, Native Americans, Latinos and those with disabilities watched as African Americans used the courts to fight the imbalances of society. Among these groups, albeit decades later, were gays and lesbians[4] who looked at what was accomplished in the courts and believed that the protections offered might (or ought) to also extend to them. Similar to the *Brown* era cases, there was (and is) a reliance on a notion that the plaintiffs were more like the dominant groups than different.

Returning to *Brown* and the rise of CRT, part of the call for desegregation was a demand for an increase in student achievement among students of color. Similar arguments have been and continue to be used by proponents of cultural pluralism (Ravitch, 1990) and liberal multiculturalism.[5] These more liberal movements do not take systemic change or social reconstruction as their project. It is enough for students to "see" themselves positively portrayed in the curriculum and view themselves as more a(part) of; the focus is on how students are more similar than different. In this pedagogic turn, finding commonalities would lead to a lack of discrimination and prejudice. Consequently, students of color who underachieve would learn more and "better" causing their achievement to rise. As with desegregation, an argument can be made that interest convergence played a part in the rise of multiculturalism, and continued usage of a liberal-leaning multicultural education that is in evidence in many schools in Canada and the United States.

By this, I mean that part of what has driven the rise of multiculturalism, particularly in the United States, is a concern about the gap in achievement between White and some student of East Asian descent and many Latino/a, African American and Native American/First Nations students. The desire to alter this achievement gap was, and is in no small part, necessary for schools to continue to be viewed as meritocratic systems. If students of color, poor kids (and/or GLBTQ students) are failing in large numbers, then the meritocracy is called into question. Therefore schools embrace a relatively "quick fix" of adding in bits of multiculturalism here and there. This appearance of multicultural education can be read through interest convergence in productive ways. Interest is most clear when some form of liberal multiculturalism is present and articulated as present or implemented with common sense discourses in and around the school. Here, multiculturalism is often pursued because it is in the interest of the system to look as if visible minorities (at the very least) are having attention paid to their needs. Too often, this attention takes the form of yearly renditions of Martin Luther King's speech, "I Have a Dream" each January for his birthday or February for Black History Month in the United States, or celebrations of Kwanzaa, Hanukah, Chinese New Year, etc. This "foods and festivals" approach of these insertions lead to a perception that schools are promoting tolerance and encouraging teachers to include more culturally relevant curricula (Ladson-Billings, 1995). Simultaneously, students of color and non-White and/or non-U.S. and Canadian cultures are exoticized and othered. In addition, the very real and complex concerns that an integrated social reconstructionist multiculturalism (Grant & Sleeter, 1989) might address remain silent. These silences lend themselves to a normalizing dominant cultures and a support for the status quo and the straw man appearance of the level playing field.

There has been debate about whether GLBTQ issues ought to be included in a social reconstructionist multicultural education. No matter where one might stand on the outcomes of foci of multicultural education, there are correspondences among the inclusion of race and ethnicity a la multicultural education, and the smattering of inclusion of gay and lesbian issues in K–12 social studies and teacher education courses. Just as there was pressure on the system to be inclusive and to alter student achievement (but not necessarily the culture of the school), similar pressures are being brought to bear on schools in relation to gay and lesbian (but necessarily bi-, transgender or queer) issues.[6] The number of bullying incidents, the death of Mathew Shepard and the unconscionably high suicide rate among students who identify as GLBTQ has forced a convergence of interests between advocates for the inclusion of gay and lesbian topics in the schools, educators at both the K–12 and post-secondary levels and a small percentage of the general public. The need to address the concerns because of the civil rights atrocities and fear leads to teachers and classrooms of social studies students, and soon-to-be social studies teachers, engaged in one-off (i.e., single day) lessons where homosexuality is the uncomfortable focus. Often, in teacher education programs this is the day that the useful and well-conceived film, "It's Elementary," is trotted out for pre-service teachers to talk about how hard gay and lesbian students (who are almost always silently marked as White) have it, and how difficult and fear-of-parent-reaction-provoking teaching about gay and lesbian issues is. This is not to say that these introductory moves are not important, but they have unintended results. In both teacher education, and in the few secondary social studies classrooms where sexualities are discussed, the Gay Person is almost always Outside the classroom.

Similar to concerns about the human relations approach to a broadly conceived multicultural education are worries about Othering GLBTQ peoples of all ethnic and/or racial backgrounds. Just as multicultural education, in its more pluralist and liberal tones, serves to reify the status quo around race, so too do teacher and student discourses about sexualities. With these more pluralistic strategies of inclusion, there are limited moves to alter schools to make them more "safe." If the lack of safety persists, it might be perceived as impacting non-queerly identified students. If the concerns (or interests) of the majority are inflamed, then more deeply rooted social changes might be demanded.[7] There are analogous desires when working with race in more essentialist or pluralistically driven programs. That is, they often leave the systems that foster racism, as well as heterosexism and homophobia, in place and unanalyzed.

In addition to concerns about pedagogies that leave the status quo unchallenged, the ways that race and sexualities are addressed when they are placed within the official curricula can also be problematic. Accompanying this can be an over-reliance on a fixed notion of who is GLBTQ (White and often middle-class) or a visible minority (of color, heterosexual and not middle class). Early on, critical race theorist Kimberlé Crenshaw (1995) reminded legal scholars that race is never merely race; rather, there are intersections of race, class, gender, sexualities, etc. Crenshaw began the move away from unitary, uncrossing constructions offering a particularly helpful mapping of intersectionality, which incorporates power and its relationships to race, gender class and sexualities. Intersectional frameworks are: "attuned to the various ways that these dynamics intersect is a necessary prerequisite to exploring how this double vulnerability influences the way that violence against women of color is experienced and addressed" (p. 112). She questions the role of binaries as placeholders for the status quo, arguing that they too have a normalizing function. Challenging the idea that identities can be viewed in isolation from each other, Crenshaw argues that the areas intersect in, and among, political and representational structures and systems. This analysis is particularly useful in exploring the many overlapping and criss-crossed identities of marginalized students.

This early work of Crenshaw's foreshadowed a number of future arguments and fracturing that would occur within CRT. It also points to ways that this more essentialized and fixed notion of race (and sexualities) works within civil right discourses and equal protection clauses which must by their nature argue that the wronged class are both different (and in need of remedy or protection because of this difference), in order that we/they may become the same as those who are not in need of protection or remedy.

SECOND WAVE AND THE MOVES TOWARD THE CONTESTED POST PLAYS

There are interesting and productive tensions within and among critical race theory, civil right discourses, gay and lesbian studies and queer theory in relation to claiming multiple and fluid identities and the continuing need for identity or group politics. It is within these tensions that queer theory and CRT (particularly first wave) sit most uncomfortably. It is helpful to start with Crenshaw since she both complicated essential notions of race and foreshadowed concerns within CRT about anti-essentialism. Crenshaw (1995) critiques "the vulgarized social construction thesis of anti-essentialism' argument" (p. 375). Restating one argument against essentialism, she notes that since this line of reasoning argues that "all categories are socially constructed, there is not such thing as say, Black or women," then if follows that "it makes no sense to continue reproducing those categories by organizing around them" (Crenshaw, 1995, p. 375). Drawing upon an exaggerated relativism, Crenshaw wonders what will happen to African Americans or women as political entities if there is not African American or Woman as identities to work within. She argues against this loss of identity categories because, in her view, it removes the political means for change.

Similarly, Guitierrez (2000) argues that "the liberal slant of postmodernism privileges individuality through the guise of 'subjectivity' and in the process reorients discussions of power away from structural forms of oppression" (p. 12). This argument is repeated within CRT literature, sometimes as if it is the only representation of postmodernism or the only critique of essentialism. In a strongly stated rebuff of post-structural rejections of identity politics and a wholly fixed subject, Cho (1997) fears,

> that we have stopped thinking ... about the political impact that critical race theory as a movement should be having. Instead of an unflinching commitment to intellectual activism, theoretically informed political resistance, and guiding ideals and principles of social justice, I sense instead a demobilizing fear of "essentialism" and a fetishization of the array of post-isms placed before us like a theoretical smorgasbord at a feast prepared by elite intellectuals whose political commitments lie who-knows-where. (pp. 434–435)

Cho offers an explication of this rift as generational at its roots. She argues that earlier scholars faced the very real experiences of identity-based oppressions and felt (and still feel) that they only way to remedy these situations is to continue to coalesce around race or sexualities in order that nothing gets lost or overlooked in the translation.

These concerns are worth noting, especially as Crenshaw reads relativism arguments as having been (mis)applied in a reactionary and over-simplistic fashion by various courts. Ironically, many theorists who advocate a social constructionist framework state, as Crenshaw (1995) does, that:

> to say that a category such as race or gender is socially constructed is not to say that that category has no significance in our world. On the contrary, a large and continuing project for subordinated people—and indeed, one of the projects or which postmodern theories have been very helpful—is thinking about the way in which power has clustered around certain categories and is exercised against others. (p. 375)

However, within the critiques of anti-essentialism, there is a sense that it must be either/or—that either you are "postie" or you are "essentialist." What is the promise of these divisions? What might the fluidity of subjectivities offer? Why might relying on notions of identity politics still have a place at the table? That is, why can't it be all and both rather than either/or? Crenshaw's use, embrace and rejection of different tenets within postmodern and post structural theories points to the usefulness of seemingly opposing theories within different contexts. As will be argued below, the same can be said for the usefulness of intersectionality and the fluidity of fixed subjects within classrooms. Williams (1995) addresses the usefulness of intersectionality when working with issues of heterosexism and homophobia arguing that:

> ... intersectionality provides a basis for reconceptualizing race as a coalition between men and women of color... race can also be a coalition of straight and gay people of color, and thus serve as a basis for critique of churches and other cultural institutions that reproduce heterosexism. (p. 377)

I would argue that the lack of intersectional frameworks in schools is, in part, what students of color and other marginalized students are reacting and often rejecting.

It is not only a sector of RaceCrits who engage in essentialist conceptions and rendering of identities. The growing field of QueerCrit often fails to highlight concerns about race, even while it appropriates (in, at times, problematic ways) the arguments and narrative methods developed by critical race theorists. For example, Robson (1997) writes of the struggles of rights with lesbian and queer narratives but fails to offer gendered or racialized analyses, and does not offer a proverbial tip of the hat to her CRT forebearers. For without the groundbreaking work of CRT, it is quite clear there would not be a QueerCrit, just as without critical legal studies, critical race theory would not have developed in the theoretical ways that it has. Without these analyses, some of the narratives of some GLBTQ peoples may be unearthed; yet, there is still an over-reliance on a foundational and silencing essentialism. Therefore, while all narrative is partial, the silencing of difference points toward exclusion and missed opportunities. As noted by Guitierrez (2000), Cho (1997), and Crenshaw (1995), and will be further discussed below, there are many who are invested, both politically and intellectually, in essentialism as the most useful method of making sense of difference.

Relying on identities as fixed and unmoving undercuts the very possibilities of intersectionalities, erasing the very real lives of queers of color. Alternatively, Valdes (1997) whose work grows out of CRT and LatCrit, theorizes across race and sexualities, pointing toward the intersectionality of race, ethnicity, class, gender and sexualities. He envisions

> a similarly powerful and empowering engagement of race and ethnicity, or, more precisely, an engagement of the interplay of racism and ethnocentrism in the formation of "sexual orientation" identity, community, and subordination—a critical investigation of the ways in which white and straight supremacy interlock to create social and legal conditions that permit or encourage the practice of permutated bigotries against the multiply diverse sexual minorities of the United States. (pp. 1296–1297)

Moving LatCrit and QueerCrit toward queer theories, Valdes (2000) calls for an end to the silences surrounding race and ethnicity in QueerCrit. He argues that "neither sex, race nor sexual orientation can "come first" in the configuration of human identities, politics and communities. I reject this notion of fixed or unitary identity politics..." (p. 336). Unlike Cho and Crenshaw, Valdes believes that relying on singular identity construction is politically naïve, because it does not take into account complex and complicating local contexts and situations. Accordingly, people are roused to political action when interest convergence occurs, even when the power differentials are less, or not evident. In order for action to develop, the needs of those from whom action is desired must be addressed. In relation to jurisprudence (and I would argue students and schooling at all levels), the complicated, intersecting and non-fixed primacies have to be utilized and made significant.

Yet, much of the conversation in GLBTQ communities does not surround intersectionalities, but on how useful or appropriate the fight for "gay" marriage might be. Queer scholars and activists wonder whether the courts are the road by which rights will be attained. Certainly, there are gay and lesbian activists and scholars who advocate gay marriage and other legal remedies as the most useful path. They agree with CRT scholars who worry about the dilution of identity politics within political, legal and intellectual spheres. What queer theory suggests is that the courts might not offer tenable and inclusive solutions, because queer folks are different than those non-queerly identified. And it is on this basis that freedoms ought be won. The focus of queer theories, as I am utilizing it, is on difference and on the fluidity of difference and identities as a central focus. Yet, in classrooms every day we see teachers and students who do not fit those tightly drawn categories and constructions. Many queer scholars, teachers and activists reject the lines of identity as singular and unchanging. This is similar to how some marginalized students view themselves in school (Loutzenheiser, 2001, 2002). How, then, does pedagogy that relies on these singular constructions meet these students? What is lost if their needs are not addressed?

FLUIDITY AND INTERSECTIONALITY— UNEVEN PARALLELS

Perhaps, it is within discussions and realities of social construction that the veering apart of queer critical theory and critical race theory is most significant. The fact that many who identify as queer are comfortable with the notion that sexuality is constructed rends apart the mutuality of the arguments. The fact that race is a constructed identity does not alter that the material salience of those identities placed upon peoples of color (queer or heterosexually identified) is very different than the identity forced upon White queers. I would argue that one relevant difference among these are that queer identities are embraced along the way.

Even if we know very early on that we are not heterosexual, the realization of sexuality is emergent. It is emergent in differing degrees for each individual, with infinite and changing variety—for some, a lifelong singular gender attraction, for others, a choice along a continuum, and yet others, an always changing and moving desire, etc. Except for those in communities of color who do not "appear" to the dominant as different, most people of color are viewed as, and often raised within family (or even institutional) structures which recognize race as an organizing category. Therefore, theorizing about essentialism and constructionism for scholars, activists, and educators, White queers and queers of color are dissimilar, and the investments are often distinctive between different groupings and constructions when interogating categories of sexual orientation and race.

For those who identify as queer (particularly for those whose queerness is their only deviation from the dominant society), the fluidity of identity is seen as an advantage and as a positive move toward rights and understandings. Fluidity invites a questioning of restrictions about how one performs one's sexualities, and/or how or what sexualities are being performed with or against. However, for many people of color there may be less freedom to choose, or even to move along a continuum in relation to sexualities, race or their congruencies. If race is fluid, then how is racism combated? How are institutional structures brought down? How are the oppressors identified? In point of fact, many scholars of color have embraced notions of intersectionality, and have noted as Crenshaw and others have, that identities collide at singular points. I would argue that this is not the same as arguing that the social construction of race leaves room for fluidity of racial selves. In fact, fluidity of racial selves is already seen in those who identify as bi and multicultural, but even then there is a push for a choice between which ethnic or racial backgrounds one affiliates with the most. Even though individuals may view their race as fluid, the dominant culture views them (if they are a visible minority) as of color.

Perhaps acknowledging a fluidity of racial constructions exposes the very real fear that the material and systemic realities of racism would remain without a focus for remedy. One might argue that race is held onto because race is; that is, it has both discursive and embodied consequence. Sexuality as an identity may be useful when GLBTQ people are reacting to the larger society. However, within Queer communities fluidity is seen by some as a political move both in reaction to gay, lesbian studies/movements which demanded an allegiance to a fixed sexuality in the name of political power, as well as the society at large. For people of color that may sound too much like the color-blind discourses that CRT very explicitly deconstructs.

Notions of intersectionality, momentary coalitions and fluidity each have something to offer social studies educators and theorists. While there is a material reality in walking down the street in Canada or in the United States as other than Caucasian, there is great fluidity and variance with racial and ethnic cultures and among race, gender, sexualities, disability and class. Fluidity demands attending to the complicated and incomplete picture that subjectivities and identities offer. Intersectionality requires that attention is paid to the places where identities join momentarily, and to the materiality of the social and political constructions that race, gender and sexualities, etc. are undergoing within local contexts. Yet, within our classrooms at both the secondary and teacher education levels we seem to lean on pedagogy that has at its foundation an attitude that not only are our students essentialized, non-intersecting and fixed, but so too is much of the curriculum. Teaching with or across difference remains a priority; however, it is often approached from a deficit model that desires to find The Answer and fill the students (and new teachers) up with feelings and experiences leading them to that answer.

EMPATHY PEDAGOGIES AND CIVIL RIGHTS DISCOURSES

What does teaching about race, racism and sexualities/gender roles mean? Speaking of add-in pedagogy, what do lessons which take as their only

GLBTQ content the highlighting of the sexualities of queer folk who represent us in academia—for example, Oscar Wilde, Virginia Woolf, James Baldwin, etc.—accomplish? Is it yet another turn that says "hey we, or they are really just like you ... they are not the Other?" Add in and stir pedagogy is the type of curriculum that merely adds in content that includes people of color and/or queer peoples without contextualizing or building interconnectedness with the rest of the content. The end result of this is often an Othering which separates out, but does not complicate. Alternatively, educators note the similarity of these Others, even while reifying the difference. In this pedagogy, neither intersectionality or fluidity are important, merely the (apolitical, historicized) inclusion of difference. But in point of fact they (Gertrude Stein, Michaelangelo, etc.) *are* the Other because students, both high school and pre-service, construct them (us) in that way.

Certainly the construction of the queer Other occurs in far more places and spaces than schools—popular culture and the media to name just two. However, curricula both hidden and explicit play a part in formulating the Other. Therefore, is saying "look at these famous folks who were White and gay, or Black and Lesbian, disabled and queer but just like you" only another turn toward assimilation? Certainly it feels like the Human Relations or "can't we all just get along" notions of multiculturalism that have come to mean so little and so much within North American curricula. Multiculturalism as a term and a movement in Canada and the United States has lost specificity of purpose. A generalized inclusion (or add-in) of role models or historical characters who were gay, lesbian or bisexual, and/or of color is often deemed enough, and again the desire to "get" along, for sameness and assimilation rule most of these projects.

The assumption within assimilationist moves is that we, educators at all levels, can *think* our way out of racism, homophobia and heterosexism. What if this is only one piece of the puzzle, and that there is always an unknown or unconscious combating of this assimilation, or sameness/difference? How would the educational project and use of empathy change? Britzman (1998) argues that empathy is dangerous because it involves the more privileged "incorporating their sense of the Other to keep their identities uncontested and immutable" (p. 87). Critical race theorists, Grillo and Wildman (1995) also note that Whites have a tendency to over-analogize which encourages a complacency in that:

> the "analogizer" often believes that her situation is the same as another's. Nothing in the comparison process challenges this belief and the analogizer make think that she understands the other's situation fully. The analogy makes the analogizer forget the difference and allows her to stay focused on her own situations without grappling with the other person's reality. (p. 564)

The focus on similarities, then, encourages and allows those within the dominant cultures to refocus the conversation on their own interests and concerns. Grillo and Wildman (1995) also note the ways this occurs when race and gender are discussed when the class is made up of predominately White (female) students. I, too, have found that when issues of race are raised, some White students feel encouraged to raise the issue of "reverse discrimination." Similarly, when discussing queer sexualities, sexual harassment or gender biases often become the focus. These examples point to the uncontrollability of dialogue and the usefulness of a CRT lens upon classroom discussion that will not render "Them" controllable, but under surveillance. This scrutiny would likely offer moments of guided analyses where students could become the analyzers of the classroom avoidances and discourses.

Ellsworth (1997) speaks of dangers of dialogue:

> What is impossible is knowledge that is based on assumptions that the mind can mirror the world, that language can reflect reality, that communication can be total, that curriculum is the territory it maps. (p. 75)

When we offer teacher education and secondary students a singular perspective or story of African Americans, First Nations members or queers, we are ignoring that "in the wake of feminisms, multiculturalisms, and postmodernisms, we are faced with a variety of multiplicities, paradoxes, and subtleties that complicate self-awareness." And this further complicates self-understanding and its implications for understanding others (Ellsworth, 1997, p. 77). In doing so, the post-understandings, disregarding fluidities *and* intersectionalities are overlooked. That this is, for example, reinscribing and encouraging students to accept that African Americans as simply comprehended, and usually heterosexual, poor, etc. Further reinforcing that peoples of color, are not complicated groups and groupings of peoples between and amongst issues of sexualities, disability, class, gender, etc. In addition, these singular tales expect that the reader is not part of the interpretation and filtering of the story. Teachers understand that students will read stories or discourses in a variety of ways, but too often there is still an expectation of the "right" way to read a text. A reading which rarely accepts the reader's positionality as an integral part of the reading.

Empathy pedagogies and discourses rarely leave large spaces to engage in the messy, scary spaces where students, teachers and texts are interrelated in varying degrees dependent on the very unknown of the players. If one embraces this, the outcomes are unknown, and can seem unknowing when it all seems to "go" wrong for the instructor. One example of this is when an instructor offers a moving, written account of racism or homophobia hoping to encourage student understanding of the predicaments of race and sexualities in North America by "placing them in their shoes." However, the students push against these readings, and in this pushing there is denial, essentialist acceptance, complication and confusion. To the instructor, it can feel as if the lesson has failed because there has not been an acquiescence to, and taking on of, the wrongs of racism and/or homophobia. Yet, students resist empathy for reasons they both understand and fail to recognize. Empathy pedagogies ask students to accept a one-size-fits-all kind of understanding that they reject without necessarily knowing why. From their very different subject positions, it may feel restrictive or unsettling.

Within one teacher education program I have worked with, students were required to take a foundations course, where all multicultural education for the program "belonged" according to program folklore. The students called it the "Isms" class, where multicultural education was "crammed down our throats." They spoke of pedagogy that seemed framed to elicit empathy as akin to a tear jerker in film. That is, it gets a reaction, a strong reaction, but the viewer rarely knows the origins of it, and ends up feeling slightly manipulated by the process. Even though this practice can sometimes feel good or elicit strong, cathartic emotion, it is rarely designed for students to construct their own knowledge. Rather, students should accept the knowledge offered to them because it is good for them and in the end, will lead to prejudice reduction. As this story goes, acknowledging teacher prejudice results in an individual reacting to his or her own racism or homophobia which ought to cause the achievement of students of color to rise since there is less prejudice in the classroom. If we can just get students to understand each other better (or teachers to understand their students better) then oppression will disappear. However, too often this essentializes the identities, discourses and experiences of constructed groups as one. In addition to the fallacy of this occurring in the classroom as if by rote, the focus on individual change also removes systemic responsibility from the equation. Relying on notions of understanding and empathy removes the individual and systemically influenced subject positions out of the picture as well. In other words, in Ellsworth's language, students refuse "the continuity of the dialogue," which "calls attention to the frame around the premapped nature of the territory within which the call to dialogue is addressed ... A refusal to participate raises the specter of loss of coherence and control—a failure" (Ellsworth, 1997, p. 89).

In a course where empathy pedagogies are employed as the major tool of understanding the Other, it is also necessary for all of the students to go along for the ride, or at the very least feign that they are doing so. Students speak of this as offering the "politically correct" answer; the answer that the empathy and rights discourses require. Students are savvy enough to know what the teacher/professor wants and either endeavor to give it, or stay silent. Empathy dialogues, "cannot tolerate ... and must exclude ... one who says 'our differences are such that you cannot understand me and I cannot understand you where understanding is a complete conscious, self-reflective by-product'" (Ellsworth, 1997, p. 107). Therefore, even when it seems as if empathy pedagogies are working because everyone seems engaged in the same happy, liberal task, the teacher/instructor cannot be sure that students are reacting because this communicative style is "really" (as if there were a really) making differences or that the silences and right answers are more about marks and teacher power than real change or learning. This is not to say that all moves toward teaching to and about others is negative, or doomed or over arching failure, as evidenced by the mass of CRT literature, stories and narratives that move courts, legal scholars and others. However, it is in the close-endedness of many of these tellings; the fact that there is only one or two "right" ways to interpret offered, and therefore little or no knowledge construction or unknowing are invited which is problematic to the entire project.

Discourses that rise from "understanding" the *feeling* and *pain of*, are similar to color blind discourse masking normalcy. Discourses, as stated above, which demand the same rights, same uncritical position in the curricula. Yet:

> How different can these different folks be and still be recognized as just like everyone else. Pedagogies of inclusion, and the tolerance that supposedly follows, may in actuality produce the grounds for normalization ... such hopes are able to offer only the stingy subject positions of the tolerant normal and the tolerated subaltern. (Ellsworth, 1997, p. 87)

Both are discourses that wish to speak and think their pedagogical way through racism, heterosexism and homophobia.

INTRODUCING CONTINGENT FLUIDITY AND INTERSECTIONALITY

Yet, I do not have to abandon the usefulness of intersectionality or fluidity, or argue that only one is the most useful construction. I would argue for a contingent notion of identity (Butler, 1992) because it can be "coherent with the post-modern comment because this moment [of identity politics] is grounded in the historical, the social and the political, and highlights the potential of the local and the limited, the multiple and the provisional" (Marshall, 1992, p. 16). I contend is that we cannot rely on knowing or understanding a single construction for those identity labels. This is true in the bodies of our students whether they are marginalized secondary students, or young White pre-service teachers that we, perhaps too often, assume are coming from privilege and/or an insurmountable ignorance in how to work across difference. It is also important when telling the stories of social studies, such as laying out the agency of Rosa Parks, the mindful resistance on the Rosebud Reservation, labor struggles in the United States and Canada, the revolt by transvestites at Stonewall, the complicated disruption of family that occurred during Japanese Canadian and American internments. The lives that we use to teach history, politics, social science, etc. are more often than not both fluid and intersecting.

Utilizing these fluid, situated notions of raced, sexed, classed and gendered things and beings does not necessarily argue that all differences are "equal or reconcilable" (Flax, 1993, p. xii). I do not speak about the necessity to swirl gender, class, ability, and sexualities with race and ethnicity, or sexualities with race, etc. because it is the (only or best) Way, or, as noted above as a "White-washing of difference." Educators will use and alter the lens and frames of fluidity and intersectionality to work within their local contexts. However, I would argue that the very process of incorporating and utilizing these frameworks requires one to interrogate dialogue and empathy and alters practices.

To be as aware as contexts allow and warrant, offers possibilities for incomplete understandings of the different relations within race and sexualities. It may push us to see teaching and research differently, and contingently. In this way, identity might be seen as partial and always contingent (to borrow from Butler), be seen as all parts of us in play rarely able to singularly point toward an identity without citing the others. Even when one identity is or has primacy in a moment, the knowledge that the others swirl in and around us, our schools, the social studies curriculum and the systems within which we live, may be a caution and may open up other questions. That is, the unitary subject may be fictive, but we reach for it because it is comforting, politically necessary, less confusing, and because we have no words for this other fragmented self.

These complicating ideas are needed to understand the experiences of complicated students, and players within and outside the theater of the social studies curricula. The stories of CRT offers this, as does the constant uncovering and dissecting that is required within ideals of intersectionality and fluidity. At particular political and pedagogical junctures the more fixed notion of the coming together of identities found in intersectionality may offer students and teachers better lens through which to read the historical, social and cultural significance. For example, understanding how moves by White women for suffrage in the United States meant that refusing support for universal suffrage for Blacks was politically expedient. What might it mean for students to read the political, economic and social times, understanding that the identity of Black women as crossing race and gender? How might it offer a fruitful set of lens from which to analyze? How might it alter their learning to explore how, in this case, the intersectionality of race, gender and class, and the material primacy of race and gender for both Black and White women was (within a White male dominated society) salient?

At other times, fluidity will offer a more helpful way to read. For example, in understanding the complicated nature of the rise of AIDS. Asking students to view sexualities, and the roles of race and sexualities in the responses by different communities, might offer students ways to construct knowledge about why White agencies were slow to respond to communities of color, and why some communities of color were less likely to acknowledge the rise of AIDS.

Many educators and theorists of all subject positions (embraced or not) are searching for ways to better teach across difference. In the case of teacher educators, there is also the drive to offer new ways for our young teachers to teach across difference. However, the gains that many of us hoped to see through the courts, education, pedagogy and curricula has largely failed to have the significant impacts that we desired. Yet, we remain committed to ways of teaching and learning that rely on reason, logic and fully conscious understandings of the Other. This seems ironic because the difficulty and ultimate failure of this approach has been demonstrated in the continued schooling difficulties for marginalized students, teachers and student teachers. In the end, if we, as educators, fail to utilize (and explain to pre-service teachers) intersected, complicated, fluid ideals and constructions, then we continue to fix students and curricula as things we can put right. This will likely continue moves geared toward changing the individuals or pedagogies to fit the norm rather than repeatedly de-centering the norm.

NOTES

1. "Queer" as a term, as opposed to gay, lesbian, or bisexual purposefully disrupts the notion that identity is fixed or immutable. Those who chose to call themselves queer, most often have embraced this notion. It is also a move to highlight the existence of, and disrupt a ubiquitous heteronormativity.

2. For example, in the United States and to some degree Canada, the *culture* in *multicultural* has often denotes a conflation of the word *culture* with race or ethnicity. In some Canadian contexts multi*cultural* also incorporates, at least superficially, the concerns of French-speaking Canadians.

3. Intersectionality (mostly from within CRT) and fluidity (from within poststructural theories) will be defined within the body of the paper.

4. I purposely exclude bisexual, trangender and queer here because these groups, and their political needs (along with poor and working class gay

and lesbians) excluded by many (middle-class) self-identified lesbians and gay men.

5. While multiculturalism has a tendency to be discussed as a singular move-ment with the interchangeable methods and desired outcomes, it is a move-ment, or movements that vary greatly. It is well beyond the scope of this chapter to review that literature; however, it is important to encourage the reader to explore this complex field for his/her self.

6. While discussion of gay men and lesbians are gaining a limited foothold in teacher education programs and some secondary schools, issues of those who identify as transgendered or queer seem to, in my experience, draw increased discomfort between pre-service and in-service teachers. Since they decide what occurs in their classrooms, it follows that this uneasiness is likely to translate into curricular silences.

7. Of course, this logic is flawed. Gay bashing is directed at those the perpetra-tors believe look "gay," "lesbian" or "transgendered." Anti-bullying measures often target the violence and teasing as negative, but may not address the homophobia and heterosexism that it under girds. This is not dissimilar to teachers setting up classroom rules that rightfully demand a lack of biased language involving race or gender in the room, but do not discuss why these words are used and harmful.

REFERENCES

Barnard, I. (1994). Anti-homophobic pedagogy: Some suggestions for teachers. *Radical Teacher, 45,* 26–28.

Bell, D. (1992). *Faces at the bottom of the well.* New York: Basic Books.

Bell, D. (1995). *Brown v. Board of Education* and the interest convergence dilemma. In K. Crenshaw, N. Gotanda, G. Peller, & K. Thomas (Eds.), *Critical race theory: The key writings that formed the movement* (pp. 20–28). New York: The New Press.

Britzman, D.P. (1998). *Lost subjects, contested objects.* Albany: State University of New York Press.

Butler, J. (1992). Contingent foundations. In J. Butler & J.W. Scott (Eds.), *Feminists theorize the political* (pp. 3–21). New York: Routledge.

Calabrese, R.L. (1986). The effects of service activities on adolescent alienation. *Adolescence, 21*(83), 675–687.

Carter, R.L. (1995). The unending struggle for equal educational opportunity. *Teachers College Record, 96*(4), 619–625.

Cho, S.K. (1997, Fall). Multiplicities and intersectionalities: Exploring LatCrit diversity: Essential politics. *Harvard Latino Law Review, 2,* 433.

Crenshaw, K.W. (1995). Mapping the margins: Intersectionality, identity politics, and violence against women of color. In K. Crenshaw, N. Gotanda, G. Peller, & K. Thomas (Eds.), *Critical race theory: The key writings that formed the movement* (pp. 357–383). New York: The New Press.

Delgado, R. (1995). Introduction. In R. Delgado (Ed.), *Critical race theory: The cut-ting edge* (pp. Xiii-xvi). Philadelphia, PA: Temple University Press.

Ellsworth, E. (1997). *Teaching positions: Differences, pedagogy and the power of address.* New York: Teachers College Press.

Evans, K. (2002). *Negotiating the self: Identity, sexuality and emotion in learning to teach.* New York: Routledge.

Flax, J. (1993). *Disputed subjects: Essays on psychoanalysis, politics and philosophy.* New York: Routledge.

Gordon, L. (1994). What do we say when we hear "faggot"? *Rethinking our Classroom: Teaching for Equity and Social Justice* [Special Issue], 208.

Grant, C.A., & Sleeter, C. (1989). *Turning on learning: Five approaches for multicultural teaching plans.* Columbus, OH: Merrill Pub., Co.

Grillo, T., & Wildman, S.M. (1995). Obscuring the imporance of race: The implication of making comparisons between racism and sexism (or other -isms). In R. Delgado (Ed.), *Critical race theory: The cutting edge* (pp. 564–572). Philadelphia, PA: Temple University Press.

Gutierrez, G. (2000). Deconstructing Disney: Chicano/a children and critical race theory. *Aztlan: A Journal of Chicano Studies, 25*(1), 7–46.

Harris, M.G. (1994). Cholas, Mexican-American girls, and gangs. *Sex Roles, 30*(3/4), 289–301.

Jennings, K. (Ed.). (1994). *Becoming visible: A reader in gay and lesbian history for high school and college students.* Boston: Alyson Publications.

Ladson-Billings, G. (1995). Toward a theory of culturally relevant pedagogy. *American Educational Research Journal, 32*(3), 465–491.

Ladson-Billings, G. (1999). Preparing teachers for diverse student populations: A critical race theory perspective. In A. Iran-Nejad & P.D. Pearson (Eds.), *Review of research in education* (Vol. 24, pp. 211–248). Washington, DC: American Educational Research Association.

Loutzenheiser, L.W. (2001). *Painting outside the lines? Tensions and possibilities of alternative programs for marginalized students.* Unpublished doctoral dissertation, University of Wisconsin–Madison.

Loutzenheiser, L.W. (2002). Being sen and heard: Listening to young women in alternative schools. *Anthropology and Educational Quarterly, 33*(4), 1–24.

Marshall, B.K. (1992). *Teaching the postmodern: Fiction and theory.* New York: Routledge.

Massachusetts Governor's Commission on Gay and Lesbian Youth. (1993). *Making school safe for gay and lesbian youth.* Boston: Author.

Matsuda, M. (1993). *Words that wound: Critical race theory, assaultive speech, and the First Amendment.* Boulder, CO: Westview.

Ravitch, D. (1990). Multiculturalism: E pluripus plures. *American Scholar, 59,* 337–354.

Robson, R. (1997, August). Continuing the civil rights struggle: Ends and means beginning from (my) experiences: The paradoxes of lesbian/queer narratives. *Hastings Law Journal, 48,* 1387-.

Rothmayer, D. (1999). Negotiating borders of consciousness in the pursuit of education: Identity politics and gender for second-generation Korean American women. In L. Parker, D. Deyle, & S. Villenas (Eds.), *Race is . . . race isn't: Critical race theory and qualitative studies in education* (pp. 1–6). New York: Westview.

Russo, C.J., Harris, J.J., & Sandidge, R.F. (1994). *Brown v. Board of Education* at 40: A legal history of equal educational opportunities in American public education. *Journal of Negro Education, 63*(3), 297–308.

Tate, W.F.I. (1997). Critical race theory and education: History, theory and implications. In M.W. Apple (Ed.), *Review of educational research* (Vol. 22, pp. 195–250). Washington, DC: American Educational Research Association.

Uribe, V., & Harbeck, K.M. (1991). Addressing the needs of lesbian, gay, and bisexual youth: The origins of PROJECT 10 and school-based intervention. In K.M. Harbeck (Ed.), *Coming out of the classroom closet* (pp. 9–28). New York: Harrington Park Press.

Valdes, F. (2000). Sex and race in queer legal culture: Ruminations on identities and interconnectivities. In R. Delgado & J. Stefanicic (Eds.), *Critical race theory: The cutting edge* (2nd ed., pp. 334–339). Philadelphia, PA: Temple University Press.

Valdes, F. (1997). Intersections of race, ethnicity, class, gender and sexual orientation: Queer margins, queer ethics: A call to account for race and ethnicity in the law, theory, and politics of "sexual orientation." *Hastings Law Journal, 48,*1293.

Williams, P.J. (1995). Reconstructing ideals from deconstructed rights. In R. Delgado (Ed.), *Critical race theory: The cutting edge* (pp. 84–95). Philadelphia, PA: Temple University Press.

CHAPTER 9

ETHNIC YOUTH PROGRAMS

Teaching About Caring Economic Communities and Self-Empowered Leadership

Jessica Gordon Nembhard and Valerie Ooka Pang

ABSTRACT

The purpose of this chapter is to explore aspects of high school social studies and economics curricula in light of the challenges posed by the post-industrial economy and the needs of communities. This chapter also explores the implications of innovative strategies for expanding the social studies and economics education of inner-city youth in the 21st century. The authors focus on the importance of integrating "caring collaboratives" (founded on principles of social justice, community, and cooperation) in the high school economic curriculum. Such collaboratives arise out of self-empowerment efforts of young people in ethnic communities who, because they were excluded from mainstream financial resources, develop their own resources by pooling their abilities and wealth. Research is presented on youth groups mostly from African American and Asian Pacific American communities who have developed economic and social resources within a caring collaborative. We find that programs which introduce students early to cooperative economics

Critical Race Theory Perspectives on the Social Studies, pages 171–197
Copyright © 2003 by Information Age Publishing

171

and other alternative community-based strategies, along with providing students with experiences working in communities, increase student understanding of viable and relevant economic and community-building endeavors. Social studies and economics curricula benefit from such innovative programs.

INTRODUCTION

One of the key aims of social studies education is to prepare students to be active and responsible citizens in a democracy (Barr, Barth, & Shermis, 1977; Ross, 2001; Shaver, 1977; Stanley & Nelson, 1994). To accomplish this broad and complex purpose in the current Information Age, individuals must be able to work collaboratively, think critically, develop leadership capabilities, and understand post-industrial economics. The purpose of this chapter is to explore aspects of high school social studies and economics curricula in light of the challenges posed by the post-industrial economy and the needs of communities. This chapter also explores the implications of innovative strategies for expanding the social studies and economics education of inner-city youth in the 21st century. We investigate approaches to and reasons why racially and ethnically diverse young people proactively create programs that are aimed at personal and community development. The first section provides a selected review of current social studies/economic curricula and describes the characteristics of the post-industrial economy particularly relevant to changing needs and concepts in secondary social studies education. We then report on youth of color who have created "social studies in action" programs. Through their self-empowered activities in community building, entrepreneurial endeavors, and leadership, these young people design collaboratives that involve them in community and are self-sustaining. We conclude with a discussion about economic education pedagogy, teaching about cooperative economics, and the potential of combining youth development and community economic development through innovative economics curricula.

We argue that programs which introduce students early to cooperative economics[1] and other alternative community-based strategies along with experiences working in communities will increase student understanding of viable and relevant economic and community-building endeavors. These experiences provide crucial skills and perspectives needed to succeed in today's economy, and help motivate particularly inner-city students to continue in school and find a place for themselves in the "new economy." Involvement in these programs also increases student skills in decision making and participatory democracy. Student collaboratives and community-based enterprises include self-governance capacities that create a hands-on, engaging process of community building. Community-based businesses are both profitable and community nurturing. In an age of increased corporate globalization and diminishing local economic control, community-based strategies keep capital local, broaden economic ownership, and increase concern for and involvement in community. These are all issues attractive to young people of color searching for their place in society and an education relevant to their concerns. We also believe the students involved in economic, community building, and leadership programs become more proactive in creating alternatives, and thus broaden their options, their motivation for school and their capacities at the same time that they contribute to their communities. We suggest that the lack of exposure to economic alternatives in high school curricula may limit the participation of inner city youth in needed economic development and community building, and lessen their enthusiasm for formal schooling.

THE POST-INDUSTRIAL ECONOMY AND HIGH SCHOOL SOCIAL STUDIES PROGRAMS

Are secondary school students learning current innovations in economics? Do students discover that many competitive businesses provide an opportunity to insert democratic skills into economic production processes such as requiring and developing learning-by-doing, team work, and other "soft skills"?[2] Do they know that viable businesses can be organized in a variety of structures that are democratically and sometimes collectively governed? Are schools preparing students to participate in such economic alternatives as cooperative consumer-owned, producer-owned or worker-owned businesses, credit unions, worker-owned or municipally-owned enterprises, and other locally-based, democratically-run endeavors? Haynes and Nembhard (1999) argue that competitive methods now used worldwide to gain market share are built on entrepreneurial strategies that combine competition and cooperation. Entrepreneurial activity is transformed from a traditional individualist focus to a more collective focus. How are high school social studies and economics curricula preparing students?

In this section we discuss the characteristics of the post-industrial economy which require certain kinds of social studies economics education, and which provide opportunities for emphasizing innovations and community focus in the high school curricula. We then analyze social studies and economics curricula to understand what is currently being emphasized and where proactive programs are having success.

Characteristics of the Post-Industrial Economy

Over the past thirty years, increased international competition and con-solidation of economic power and ownership into fewer hands at the same time that industrial economies changed from manufacturing- to service-based has led corporations to follow low road strategies. These strategies include cutting costs, particularly labor costs (wages and usually benefits); increasing contingent or temporary work; breaking unions; lobbying for decreased government regulations; and polluting low status and disenfran-chised communities without taking responsibility for the consequences, costs or clean up. These transnational, footloose companies keep workers in fierce competition with one another and with the lowest paid jobs in the world, giving up any loyalty to location or locality. This has created a period when growth "generates inequality" (Williams, 2000). The increased importance of the service sector—now the fastest growing sector—and of knowledge production and technological change, and the decreasing importance of the manufacturing sector, have also changed the reward structure in terms of the types of jobs that are favored and provide high wages. Jobs that require knowledge of production and highly technological skills receive a high premium. Many middle-wage jobs, especially in the ser-vice sector, no longer exist. Therefore, if an individual does not qualifying for a high wage job in the service sector, the only other option available is a low paying job with little mobility, and often few benefits.

Between 1974 and 1993 the returns to a bachelors degree were much higher than the returns to a high school diploma. The ratio between what a high school graduate earned and what a college graduate earned decreased from 70% in 1974 to 57% in 1993 (Rodgers, 1999; also see Uchi-telle, 2000); and increased slightly to 60% in 2000.[3] Uchitelle (2000) observes that:

> ... in the high-technology economy, employers say they value a college degree as evidence that a job applicant has learned to think and to master new ways of working, and is also sufficiently disciplined to work hard. The high school diploma no longer sends that message to employers.

Meanwhile, White, non-Latino students in 1996 had high school drop out rates of 7.3%; African American students, 13%; and Latino students, 29.4% (Ball, 2002, p. 96). Williams (2000) notes that "Wage inequality increased [particularly from the mid 1970s through the early 1990s] because wage growth slowed or reversed for many U.S. workers, particularly those who are young, without a college education, and/or are Black and Latino."[4]

Similar findings can be seen in some Asian American communities. Dis-aggregated statistics must be used in order to accurately examine the diverse economic realities that exist within this population (Pang, 1995; Pang, Kiang, & Pak, forthcoming). For example, less than 6% of Cambodian American, Laotian Americans, and Hmong Americans have earned a college degree (Interim Report of the White House Initiative on Asian Americans and Pacific Islanders, 2001). In addition their poverty rates are extremely high. The President's Advisory Commission on Asian Americans and Pacific Islanders (2001) states that although the general U.S. poverty rate for all Americans is 10%, Hmong Americans have a rate of 66%; Cambodians, a rate of 47%; Laotian Americans, 67%; and Vietnamese Americans, 34%. These statistics indicate how difficult it is for some Asian Americans to earn a college degree and become competitive in this post-industrial society.

In addition, wage inequality grew even among workers with the same level of education (Rodgers, 1999). While high wage jobs increasingly depend on a college degree, the greatest growth in employment is not necessarily in high wage industries or occupations, particularly for African Americans, Latinos, Cambodian Americans, and Laotian Americans. This means that the greatest demand for workers is not in areas that reward high educational attainment. According to projections by the U.S. Bureau of Labor Statistics, retail trade, health services and business services will account for half of job growth between 1992 and 2005 (from Williams, 2000). Of the nine jobs expected to show the most growth in employment,[5] only two require college diplomas, some do not require a high school diploma, and 7 of 9 are low wage jobs. Professional, technical and managerial jobs, which pay the highest wages in the service sector and employ college educated workers, accounted for 23% of job growth in 1992 (and are expected to account for 24% by 2005) (see Williams, 2000). Here modest growth is projected to continue but not increase. Since the high wage jobs are not growing as fast, not having the credentials to qualify for employment in the favored sectors has serious consequences.

Moreover, a very large wealth gap persists between African Americans and White Americans, and also other communities of color and Whites (Oliver & Shapiro, 1997; also see Conley, 1999; Kunjufu, 1991; Wolff, 2001). Recent data from Wolff (2001) finds that the ratio of median wealth holdings between non-Latino White and non-Latino Black households is 0.12. Even when Black and White households are matched for similar income levels, occupational status and educational attainment the wealth gap is large. Since the wealth gap has persisted and changed very little in 30 years, those who study wealth inequality have begun to suggest that wealth holdings may be an important missing variable in our understanding of racial and ethnic economic inequality. This means that asset building strategies and economic development that creates wealth for broader portions of the community have added importance. More research is needed (see Conley, 1999; Nembhard, forthcoming).

While those who can will continue to make superhuman achievements in education to cash in on higher returns in the labor market, we continue to live in a world where they also need to do so to compensate for continued discrimination. Increased education and better test scores are necessary but not sufficient conditions for increased economic well-being, particularly for young people of color. Rosenzweig (2000), for example, suggests that:

> There is emerging evidence that schooling does not always have payoffs, and just where and when schooling does augment productivity suggests some answers to our puzzles. One long-standing hypothesis is that schooling augments productivity by enhancing the ability to learn, which implies that where profitable learning opportunities exist, schooling is most productive. (p. 229)

Current innovations in many competitive businesses provide an opportunity to insert the democratic process into economic production processes, requiring and developing learning-by-doing, team work, and other "soft skills." This would be an example of Rosenzweig's "profitable learning opportunities," and increased possibilities for meaningful work, returns to schooling, and economic security.

High School Social Studies and Economics Curricula

High school social studies goals include developing citizenship to build democratic societies. As civic participation and political participation decline in the United States, high schools have a more difficult and more important task, particularly in a global age when local and national participation increase in importance to counteract the power and influence of global players (see Nembhard & Blasingame, 2002). Economics education in secondary schools has grown in importance as economic policy discussions permeate society. High school economics education can help students to make decisions about their economic lives and future, decide on college, teach how to enter the workforce, explore various options for entrepreneurship, and even learn how to raise money to afford college or graduate school. James Tobin, 1981 Nobel Prize laureate, argues that

> The case for economic literacy is obvious. High school graduates will be making economic choices all their lives, as breadwinners and consumers, and as citizens and voters. A wide range of people will bombard them with economic information and misinformation their entire lives. They will need

some capacity for critical judgment. They will need it whether or not they go
on to college. (Tobin, 1986, p. 22)

Recent economics education guidance given to secondary instructors
stresses the economic discipline as a way to think about problems, rather
than a study of past and current economic thought or a course in financial
literacy. Economics asks questions about what to produce, how to produce
it, who controls the process of production, how to distribute goods and services and the wealth created through the exchange of goods and services.
Economics education values viewing economics as "a way of thinking"; and
treating the learning of economics more like learning a language (Klamer,
1995). Most new thought in economics education urges economics in this
context. A society adept in a logical form of problem solving is certainly an
asset both publicly and privately. Evidence that hands on economic curricula immerse students in active economic role playing and problem solving,
and effectively motivate and teach economics to students in a variety of
ways is found in the volumes of *Economic Education Experiences of Enterprising
Teachers* (see, e.g., Nappi & Suglia, 1992).

The National Assessment of Educational Progress (2002) notes that thir-
teen states currently require students to take an economics course before
graduating from high school and that in 1998 the National Center for Education Statistics found that about 1.3 million high school seniors (47%)
had actually taken a course labeled "economics" (p. 6). According to
NEAP, except for the Advanced Placement Economics or International
Baccalaureate courses which tend to be standardized, the high school economics curriculum is quite varied—"there is no standard agreement on the
content of a high school economics course, which tends to be a one-semes-
ter course" (p. 7). The NEAP Steering Committee for the new Economics
Framework suggest the following among their rationale for economics
education (p. 8):

- the increasing complex financial and political environment;
- the role of economics education in accessing opportunities to create
  wealth;
- information management of financial news; and
- fully functioning citizens, employees, employers, personal consumers.

The concepts and themes they recommend include scarcity, takeoffs,
opportunity costs, comparative advantage, incentives, dynamics of economic growth, the price system, sources of income and profit, interactions
between economic institutions and markets, the role of money and interest
rates, business cycles, the role of government policy, and international economics (also see National Council for the Social Studies, 1994).

High school economics education as a component of the social studies curriculum can help students to make decisions about their economic lives and future, decide on college, how to enter the workforce, explore various options for entrepreneurship, and learn problem solving. However, many school curriculums lack examination of the pervasive and powerful impact of race and class on issues in economics education and other disciplines within social studies (Vinson, 2001). Researchers (Nelson, Palonsky, & Carlson, 2000; Ross, 2001; Vinson, 2001) recommend that teachers teach issues such as production, labor, and distribution of goods within social contexts. Issues of race, class, gender, nationalism, and imperialism are powerful forces that shape the economic opportunities and successes of people. Vinson (2001) recommends that teachers include the following contemporary issues that impact students and their neighborhoods: the income and wealth gap in underrepresented people, continuing commercialization of children and schools due to corporate advertising, abandonment of inner city communities, marginalization of people from inner city neighborhoods, and assault on organized labor (pp. 58–59). Vinson contends that social structures that are oppressive must be addressed in citizenship and economics education. In addition, teaching students of color about economics assists them in better understanding the society they live in and how the social realities of communities are shaped (Nelson et al., 2000).

Economics education appears to have increased benefits for students of color and low income students. Economics education can be an entree into the traditionally White male world of business. Walsted and Rebeck (2000, p. 99) note,

> In 1994, a significantly higher percentage of high school graduates who were black, Hispanic, or Asian/Pacific Islanders took economics relative to those who were White. These percentages increased dramatically over the years, especially for Hispanic students. A likely reason for this increase is that the states that have mandated economics (such as New York or California) have higher proportions of these racial or ethnic groups relative to states that have not mandated economics courses.

Further, currently the public schools, which are more likely to have a significant population of students of color, are more likely to include economics education in the curriculum. "The results suggest that students in public schools may learn more economics than students in private schools (holding everything else constant, including student ability, aptitude, and prior exposure to economic concepts.) Thus, public schools appear to be doing a better job in the teaching of economics than private schools do..." (Grimes, 1994, p. 27). In addition, economics education may aid traditionally oppressed and marginalized groups to understand the forces that maintain the status quo, and learn strategies and skills that will help them find a place in or change the prevailing paradigm.

We next explore ways that high school and college students of color bring social studies to life and engage in community-building activities. We end by discussing the potential of education about cooperative and community-based economic development to empower students of color and enhance their high school curriculum.

SOCIAL STUDIES AND ECONOMIC EDUCATION IN ACTION: SELF-EMPOWERED COMMUNITY BUILDING AND LEADERSHIP DEVELOPMENT

Social studies education is more than the transmission of ideas and knowledge. Scholars in the field also believe it must include involvement in challenging the status quo and addressing inequities in society (Stanley & Nelson, 1994). What do students of color do when they want to build a strong ethnic community, but there is no program or organization that they feel addresses their needs and goals? Can young people be proactive and create an organization? High school students do take leadership. They identify critical social and racial issues and design collaboratives that address these needs. Within these organizations they also create infrastructures that include economic development goals.

Pang examined three student collaboratives created by Asian Pacific American youth. She was particularly interested in proactive Asian Pacific American (APA) organizations since in much of the educational literature, APA students are invisible and rarely discussed (Pang & Cheng, 1998). In addition, along with the often invisibility of APA youth is the stereotypical misconception that these young people do not have leadership capabilities and/or are not leaders.

Developing leadership and entrepreneurial skills in youth not only can assist young people in developing their personal talents, but also builds future community leaders. In the three organizations studied, the young leaders recognize social issues and then create a mission of how to address those needs. A common value found in all three collaboratives was that the members cared about others and wanted to address issues of exclusion, prejudice, and social justice. As problem solvers and leaders, the founding members had the ability to gather others together with similar concerns. They also communicated well with others and built a core team of young people who had strong ethical principles and commitment to the community. In the organizational process, the leaders also developed effective speaking and listening skills. The leaders had a sense of personal competence and were risk takers. The organizations were also places where these leadership skills were taught to new members. The three collaboratives have existed for as few as three years and as many as eleven years. The leadership skills the members hold ensure the continuation of these groups and their existence is critical in today's post industrialized context.

The three APA youth organizations developed entrepreneurial programs as part of the community structures they put in place. They effectively pooled their individual human resources because the young people knew they needed assets in order to create effective social programs. For example, the founders of these organizations were sensitive to the aggressive nature of society and understood the importance of working toward building a culturally sensitive community that fought to eliminate prejudice and discrimination. To support their activities such as guest speaker bureaus and workshops, they needed resources. This led the organizations to have branches within the groups to write grants, conduct fund-raising activities, and solicit contributions from large foundations.

The members of these collaboratives applied the principles of democratic citizenship and put into practice what Dewey (1914) characterizes as "associated living." Dewey carefully describes democracy as more than a system of government. Democracy is a system of living where individuals develop common goals and work collaboratively and actively in pursuit of those goals. Social justice must be a component of the system of associated living (Ross, 2001).

These three collaboratives developed out of the belief in proactive citizenship and share the following characteristics:

1. Each organization was created by students themselves because there were no existing organizations that addressed their ethnic issues of identity and community;

2. Each organization addresses issues of inequity through a variety of community service projects because making contributions to the community is a key purpose;

3. Each organization is financially supported by the entrepreneurial actions of its members which provides youth collaborative economic experiences;

4. Ethnic/racial membership is an important component of each organization and there is a common understanding of the social prejudice based on race/ethnicity that exists; and

5. Each organization has leadership, academic, and identity development skill activities for its members in order to grow intellectually, socially, and personally.

Individuals were interviewed from three organizations: Alpha Psi Rho, An Asian Pacific American fraternity in Southern California; Coalition for

Asian Pacific American Youth, a statewide student organization in Massachusetts; The Mavin Foundation, a national interracial organization founded by a Korean American male in the state of Washington.

Three APA Youth Organizations

Alpha Psi Rho

Alpha Psi Rho is an Asian Pacific American fraternity at San Diego State University. Alpha Psi Rho was founded by ten young men in 2000 to provide Asian Pacific Americans on campus with a brotherhood and family away from home. Ethnicity was important to the members of this fraternity. Their Asian Pacific American ethnicity was an important bond. The founding members of the fraternity identified racial prejudice and struggles that their ancestors endured in this country as important contexts for their organization. In addition, the members felt that Asian Pacific Americans were severely underrepresented in the Greek system. The young men wanted to provide Asians opportunities to get more involved in the local community and create ways to meet people.

Their mission statement reads:

> We the gentlemen of Alpha Psi Rho, strive to achieve Brotherhood through active participation in the community by promoting Asian/Pacific Islander awareness. By fostering scholastic achievement, we shall mold future leaders who will actively pursue the apex of life. Our cultural backgrounds shall provide us with the strength and unity to attain greatness. Through Brotherhood, we will produce high caliber men who will be triumphant in the face of perseverance. We are the gentlemen of Alpha Psi Rho.

Alpha Psi Rho is the smallest APA organization studied with approximately 35 members.

CAPAY: The Coalition for Asian Pacific American Youth

The Coalition for Asian Pacific American Youth (CAPAY) is a statewide collaborative. CAPAY was founded by a group of Asian Pacific American high school students who initially were concerned with racism in schools. The move toward the collaborative came with the proactive leadership of Vira Douangmany, a Laotian American high school senior, who organized a walkout of students from her school in the Boston area. Vira and other students protested the harassment of Asian Pacific American students. School administrators threatened to suspend Vira and other Asian Pacific American students. Although the walkout was cancelled, Vira and the other students stipulated that school personnel and students engage in a cultural sensitivity seminar. School administrators were extremely reluctant to do anything about the racism that Vira and her colleagues identified.

The unwillingness of school authorities to address the continual harassment of Asian Pacific American students led to the development of a group of students and community people who began with summer internships and the planning for a statewide conference. The first conference was held in December of 1993 and celebrated Asian diversity. Though 300 students were expected, more than 600 attended. Sessions included international dating, "gangs," race relations, intergenerational conflicts, classroom curriculum, and dynamics in schools. Following this conference, students met for five months and an APA network of youth was established. This collaborative of young people used democratic principles of consensus and group decision making. They developed their own mission statement, governance structure, and adopted a name. They became known as the Coalition for Asian Pacific American Youth (CAPAY).

Here is the mission statement they adopted:

> We believe that youth united by a common purpose can make a difference. We aim to establish and maintain a forum for free dialogue and for positive change in our communities. Our initiatives are diverse and include avenues to abolish stereotypes, to educate ourselves and others about Asian Pacific Americans, to celebrate our heritage, and improve race relations. Our hope is for all to be able to contribute to society. (CAPAY, 1994)

CAPAY requested that schools include courses in Asian American history at their high schools. They also wanted issues of prejudice and name-calling to be addressed by school personnel and students. Prejudice also impacted their developing ethnic identity and self-development. These were important goals and took much effort to implement in public schools across the state.

Today, CAPAY is governed solely by high school students. Members write grants to fund their daily operations and the position of a coordinator. They provide a speaker's bureau for high schools who provide seminars on Asian Pacific American history, race relations, leadership skills, Asian Pacific American culture. CAPAY also is a peer support network that publishes the AS.I.AM Newsletter. In addition, the collaborative has a program called "Empowering Us." This portion of the organization sponsors a series of workshops in which members train other youth in leadership and organizational development. The sessions have included public speaking, professional writing, grant writing, and political action training. In order to put into place some of these skills, members of CAPAY often work as interns in community-based organizations and develop their own community-service project. In these projects, students become involved in organizing events and activities in support of Asian Pacific American communities.

CAPAY is also a collaborative where young people are educating themselves about Asian Pacific American communities. They have networked with 21 organizations like the Massachusetts Immigrant and Refugees Advocacy Coalition, the Asian American Resource Workshop, and the Massachusetts Asian American Educators Association.

The MAVIN Foundation

The Mavin Foundation is another grassroots community collaborative run by young people. The foundation was created by Matt Kelley, a young interracial Asian American, who believed there was a need for an organization that focuses on issues of mixed race individuals. The organization began with Kelley's creation of the magazine called MAVIN in 1998 when he was a freshman at Wesleyan University. Kelley found most people did not understand multiracial issues. He was tired of being asked "What are you?" Kelley founded MAVIN, a collaborative that celebrates multiracial persons and families, based on his belief that it is important for multiracial people to be proactive. The word, mavin, has roots in Hebrew and refers to a person who understands. The mission of the MAVIN Foundation is as follows:

> The MAVIN Foundation redefines diversity through innovative projects celebrating multiracial youth and families. (Mavin Foundation, 2003)

The MAVIN foundation is the nation's largest nonprofit organization dedicated to redefining diversity by celebrating multiracial and transracially adopted youth. Through their programs, MAVIN desires to create a cohesive, multicultural society. The organization has been recognized by Presidents Bush and Clinton for its innovative approach to race and diversity issues. Educating oneself and others is a major goal of the foundation. The organization has developed several products in their educational efforts. One of their first products is a magazine called MAVIN. The magazine discusses various multiracial issues such as identity, transracial adoptions, and monoracial bias. This magazine can be ordered by mail and is found in bookstores. The organization also edited and published a book for parents, teachers, counselors, and other service providers. The *Multiracial Child Resource Handbook* includes unique information about multiracial youth, chapters on multiracial childhood development, and a compilation of resources. In order to fund these projects, Kelley and his staff wrote numerous grants and engage in continual fund-raising. In the past, the foundation received contributions from the K&F Baxter Family Foundation, the Educational Legacy Fund, The Harvest Foundation, The Seattle Foundation, Microsoft Corporation, and the J.C. Penny Company Fund. Funding is an important component of the foundation because funds are needed to support their many community-building activities.

One of their community-based projects is called Matchmaker. Their program is the only national bone marrow program dedicated to registering multiracial marrow donors. Kelley and his staff decided to create this program because of the plight of a four-year-old interracial girl named Nicole Howard who has leukemia and was in need of a bone marrow transplant. Matchmaker is an important commitment to the needs of multiracial people. Only 1.9% of donors registered on the National Bone Marrow Registry are interracial, so it is exponentially more difficult to find bone marrow transplants for mixed-race people. MAVIN's Matchmaker is a crucial piece in the health of many interracial individuals. Their recruitment efforts are national and the organization has recruited donors on college campus like Cornel University, University of Washington, Yale University, San Diego State University, and Arizona State University.

An Intergenerational Program

Youth Warriors

In her work, Nembhard finds that youth development and intergenerational participation in community advocacy and economic development activities are essential to the sustainability and success of most alternative strategies. The Youth Warriors Environmental Justice After School Program in Baltimore, MD, for example, provides predominantly Black students from 13–18 years of age with an after school program that focuses on learning about and becoming active in addressing local environmental injustices. Youth Warriors was founded by a young African American woman, Lynn Pinder, who wanted to help young people learn how to be advocates in their community, and proactively address inequalities and injustices. Students are involved in community service and leadership development, get their homework done, and also learn environmental science and communication skills. The activism and involvement appear to positively impact these youth's school attendance and academic attitudes. Such a program develops leaders, while increasing their academic and advocacy skills, and can be a stepping stone to involving students in community economic development activities and motivating them to stay in school in order to do so more effectively.

ECONOMIC INNOVATION, WORKPLACE DEMOCRACY, AND COOPERATIVE ECONOMICS

In each of the above organizations, issues of race, social exclusion, and social injustice are seen as powerful forces in society. The members of the collaboratives work to better understand the social forces that impact them and attempt to address social oppression in their own lives through activism and advocacy. They understand how prejudice and cultural imperialism have impacted their lives and the lives of others. They work toward elimination of prejudices and the building of a cooperative and caring community. They see urgent problems that teachers, professors, and other adults are ignoring. They believe the legacies of segregation and racism are active forces in society. The members of these groups address the disempowerment and labeling of racism through proactive collaboratives.

The above examples show that students take principles from their social studies and economics education classes and put them into action. They expand efforts into the community helping others particularly around issues of racial and ethnic justice, and community development and health. Another way to fill the gap between what teachers are teaching and what students want to learn is to change the way educators teach economics. In this section we suggest that the high school economics curriculum can add value to the studies and lives of youth of color, increase their knowledge of alternatives and their capacity to create change in their communities.

Haynes and Nembhard argue that competitive methods now used worldwide to gain market share are built on entrepreneurial strategies that combine competition and cooperation (Haynes & Nembhard, 1999). Today's successful industries, for example, use different methods of production and organization both between firms and within firms. The strategy is production-based, focused on organizational practices that facilitate continuous improvement in methods, products, and processes. Entrepreneurial activity is transformed from a traditional individualist focus to a more collective focus. Within the firm, flexibility and varying degrees of worker participation transform worker-management relations: labor may be consulted directly, or labor may be in control of the production process. Democracy, particularly workplace democracy or democratic governance, stimulate effectiveness in democratic firms, and can increase the competitiveness of enterprises that practice flexibility, teamwork, decentralized control and participatory governance.

Economic benefits of various forms of democratic economic participation include: giving workers a stake in expanding company productivity; promoting feelings of ownership and pride in high quality workmanship; fostering creativity and critical thinking; increasing productivity and professionalism; improving self respect, happiness and personal growth; preserving and creating jobs and wage security; income and wealth generation; family and community orientation because of interdependencies with both; and increased concern for environmental and health issues because they live and work in those places (see Nembhard, 2000). Democratic enterprises such as cooperatives and worker-owned companies often

give women control of economic resources, more leadership and managerial training and opportunities (see Weiss & Clamp, 1992). "Perhaps more
important, worker ownership and control offer communities ... the hope
of a greater voice and control in their economic destinies" (Krimerman &
Lindenfeld, 1992, p. 8).

A characteristic of the post-industrial economy, what we broadly call economic innovation, has important implications for how we educate young
people. Participation in such alternatives and cutting-edge economic processes such as cooperative businesses require both opportunity and preparation, formal and informal education. Cooperative businesses need their
participants to be ability to be flexible, to engage in critical thinking, use
good communication skills and nurture continuous learning habits. Standard achievement measurements are often a proxy for such "skills." Here
again lack of high achievement can put students and people of color at a
disadvantage. However such "skills" are not just learned in a formal education setting and can be acquired, developed, and nurtured through a variety of experiences, particularly innovative entrepreneurship opportunities
in cooperative settings.

Cooperative economics provides an innovative approach to teaching
economics and community building. Cooperatives operate according to
principles of shared ownership and democratic governance, particularly
one member, one vote (as opposed to the traditional investor model based
on a vote for every share owned). Members pool and share resources, risks,
and profits. Cooperatives serve their members' needs through the production, distribution and/or acquisition of goods and services. Because they
are based on democratic participation cooperatives are a unique form of
business. Cooperatives combine the requirements of a business with the
requirements of an association or collective—the traditional economics of
supply and demand and business planning melded with group needs, democratic participation and ownership, and concern for community. As of
2000 more than 100 million people were members of 47,000 cooperatives—some producer-owned, some worker-owned and some consumer-
owned (see National Cooperative Business Association website,
www.ncba.coop). About 30% of agricultural products are sold by cooperative marketing associations in the United States. More than 50 million
Americans use insurance companies that are owned by (or closely affiliated
with) cooperatives. More than 67 million people are members of credit
unions (cooperative financial institutions), with combined assets of more
than $100 billion. More than 20 cooperative businesses make more than $1
billion in annual sales (see National Cooperative Business Association).
More than 1.5 million families live in cooperative housing.

The reasons to provide students of color with cooperative education are
compelling. Students of color often come from families with low net worth

and communities that lack economic opportunity. Many inner-city neighborhoods suffer from market failures and the overestimation of the risks of doing business in these neighborhoods. With their more accurate risk assessment, local students will be poised to take advantage of these market opportunities. Exposure to cooperative models may enable these young people to start their own community-based businesses and bring income and wealth to their communities; or inspire them to study more and specialize in community economic development. Lessons from the past and present, such as the Federation of Southern Cooperatives in the United States, and the Mondragon Cooperative Corporation in Northern Spain, both successful cooperatives managed largely by members of racial or ethnic subaltern populations, can serve as both inspiration and template.[6]

The Federation of Southern Cooperatives/Land Assistance Fund (FSC/LAF) is a network of rural cooperatives and cooperative development centers in the southern United States. For 35 years the organization has pursued goals to retain Black-owned land, and use cooperatives for land-based, self-help economic development to increase income and wealth in low-income communities. Strategies used by the FSC/LAF in their cooperative education workshops for young African Americans provide an example of how to teach youth about cooperatives. One strategy used is to call attention to culturally familiar ideas and apply them to economics, to help participants feel comfortable with the topic. Federation/LAF education workshops point out quotes and activities by famous African Americans supportive of cooperative economic development. The workshops refer to the principles celebrated during the Kwanzaa festivals (in particular "Ujamaa" or cooperative economics). This helps the participants make a connection between the democratic economic concepts and their own culture and family values (see Nembhard, 2002). In addition, the facilitator illustrates familiar paradigms and easy, safe ways to change or alter familiar systems. For example, the first system we all learn is the system of letters, the alphabet. We all know it so well we can recite it with our eyes closed. But how easy is it to recite it backwards? We are not comfortable at first but can learn with practice to be as comfortable with Z-A as we were with A-Z (see Nembhard, 2002). Economic systems can also be changed.

A recent Federation of Southern Cooperatives/Land Assistance Fund cooperative economics workshop used a human pyramid to illustrate class structure and economic inequality in our system. Three teen-aged participants were asked line up side by side on their hands and knees on the floor in the middle of the group. They represented the masses of people. Two more teenagers representing the middle class climbed on top of them on their hands and knees. The last lone participant climbed up to the top finishing the pyramid—representing the rich. While the participants held that position (and moaned and groaned at the bottom with all the weight on them) the facilitator led a discussion about inequality and fairness—who is bearing the weight for whom and the status of each level of the pyramid. Once the pyramid was dismantled, the facilitator asked what might be a better distribution, or how might we avoid such inequality. Many good suggestions were made, and the participants are led to consider cooperative structures and the principles of cooperative enterprises (see Nembhard, 2002).

Similarly, the Six Nation's Politechnic of Ontario, Canada's (with other sponsors) "Cooperative Entrepreneurship Curriculum" early on explores synergies between the values of First Nations (Amer-Indians) and cooperative principles and values. They draw out traditional First Nation's values of peace, power, righteousness, honesty, sharing, caring, fairness, self-determination and community with cooperative values and principles of openness, self-help, honesty, equality, caring, social responsibility, solidarity and democracy. They use quotes from indigenous people, and provide examples of cooperatives developed in First Nations communities. Only after this kind of introduction do they move on to training in entrepreneurship, and cooperative business development.

The Urban Nutrition Initiative (UNI) is a school-based community health promotion collaboration between the University of Pennsylvania, the West Philadelphia Partnership, and public schools in Philadelphia. It combines an interdisciplinary pre-K through 16 community health curriculum, school-based gardens, and entrepreneurial and business development into a "dynamic educational process based on experiential learning and community problem-solving" integrated with public service (UNI, 2002, p. 3). The programs goals are to:

- create and sustain an interdisciplinary pre-K through 16+ curriculum that focuses on improving community health and simultaneously results in increased educational skills and abilities;
- work with university faculty, public school teachers and community residents to effectively engage students as agents of school and community change; resulting in;
- students' increased sense of control over their lives and their futures, and in
- mobilization of substantial and effective resources (youth) to improve community health (Center for Community Partnerships, 2003; UNI, 2002).

The project enables students (mostly African American) at all levels to combine learning about nutrition, teaching it to others, growing healthy food, and creating businesses to sell and market the food. This is an innovative comprehensive program that helps students make connections between what they learn, how they live their lives, problems and issues in their communities, food production, and socially responsible entrepreneurship. Students are not just volunteers or tutors or even gardeners, but become all that and in addition become community builders, activists and business developers.

EcoTech, at University City High School in Philadelphia, is a communications, technology and environmental studies program sponsored by the UNI. It includes projects with peer horticulture education, peer nutrition education, a farmer's market, and a winter harvest (cooperative purchasing) club. High school students learn about horticulture and nutrition from college students and university faculty. They in turn teach students at Drew Elementary School, grow fruits and vegetables in urban school-based gardens, sell fruit and healthy snacks at student-run after-school fruit and vegetable stands (which even first graders run), set up Saturday farmers' markets, and develop microbusinesses. Martin Galvin, the Program coordinator, notes in reference to the tutoring that both the high school and the elementary students benefit: "You're saying to 15- and 16-year-olds that we believe you are capable of going over into a classroom, delivering that lesson plan, and having smaller students learn (from) you—an incredibly powerful message" (National Public Radio, 2003). Students also gain self-esteem and confidence from both the tutoring and the economic activities. The program uses entrepreneurship to engage young people in skill-building activities and school and community service through a "democratic collaborative process" (UNI, 2002, pp. 8, 3). In addition, early data analysis suggests that students are beginning to change their eating habits. Thousands of food frequency surveys taken at Drew Elementary show that the students "consume relatively higher proportions of fresh fruits and vegetables as after school snacks as compared to children at control schools in West Philadelphia" (UNI, p. 19).

In the past year the high school project also began to develop a food cooperative, starting with the development and support of buying clubs. Buying clubs enable students and community members to "pool their resources to buy quality and organic groceries and produce at wholesale prices" (UNI, 2002, p. 16). The fruit stands, farmers' markets, and harvest and buying clubs make healthy alternatives available in inner cities and connect low-income communities with fresh farm products, and the local farmers that grow them, including some of the students. These enterprises provide the students with entrepreneurial skills and business experiences, and expose them to models of local sustainable food production (UNI, p. 14), while giving them experience with owning and running cooperative enterprises. Community development, health and nutrition, leadership, entrepreneurship, and cooperative development are learned and nurtured through this integrated curriculum.

CONCLUSIONS

We began by exploring the characteristics of the post-industrial global economy and the kinds of skills that are rewarded (technological as well as "soft" skills). Understanding and recognizing the characteristics of the post-industrial economy indicates that the typical high school social studies curriculum may be irrelevant or inadequate to the tasks at hand. This is particularly an issue for traditionally marginalized students of color and low-income students attempting to gain skills and find their place in the "new economy," and formulate a viable plan for their future. Teachers and students need to understand the changing economy, how young people fit into it, and how they can be more proactive in addressing 21st century needs. Youth can learn to be economic innovators in a changing economy that relies more on information, technology and technological change, problem solving, and team work and collaboration than ever before. At the same time they can be exposed to new forms of economic organization and management that put people and communities more in control. We are beginning to find examples of such programs and curricula.

In analyzing current social studies and economics curricula for high school students, we find that most programs focus primarily on the transmission of specific knowledge, and are based on traditional and conventional models of economic activity and civic engagement. Many programs moved too slowly to be relevant to the experiences of the youth on which we focus. We critique social studies and economics curricula from the perspective of engaging students of color in thinking about and participating in new economies and alternative democratic community-based economic development and leadership strategies. We also critique traditional curricula from the perspective of teaching about caring community (Pang, 2001) in addressing issues of community development and justice, as well as pedagogy and achievement. We find that it is important for youth to examine the social structure in order to understand how social and economic oppression may shape their experiences, belief systems, and ability to support themselves.

We describe programs that have been initiated by ethnic youth (and/or give them significant control), which help to fill in the gaps between what they are learning and doing in school, and what they need and want to do in real life and with their communities. These student programs include entrepreneurial components; community-building goals; community-service, social justice, and health and nutrition aims; and leadership development. They demonstrate that young people can be proactive in understanding the needs of communities and rising to address those needs. These are examples of organizations which are collaboratives—designed, implemented and governed by young people.

The learning about alternatives that are relevant to community economic development and oriented toward caring community can be motivating and have spill over effects on other academic and non-academic activities of youth, particularly youth of color. Similarly, the engagement in community-based activities that are collective, develop leadership, and address racial and ethnic inequality and injustices positively affects students' immediate communities. Such engagement gives young people reasons to become more involved, and capacities to feel confident about their involvement both in the community and in school. However, there are few examples where the curriculum focuses on teaching leadership skills.

Although attention in the social studies and economics education communities has been around issues of social justice, educators have failed to focus adequate attention on the development of leadership skills in youth, and the social context of racism and classism. Teachers want students to be able to work collaboratively and build a strong community, however few students are formally taught leadership principles and skills, or given the opportunity to experiment with or experience leadership. Most leadership skills are taught through student government activities, though leadership principles can be included throughout the school curriculum and through economics instruction. Not all students are included in student government activities and so they may not have the chance to develop organizational and leadership skills. In addition, students often lack the opportunity in class to discuss the impact of social oppression such as racism and classism on economic status. Discussing economics without mention of issues of economic marginalization and exploitation prevents students from examining underlying social forces that are powerful influences in our post-industrial society.

The experiences of the students in the examples of the student-run collaboratives that we highlight suggest that community service and advocacy develop leadership. The Urban Nutrition Initiative (2002) finds that entrepreneurship and involvement in business development along with the production of food all develop leadership in young people. Engagement of youth in cooperative economics addresses some of these issues as well. We explore the ways in which cooperative business development teaches collective action, networking, business planning and collaboration. Also valuable is the creative thinking cooperative activities encourage and require, and the applicability of the cooperative model at the neighborhood level. Students' strong peer bonds and concern for community can be important assets to bring to the development of a cooperative, a collective and other community-based organizations and activities. Students find that they are able to help themselves, their peers, their family and community when they engage in collaborative relationships and form community-based, socially responsible local businesses. The few high school curricula that combine these attributes are creating innovative integrated programs which show positive results.

We worry that in some communities the connections between academic achievement or scholarship, leadership, and economic reward and success are so remote that young people in racial/ethnic and low-income communities are making pragmatic even rational decisions not to invest in schooling. Current economic inequalities and hierarchies often privilege other attributes. However, our vision of a caring community practicing economic democracy requires learned and thinking participants. Social studies and economics curricula which expose students to alternatives and give them experiences working in communities and developing leadership can help to prepare students to be active, responsible, and productive participants in and builders of a democratic society.

ACKNOWLEDGMENTS

The authors would like to thank T.J. Lehman, Dan Taylor, Peter Kiang, Kimi Kawabori, and Matt Kelley in the preparation of this chapter.

NOTES

1. American Educational Research Association's (AERA) CORIBE Initiative definition of Cooperative Economic Development is that it "Promotes pooling of resources, shared wealth, economic and political enfranchisement that puts community members in control over economic activity and wealth creation through noncompetitive business practices for the collective benefit of all local residents. This parallels one of the seven principles of the African American value system celebrated as KWANZAA that encourages African Americans to build and maintain stores, shops and other businesses and to profit from them together." This is similar to Nembhard's definition in previous work (see Nembhard 1999 and forthcoming).

2. "Soft skills" is a term used in opposition to "hard skills" which refer to highly technical knowledge and capacities, and industry-specific skills and expertise. Soft skills tend to refer to social , interpersonal, and communication skills (similar to "bedside manner" and "people skills") including speaking and listening, negotiation, team building and collaboration, problem solving, learning by doing, and leadership skills, as well as attributes such as adaptability, flexibility, and creativity (see Houghton & Proscio, 2001; ACEnet, 1994; Carnevale ,1989, for example).

3. Author's calculations from U.S. Census 2000 data on income by educational attainment.

4. Much of the information in this section refers to the decade of the 1980s (from Williams, 2000, calculated from 1980s Census data that is sector specific; also see Nembhard, forthcoming). Current trends appear similar, although the 1990s eventually saw wage growth and a stable economic expansion after 1992. On the other hand, workers of color benefitted little until the last few years of the expansion of the 1990s, and similar issues about job quality and job segregation pertain (see Darity & Mason, 1998; Persuad & Lusane, 2000; Staveteig & Wigton, 2000).

5. The nine occupations are: retail sales workers, registered nurses (college), cashiers, truck drivers, waiters and waitresses, nursing aides, janitors, food preparation workers, systems analysts (college).

6. The Mondragon Cooperative Corporation is based on a system of interlocking networked worker-owned cooperatives, several of which are educational institutions which support cooperative development and new business start-ups, youth development in general, management training, research and development, and continuous education of cooperative members (see Mondragon's website: www.mondragon.mcc.es).

REFERENCES

ACEnet. (1994). *Creating high performance communities through the development of learning consortia.* Athens, OH: Appalachian Center for Economic Networks.

Ahituv, A., Tienda, M., & Hotz, V.J. (2000). Transition from school to work: Black, Hispanic, and White men in the 1980s. In R. Marshall (Ed.), *Back to shared prosperity: The growing inequality of wealth and income in America* (pp. 250–258). Armonk, NY: M.E. Sharpe.

Ball, A.F. (2002). Three decades of research on classroom life: Illuminating the classroom communicative lives of America's at-risk students. In W.G. Secada (Ed.), *Review of research in education* (Vol. 26, pp. 71–111). Washington, DC: The American Educational Research Association.

Barone, C.A. (1991, Winter). Contending perspectives: Curricular reform in economics. *Journal of Economics Education, 22*(1), 15–26.

Barr, R.D., Barth, J.L., & S. Shermis, S. (1977). *Defining the social studies.* Arlington, VA: National Council for the Social Studies.

Bartlett, R.L. (1997). Reconstructing economics 190 R&G: Introductory Economics course from a race and gender perspective. In R. Bartlett (Ed.), *Introducing race and gender into economics* (pp. 3–27). New York: Routledge Press.

Benello, G. (1992). Economic democracy and the future. In L. Krimerman, F. Lindenfeld, C. Korty, & J. Benello (Eds.,) *From the ground up: Essays on grassroots & workplace democracy by C. George Benello* (pp. 81–88). Boston: South End Press.

Bowles, S., & Gintis, H. (1998). *Recasting egalitarianism: New rules for markets, states, and communities.* London: Verso.

Buckles, S. (1991). Guidelines for economic content in school programs. In W. Walsted & J.C. Soper (Eds.), *Effective economic education in the schools.* New York: The Joint Council on Education and The National Education Association.

Carnevale, A.P. (1989). *Workplace basis: The essential skills employers want.* Washington, DC: U.S. Department of Labor.

Center for Community Partnerships. (2003). *The urban nutrition initiative project.* www. upenn.edu/ccp/uni.shtml (accessed 1–13-03).

Coalition for Asian Pacific American Youth. (1994). *CAPAY: Coalition for Asian Pacific American Youth.* http://omega.cc.umb.edu/~capay/history.html.

Cobbs, J.L. (1976). A job that badly needs doing—A business editor looks at economics education. *Journal of Economics Education, 8*(1), 5–8.

Conley, D. (1999). *Being Black, living in the red: Race wealth, and social policy in America.* Berkeley: University of California Press.

Daly, H.E., & Cobb, J.B., Jr. (1994). *For the common good: Redirecting the economy toward community, the environment, and a sustainable future.* Boston: Beacon Press.

Darity, W.A., Jr., & Mason, P.L. (1998, Spring). Evidence on discrimination in employment: Codes of color, codes of gender. *Journal of Economic Perspectives, 12*(2), 63–90.

Dewey, J. (1914). *Democracy and education.* New York: The Free Press.

Frey, B. (2001). *Inspiring economics, human motivation in political economy.* Cheltenham: Edward Elgar.

Gilliard, J.V. (1993). Economics in elementary and secondary schools. In V.S. Wilson, J.A. Litle, & G.L. Wilson (Eds.), *Teaching social studies* (pp. 158–171). Westport, CT: Greenwood Press.

Grimes, P.W. (1994, Winter). Public versus private secondary school and the production of economics education. *Journal of Economics Education, 25*(1), 17–30.

Haynes, C., Jr., & Nembhard, J.G. (1999, Summer). Cooperative economics—A community revitalization strategy. *The Review of Black Political Economy, 27*(1), 47–71.

Hill, R. (2000, Summer). The case of the missing organizations: Co-operatives and the textbooks. *Journal of Economic Education, 31*(3), 281–300.

Houghton, T., & Proscio, T. (2001, October). Hard work on soft skills: Creating a "culture of work." In *Workforce development. Working ventures.* Philadelphia, PA: Public/Private Ventures.

James, E.J. (1899). Educational value—Economics as a school study. *Economic Studies* (Vol. 4). Ithaca, NY: Andrus and Church Press.

Jenness, D. (1990). *Making sense of social studies.* New York: Macmillan.

Klamer, A. (1995). Rhetorical obstacles in the teaching of economics. In W. Gijselaers, D. Tempelaar, P. Keizer, J. Blammaert, E. Bernanrd, & H. Kasper (Eds.), *Educational innovation in economics and business administration* (pp. 8–19). Dordrecht: Kluwer.

Krimerman, L., & Lindenfeld, F. (1992). *When workers decide: Workplace democracy takes root in North America.* Philadelphia, PA: New Society Publishers.

Krimerman, L., Lindenfeld, F., Korty, C., & Benello, J. (1992). *From the ground up: Essays on grassroots & workplace democracy by C. George Benello.* Boston: South End Press.

Kunjufu, J. (1991). *Black economics: Solutions for economic and community empowerment.* Chicago: African American Images.

Marshall, R. (2000). *Back to shared prosperity: The growing inequality of wealth and income in America.* Armonk, NY: M.E. Sharpe.

MAVIN foundation. (2003). MAVIN Foundation. http://www.mavinfoundation.org.

Mondragon Cooperative Corporation. www.mondragon.mcc.es.

Nadeau, E.G., & Thompson, D.J. (1996). *Cooperation works!* Rochester, MN: Lone Oak Press, Ltd.

Nappi, A.T., & Suglia, A.F. (Eds.). (1992). *Economic education experiences of enterprising teachers* (Vol. 29). New York: Joint Council on Economic Education.

National Assessment of Educational Progress. (2002). *Economics framework for 2006.* Washington, DC: National Assessment Governing Board [draft May, 2, 2002].

National Cooperative Business Association. www.ncba.coop.

National Council for the Social Studies. (1994). *Expectations of excellence: Curriculum standards for social studies.* Silver Spring, MD: National Council for the Social Studies.

National Public Radio (NPR). (2003). *Civics lessons beyond the classroom.* Based on Nancy Solomon's report on *Morning Edition,* January 7, 2003. http://discover.npr.org/features/feature.jtml?wfld=905341 (accessed 1–13-03).

Nelson, J.L., Palonsky, S.B., & Carlson, K. (2000). *Critical issues in education.* Boston: McGrawHill.

Nembhard, J.G. (Forthcoming). Toward democratic economic participation. In J. King (Ed.), *Facing the new millennium: A transformative research & action agenda in Black education.* Commission on Research in Black Education, American Educational Research Association.

Nembhard, J.G. (2002, July-October). Education for a people-centered democratic economy. *GEO Newsletter,* (53–54), 8–9.

Nembhard, J.G. (2000). Democratic economic participation and humane urban redevelopment. *Trotter Review,* pp. 26–31.

Nembhard, J.G. (1999). Community economic development: Alternative visions for the 21st century. In J. Whitehead & C.K. Harris)Eds.), *Readings in Black political economy* (pp. 295–304). Dubuque, IA: Kendall/Hunt Publishing Company.

Nembhard, J.G., & Blasingame, A.A. (2002, December). *Economic dimensions of civic engagement and political efficacy.* Democracy collaborative-Knight Foundation civic engagement project (Working Paper). University of Maryland, College Park.

Oliver, M., & Shapiro, T. (1997). *Black wealth/White wealth: A new perspective on racial inequality.* New York: Routledge.

Pang, V.O. (2001). *Multicultural education: A caring-centered, reflective approach.* Boston, MA: McGrawHill.

Pang, V.O. (1995). Asian Pacific American students: A diverse and complex population. In J.A. Banks & C.M. Banks (Eds.), *Handbook of research on multicultural education* (pp. 412–424). New York: Macmillan.

Pang, V.O., & Cheng, L.L. (1998). *Struggling to be heard: The unmet needs of Asian Pacific American Youth.* Albany: SUNY Press.

Pang, V.O., Kiang, P.N., & Pak, Y.K. (Forthcoming). Asian Pacific American students: Challenging a biased educational system. In J.A. Banks & C.M. Banks (Eds.), *Handbook of research on multicultural education.* San Francisco: Jossey-Bass.

Persuad, R.B., & Lusane, C. (2000, July-September). The new economy, globalization and the impact on African Americans. *Race & Class, 42*(1), 21–34.

President's Advisory Commission on Asian Americans and Pacific Islanders. (2001). Asian Americans and Pacific Islanders: A people looking forward: Action for access and partnerships in the 21st century. In D. Nakanishi & J. Lai (Eds.), *2001–02 National Asian Pacific American Almanac* (pp. 65–79). Los Angeles: UCLA Asian American Studies Center.

Rodgers, W.M., III. (1999). A critical assessment of skills explanations of Black-White employment and wage gaps. In W. Spriggs (Ed.), *The state of Black America 1999* (pp. 167–184). New York: The National Urban League.

Rosenzweig, M.R. (2000). Schooling, learning, and economic growth. In R. Marshall (Ed.), *Back to shared prosperity: The growing inequality of wealth and income in America* (pp. 229–237). Armonk, NY: M.E. Sharpe.

Ross, E.W. (2001). The struggle for the social studies curriculum. In E.W. Ross (Ed.), *The social studies curriculum: Purposes, problems, and possibilities* (rev. ed., pp. 3–15). Albany: SUNY Press.

Shaver, J. (1977). The task of rationale-building for citizenship education. In J.P. Shaver (Ed.), *Building rationales for citizenship education* (pp. 96–116). Arlington, VA: National Council for the Social Studies.

Sigler, G. (1983, Summer). The case, if any, for economic literacy. *Journal of Economics Education, 15*(4), 60–66.

Stanley, W.B., & Nelson, J.L. (1994). The foundations of social education in historical context. In R. Martusewicz & W. Reynolds (Eds.), *Inside/out: Contemporary critical perspectives in education* (pp. 266–284). New York: St. Martin's Press.

Staveteig, S., & Wigton, A. (2000). *Racial and ethnic disparities: Key findings from the national survey of American's families.* Urban Institute, paper B-5 in New Federalism: National Survey of America's Families Series.

Tobin, J. (1986, July 19). Economic literacy isn't a market investment. *The Wall Street Journal*, Eastern Edition, Sec. A, p. 22.

Turner, C. (interview). (1992). Empowering communities of color. In L. Krimerman, F. Lindenfeld, C. Korty, & J. Benello (Eds.), *From the ground up: Essays on grassroots & workplace democracy by C. George Benello* (pp. 185–192). Boston: South End Press.

Uchitelle, L.(2000, July 23). The classroom ceiling: Making sense of a stubborn education gap. *The Week in Review, The New York Times.*

Urban Nutrition Initiative. (2002). *Annual Report May 2001-May 2002.* Philadelphia: University of Pennsylvania, Center for Community Partnerships. www.upenn.edu/ccp/uni.shtml (accessed 1/13/03).

Vinson, K. (2001). Oppression, anti-oppression, and citizenship education. In E.W. Ross (Ed.), *The social studies curriculum: Purposes, problems, and possibilities* (rev. ed., pp. 57–84). Albany: SUNY Press.

Walsted, & Rebeck, (2000, Winter). The status of economics in the curriculum. *Journal of Economics Education, 31*(1), 95–101.

Weiss, C., & Clamp, C. (1992). Women's cooperatives: Part of the answer to poverty? In L. Krimerman & F. Lindenfeld (Eds.), *When workers decide: Workplace democracy takes root in North America* (pp. 229–232). Philadelphia, PA: New Society Publishers.

Williams, R.M. (2000, May). *If you're black, get back; If you're brown, stick around; If you're white, hang tight: Race, gender and work in the global economy* (Working Paper). Preamble Center. Washington, DC.

Williams, W.E. (1982). Economic education and minorities. In W.H. Peterson (Ed.), *Economic education* (pp. 74–86). Knoxville: University of Tennessee Press.

Wolff, E.N. (2001). Recent trends in wealth ownership, 1983–1998. In T. Shapiro & E. Wolff (Eds.), *Assets for the poor: The benefits of spreading asset ownership* (pp. 34–73). New York: Russell Sage Foundation.

CHAPTER 10

TO GREET THE DAWN WITH OPEN EYES

American Indians¹, White Privilege and the Power of Residual Guilt in the Social Studies

Frances V. Rains

ABSTRACT

In the age of accountability, the selective way that Native Nations have been portrayed in the social studies warrants critical examination. This chapter argues that the residual guilt and privileges generated from 500 years of brutality and oppression have worked in tandem to maintain a very narrow, and inaccurate history that begins in 1492 and ends in 1891, and relegates Indian representation to little more than stereotypes. This chapter offers a broader time frame, with detailed examples of missing history, and Indigenous perspective, and a call for a more honest and accurate representation of Native Peoples, both past and present.

Critical Race Theory Perspectives on the Social Studies, pages 199–227

INTRODUCTION

You must speak straight so that your words may go as sunlight into our hearts.
(Cochise [Chiricahua Apache], Nerburn & Mengelkoch, 1991, p.10)

On my office door, there is a photograph of Tatanka Yotanka [Sitting Bull], the Hunkpapa Lakota leader, with a caption beneath which reads: "American history did not begin in 1492." It is a simple statement, and yet it is profound in its implication. The purpose of this chapter is to "speak straight" about what the caption on my door really means.

American Indians present an interesting dilemma to the social studies. The dilemma is how to teach about "core values" such as "freedom," "liberty" and "justice for all" in a country that has a *continuing* legacy of oppression and intimidation within its own boundaries.

For generations this dilemma has been skirted in social studies by a limited exposure that often produces some sympathy and, on occasion, identity with the "noble savage," while maintaining a minimum of detail. For example, the "Trail of Tears," the forced removal and relocation of the Cherokee Nation from their homelands to Indian Territory[2] are often mentioned as an isolated episode of our history. Their valiant effort to retain their homelands through their successful case in the United States Supreme Court may also be mentioned, thereby making their circumstances all the more noble, if not tragic. Then, Indians are typically made invisible until the topic of Manifest Destiny is broached, replete with "bloody" Indian uprisings, and pitched battles to save the lives of "innocent" White settlers on their westward trek through hostile Indian territories. In turn, this savagery becomes the impetus for the last of the Indian Wars. Conveniently, like a final chapter in a book, this becomes the end of any study of American Indians in social studies. The twentieth century becomes the exclusive domain of non-Indians.

As a Native [Choctaw/Cherokee] educator, I have had the opportunity to witness, first hand, the consequences of this coverage of American Indians. For more than twenty years, I have been invited to speak about American Indians between Halloween and Thanksgiving, in countless elementary classrooms in whatever state I have lived. The teachers in these classrooms have been weaned upon this coverage, and have been very well intentioned. Often, there has been a tipi erected in the back of the classroom, despite the longhouse and wigwam structures that were prevalent among the northeastern Native Nations. The "generic" Indians are invited to meet the Pilgrims for a big dinner. The children may even have made headdresses with brightly colored paper feathers and headbands, and/or brown paper "buckskin" clothes, which they may have displayed, to honor the Indians of the first Thanksgiving. My experience has taught me that there is an incredibly strong, blind loyalty to these stereotypes, and my efforts to insert fact and accuracy, in the face of myth and fiction, is a consistently uphill struggle.

Additionally, for more than 18 semesters, at Research I institutions, in my social studies methods courses, I have witnessed the consequences of this coverage with non-Indian college seniors. Aside from being able to name the "good" Indians that aided white survival (Pocahontas, Squanto, and/or Sacajewea), and an occasional "war chief" (e.g., Sitting Bull, Geronimo), most of these students have not been able to offer any accurate information about Indians from their past learnings. However, they often have brought many stereotypes into our classroom, which I have worked to dispel through readings and class discussion. But the misinformation is great. For example, many of the students are shocked to learn that Indians used to live all across the land east of the Mississippi River. "You mean, they lived in [insert any eastern/midwestern state], too?" is a surprisingly consistent question, each semester. My students, who have been predominantly White, have persistently demanded, "*Why* haven't we learned about this *in school? Why* are we *college seniors* and only learning about this for the *first time?*"

Interestingly, I now teach in a reservation-based program and all of my students are American Indian college students. They have gone to public schools and residential Indian boarding schools where the social studies curricula is the same curricula that is used with non-Indian children in other parts of the country. The question these Indian college seniors ask is the same one as their white counterparts. "*Why* haven't we learned about this *in school?* Why are we *college seniors* and only learning about this for the *first time?*" It is the collective query of my non-Indian and Indian students, coupled with my own concerns and experiences, that drives the writing of this chapter.

This chapter has two main objectives: first, is to offer some insights and accurate information that may expand the knowledge base for teaching about American Indians. As a sage old African American man once told me, "You can't teach what you don't know, any more than you can come back from where you ain't been." Accurate information is necessary for educators, teachers, and their students. However, knowledge alone is insufficient for a change in paradigms of how we teach about American Indians. For a change in paradigms requires more than facts alone. A change requires different ways of seeing and different ways of thinking. So, a second objective for writing this chapter is to deconstruct how white privilege and residual guilt (Deloria, 1997) have operated to maintain the status quo regarding the misrepresentation of Native Peoples. It is hoped that through examples and Native insights, a more honest and sophisticated understanding of Manifest Destiny's role in both the guilt and in the privileges will emerge. Further, it is hoped that the current "second coming" of

Manifest Destiny on the remaining 4% of the original land base (LaDuke, 1999) of the sovereign Native Nations will serve to stretch and further the possibility of different ways of thinking about and teaching about American Indians.

Finally, each semester/quarter, I remind my students of the need to 'make a difference' with what they learn. Writing this chapter is one of my efforts to make that sort of difference. In that sense, it becomes important for me to acknowledge that I stand on the shoulders of the American Indian and Alaska Native children who were removed from their homelands, languages, customs, and cultures to endure, and sometimes die, in distant boarding schools. It is because of their stamina and courage in the face of formalized education, used as a tool of oppression, that I now have an opportunity to write such a chapter. Therefore, I dedicate this chapter to the American Indian and Alaska Native children, buried in the cemeteries of Indian boarding schools, who never got to see their families or homelands again.

MISSING HISTORY AND MISREPRESENTATIONS OF AMERICAN INDIANS

> The realities of Indian belief and existence have become so misunderstood and distorted at this point that when a real Indian stands up and speaks the truth at any given moment, he or she is not only unlikely to be believed, but will probably be contradicted and "corrected" by the citation of some non-Indian and totally inaccurate "expert." ... In this way, the experts are perfecting a system of self-validation in which all semblance of honesty and accuracy is lost. This is not only a travesty of scholarship, but it is absolutely devastating to Indian societies. (Deloria, as cited in Rose, 1992, p. 404)

Basically, American Indians have been relegated to being the backdrop for the White American landscape—a landscape forged of "justice," the Bill of Rights, and "freedom from tyranny." Native Peoples have been depicted as two dimensional savages, either bloody or noble. Missing from such a stereotypical and narrow portrayal is the Native struggle, past and present, for "Homeland Defense" to protect their Homelands from invasions. Missing from such a history are the realities of the multiple, long range affects of White interactions with Native Nations, both for White Americans and for Native Peoples. Missing from such a history are the failures to live up to the ideals of "justice" and "liberty" that are held so dear. Missing from such a history is how the tyranny of Europe was overthrown, only to be imposed, with a blind sense of righteousness, upon the sovereign Native Nations here.

American Indians are not two dimensional stereotypes. Besides having survived a holocaust (e.g., Churchill, 1997; Cocker, 1998; LaDuke, 1999; Stannard, 1992) on a scale comparable to the one initiated by Hitler's Nazis in World War II, American Indians are still alive today. It sounds almost trite to have to assert that. But countless American children, White and of Color, are weaned on social studies that implies American Indians died a long time ago, and in regions where there are few reservations, or where the Native populations are small, there is little to counteract that assumption. In almost every single classroom where I was invited to address American Indian topics, I was told by students that I "couldn't be a *real* Indian because they're all *dead*."

I posit that the residual guilt over how this country has evolved, where "Native peoples have been massacred and fought, cheated, and robbed of their historical lands" (LaDuke, 1999, p. 2), coupled with the privileges that accrued from that evolution, creates an unwillingness to look past the stereotypes and misinformation, to a more realistic, accurate portrayal of this country's past. Residual guilt becomes a form of anesthetic, immobilizing and blinding as it progresses. Over time, immunity from scrutiny builds (Rains, 1998) and a disconnect occurs. The connection of how the past affects the present can be totally denied. As a White male college senior reminded me, "Aw, get over it. That was then, THIS is now." Clean, homogenized, and sanitary—the past is the past, after all, right? We can do nothing to change the past, right? The unsaid portion being, "so, do not make me look at the horrors of the past, they are too discomforting, too unsettling." Besides, as my White students continue, *"we* did not do any of it, so what's the big deal?"

The simplicity of avoidance, coupled with the lack of information, is almost overwhelming. And were the colonization of Indian Country not continuing at an exponential rate today, I might . . . might be able to agree.

True, the past *is* the past, but the blindness of guilt, denies not merely culpability for past misdeeds, but also *ignores* the *benefits that have accrued over time* as a *consequence* of those misdeeds (e.g., Macedo & Bartolome, 1999; McIntosh, 1992; Robinson, 2000). It discounts, no, *dismisses* any connection of past treatment and policies of extermination, as the foundation for the policies and legislation of termination and exploitation that continue to haunt Indian Country today. It makes me wonder . . . has 500 years taught us nothing? Have we not matured enough as a country to be able to examine our past with honesty and integrity? Worse, what messages and lessons do our future citizenry learn, when we teach about "liberty" and "justice for all," while the *in*justices, and *denials* of liberty and rights, of some are lost behind the maintenance of two-dimensional stereotypes and the status quo?

The power of residual guilt creates a hegemonic barrier to how we think and understand the past and present location of American Indians in this societal hierarchy. My focus here is to break through this barrier by examining how omissions and misrepresentations have operated to help maintain the status quo. Examples will be offered to support each area, and implications for teaching will be offered.

Early History

> I am Dekanawidah, and with the Five Nations confederate I plant the Tree of the Great Peace ... Roots have spread out from the Tree, and the name of these roots is the Great White Roots of Peace. If any man of any nation shall show a desire to obey the laws of the Great Peace, they shall trace the roots to their source, and they shall be welcomed to take shelter beneath the Tree of the Great Leaves. The smoke of the confederate council fire shall pierce the sky so that all nations may discover the central council fire of the Great Peace. I, Dekanawidah, and the confederate lords now uproot the tallest pine tree and into the cavity thereby may we cast all weapons of war. Into the depth of the earth, down into the deep under earth currents of water flowing into unknown regions, we cast all weapons of war. We bury them from sight forever and plant again the Tree. [The Peace Maker, Dakanawidah, 1000 A.D., The Opening of their Constitution] (Hill, 1994, p. 45)

When we study the history of this land, we often begin with 1492. The hegemony is so great that most non-Indians do not consciously consider that Indians "had" history before the coming of the White man. But from a Native viewpoint, history here did not begin with Columbus (or Leif Eriksson).

Native people have existed on this land for more than 20,000 years (e.g., Jennings, 1993; Nies, 1996). But even if one begins with a more conservative estimate of 10,000 years ago that is more than 10 millennia—not ten centuries, but *more than 100* centuries ago—it is long before "Europe" was even a twinkle on the political landscape. Native history here on this land existed long before the Great Pyramids of Egypt or the Hanging Gardens of Babylon. Yet, to begin American history with 1492, and to relegate the longer history of Natives here to "prehistory," as if they existed outside the boundaries of human history, denies their sustained stewardship of the ecological balance and cultural relationship with this land mass for more than 9,500 years. Being relegated to "prehistory" ignores the laws and social, political and cultural institutions "which maintained the peace within a given Native Nation, without courts, police officers and prisons" (Jackson, 1992, p. x).

The quote from Dakanawidah is an example of that early history. Peace Maker was an inspiring leader that united the Seneca, the Cayuga, the Onondaga, the Oneida, the Mohawk together in what became known as the League of Five Nations. Located on the lands to the south and east of the lake now known as Ontario, in what is now called New York state, this League of Five Nations was also known as the Iroquois Confederacy.[3] This confederacy was forged a thousand years ago [and still exists today], complete with a constitution, formal representatives, and a system for administering needed laws and justice. Citizens within this confederacy, such as the women, had rights a thousand years ago, that would be denied White women until 1920 (Roesch Wagner, 1992, 2001).

In 1722, the Tuscarora Nation, asked for refuge, as their homelands in what is now known as the Carolinas was under attack and invasion by multitudes of colonists. The Cayuga Nation offered some of their land, and so from that time onward, together, they all became known as the League of Six Nations. They also are known as the Six Nations Confederacy. But in the Iroquois language, they call themselves the Haudenosaunee.

Less discussed in social studies is that fact that forming political confederacies was not unusual in the northeast and midwestern regions. One of the more well known, certainly, by the English, was the Powhatan Confederacy (of Captain Smith and Pocahontas fame). It comprised "32 Bands and 200 villages in the Chesapeake Bay region" (Waldman, 2000, p. 108). However, there were others, formed by smaller tribes uniting to form large alliances. There was, for example, the Abenaki Confederacy (e.g., the Abenaki, the Passamaquoddy, the Penobscot, the Maliseet, the Micmac, the Pennacook) in what is now the New England region and the Wappinger Confederacy formed near the river known as Hudson (e.g., Josephy, 1994; Waldman, 1999, 2000). In the midwest, "in 1763, Chief Pontiac [Ottawa] organized a confederacy of Ottawa, Wyandot, Potawatomi, Miami, Kickapoo, Wea, Peoria, Ojibway, and Senecas" (Wilson, 1992, p.5).

While this is only a glimpse into the north east and midwest, there were Native Nations all across the land mass.[4] Despite the Bering Straits "theory,"[5] the various Native Nations of what is now the "lower 48," often trace their ancestry back in time to the beginning, and that beginning always is located here on this land mass (Rains, Archibald, & Deyhle, 2000).

When such early history is omitted, it attempts to sever the bonds that 10,000 years of rooted connections to the land provides. Instead, it casts the Native Nations here as temporal. And with that illusion of a temporal existence, comes a power to remove, destroy, or eliminate without conscious. As Deloria (1997) points out,

Five centuries of brutality lie uneasily on the conscience, and consequently two beliefs have arisen which are used to explain away this dreadful history.

People want to believe that the Western Hemisphere, and more particularly North America, was a vacant, unexploited, fertile land waiting to be put under cultivation according to God's holy dictates.... . Coupled with this belief is the idea that American Indians were not original inhabitants of the Western Hemisphere but latecomers who had barely unpacked before Columbus came knocking on the door. If Indians had arrived only a few centuries earlier, they had no *real* claim to land that could not be swept away by European discovery. (italics in original, pp. 67–68)

In essence, the omission of the existence of an earlier history of a peoples, offers blindness and immunity from accusations of theft. "To justify [the] breaches of the "permanent Indian frontier," the policy makers in Washington invented Manifest Destiny, a term which lifted land hunger to a lofty plane. The Europeans and their descendants were ordained *by destiny* [italics added] to rule all of America" (Brown, 1971, p. 8). The divinely sanctioned right, coupled with omission of the Indigenous roots, then perpetuate the status quo.

On July 15, 1997, a video aired on PBS television. In this video, *In Whose Honor? Indian Mascots in Sports* (Rosenstein, 1996), the retort "of "If you don't like it here, why don't you go back where you came from" was viciously hurled at the lone American Indian woman, Charlene Teeters (Spokane/Colville[6]). Charlene, a new Indian graduate student at the University of Illinois was horrified to attend a basketball game with her children, and see the barefoot, blond, doing a form of Russian kick dancing, splits, and other acrobatics, while wearing an authentic eagle feather headdress, and full buckskin regalia. The eagle feathers, in the midst of all the hoopla, were often dragged across the floor.

For many Native Nations, eagle feathers hold sacred significance, and the dragging of eagle feathers on the ground, would be akin to dragging the United States' flag through the dirt. In the case of eagle feathers, a ceremony is often required when a single feather has fallen to the ground. So, to see the feathers in constant casual contact, and in such a cavalier manner was spiritually and culturally offensive.

In addition, the Russian style kick dancing, and other acrobatics of the fraudulent Chief Illiniwek transformed the ritual dancing of traditional peoples into a form of mockery and half time entertainment. But to have her children see this, a symbol of the university where their mom was getting her education, that was the most horrendous part of all. Her Native children, who had been taught their traditions, were now confronted with how an institution of higher learning regarding them as a People. The title asked the question, in whose honor, because the university officials, including the president, insisted that Chief Illiniwek and his dance, *honored* Native Americans.

When Charlene began her one woman protest, she was spit upon and screamed at, with such retorts as the one above by the alumni who loved their mascot. Charlene even received several death threats. She was so culturally assaulted by such a racist caricature, however, that even when so confronted by very angry white alumni, she stood her ground. "My people *paid with their blood. . . .* And so I have to guard and protect it [the sacred aspects of her culture] for generations yet unborn. And I owe it to those people and I owe it to my children. I owe it to myself" (Rosenstein, 1996)

Ironically, her protest garnered more financial support by alumni to the institution to *keep* their beloved Chief Illiniwek mascot. Alumni support was so strong that one alumnus, Rick Winkel, an Illinois State Representative, "proposed a law that would guarantee Chief Illiniwek as the official symbol of the University of Illinois" (Rosenstein, 1996). While it passed the majority, the governor later vetoed the bill. And although State Representative Winkel attempted to override the veto, he was eventually unsuccessful.

No doubt the mascot issue will continue. What is at stake, and what this is an example of, is how that disconnect of past to present, that disconnect through the omission of an earlier and longer history, can allow a White person, with only 500 years under his/her historic belt, to retort that a Native woman, with a 10,000 year history, should go back where she came from. The hegemonic barrier is alive and well.

Colonial Invasions

> The great man wanted only a little, little land, on which to raise greens for his soup, just as much as a bullock's hide would cover. Here we first might have observed their deceitful spirit. [Delaware view of the first arrival of the Dutch on Manhattan Island, about 1609] (McLuhan, 1971, p. 69)

When we learn about the colonization of "America,"[7] the focus is most readily on the eastern seaboard. Commonly, the emphasis is on the English, French, and the Spanish. The Dutch and the Swedish, who also fought to maintain a foothold here, are often not discussed. Nor do we look to the north, where the French had a strong foothold in the land now known as Canada. They followed the river systems southward from there to enter what is now the United States. The Russians invaded from the west, entering what is now known as Alaska. The assault came from all four directions, and the fury of the conquest and invasion was brutal and intentional. This continent, much like the continent of Africa, was seen as an untapped land of resources and possibilities, to be carved up like a piece of meat.

The Spaniards are often discussed as invading from the Florida coast. And while the Spanish invasions (e.g., Hernan Cortes) into what is now Mexico are sometimes studied, less focus is given to how that invasion extended as far north from Mexico to what is now Kansas, Colorado and Utah (e.g., Josephy, 1994; Waldman, 2000). The Spanish also traveled in a north westerly direction from Mexico, both toward what are now Arizona and New Mexico, as well as along what is now the California coastline.

The Spanish made no pretense of their intentions. They had, after all, through Columbus' infamous navigational error, begun conquest of the Caribbean islands first. The Arawaks and the Tainos suffered under the reign of terror, torture and mutilation that the Spaniards inflicted with a greed fueled by a 20-year war with the Moors that had depleted their war chests(e.g., Hurst Thomas et al., 1993; Josephy, 1994; Weatherford, 1988). When no spices could be found (since this wasn't really India), the Awarak and the Taino were taken as slaves and shipped back to Spain to be sold at auction.

Slavery, then, began on this continent with the exportation of slaves to Europe. However, it was not lucrative for too many of the Arawaks and Tainos died before ever seeing the European shores. Gold, then, replaced slavery, as the main obsession.

The Conquistadors (the Conquerors) traveled to the isthmus, south of our current borders, in their quest for gold. Entire armies left Spain, with full armor, and weapons of war. The Doctrine of Discovery, the "divine law" as sanctioned by the Pope, had, after all, originated in Spain, granting entitlement of all lands they set foot on as "theirs" (e.g., Blaut, 1993; Deloria, 1997; Venn, 1998). This was to be the "law" used by the remaining European nations in their rivalistic rush to enter into the opportunistic fray of conquest and division of the "New World."

When we are taught about the colonies, we often look to the east coast, but the Spaniards also were colonizers. As early as 1598, the Spaniards had made wide inroads into what is now New Mexico. The Pueblo Nations were small, and aside from mesa top defenses, had little with which to defeat the large armies of Spaniards.

> The soldier-colonists, unable to extract their own food and clothing from the hard land, extorted corn, beans, squash, clothing, and supplies for themselves and their livestock from the increasingly hard-pressed Pueblos—by means of wholesale torture, murder, and rape. Active resistance was immediately and savagely suppressed.

> When the people of Acoma, whose adobe houseblocks were built high atop a rock mesa in western New Mexico, attacked a force led by one of Onate's nephews, killing eleven Spaniards, including the nephew, Onate's retaliation was swift and brutal. He stormed and burned the entire pueblo, killing in the

> process some five hundred men and three hundred women and children, then sentenced the survivors to twenty years of labor, and ordered every man among them over twenty-five years old to have a foot cut off. (Hurst Thomas et al., 1993, p.147)

So, for almost one hundred years, the Pueblos endured the Spanish occupation and exploitation. There were many acts of resistance, as each of the twenty-two Pueblos attempted to break free of the yoke of oppression under which they existed. But each time, the outcome was the same, horrific punishment for those that survived.

Finally, in 1680, under the leadership of Popé, a Native priest from San Juan Pueblo, a revolt took place. What made this revolt different, was that an alliance had been secretly formed, so that the various Pueblos acted in unison from their respective locations. Runners carried "cords of maguey fibers telling the number of days until the general uprising [sic.]" (Waldman, 2001, p. 302). The revolt was set for August 13, but due to leaks of information, Popé changed the date to August 11 (Waldman, 2001). And although the Spanish were to return by 1692, they never regained the complete domination they once had. In 1980, the various Pueblos held their *tricentennial* celebration of freedom from Spanish rule.

While this is but one example, it offers what is often missing history. The emphasis upon the eastern seaboard has arbitrarily taken precedence, so that the wider, and often earlier conquest is omitted. This sort of omission frames the conquest as if it was in an east-to-west direction only, which in turn, limits students' understanding.

This east-to-west bias becomes more apparent with regards to western settlement by non-Indians. For example, Mexican Americans often, due to the early colonization of the west, first by Spain, and later by Mexico, "pioneered" and settled in what is now Colorado, as early as 400 years ago. But many White students are surprised to learn this fact, even students who are *from* the state of Colorado.[8] Because these facts are often omitted, contemporary race issues are sometimes affected. Certainly, a broader historical understanding is no guarantee that conflicts around race will be avoided. However, it might shed light on how the "why don't you go back where you came from" retort, which is typically grounded in the "who got here first" strategy, is absurd, given the facts.

Schooling as a Tool of Oppression

> We know that you highly esteem the kind of learning taught in those Colleges [e.g., Harvard, William and Mary's College], and that the Maintenance of our young Men, while with you, would be very expensive to you. We are convinced, that you mean to do us Good by your Proposal; and we thank you

heartily. But you, who are wise must know that different Nations have different Conceptions of things and you will therefore not take it amiss, if our
Ideas of this kind of Education happen not to be the same as yours. We have
had some Experience of it. Several of our young People were formerly
brought up at the Colleges of the Northern Provinces; they were instructed
in all your Sciences; but, when they came back to us, they were bad Runners,
ignorant of every means of living in the woods, unable to bear cold or hunger, knew neither how to build a cabin, kill a deer, or kill an enemy, spoke
our language imperfectly, were therefore fit for neither Hunters, Warriors,
nor Counsellors, they were totally good for nothing.

We are, however, not the less oblig'd by your kind Offer, tho' we decline
accepting it; and, to show our grateful Sense of it, if the Gentlemen of Virginia will send us a Dozen of their Sons, we will take Care of their Education,
instruct them in all we know, and make Men of them. [Canassatego, Onondaga, 1744 (spelling and punctuation original)] (McLuhan, 1971, p. 57)

Native people educated their children for centuries upon centuries
before the Whites came. Native children learned the ways of survival and
the skills necessary for adult living. Children learned by observing, imitat-
ing, and practicing the ways necessary to become successful adults. While
the methods within each Native Nation, Band, or Community might differ
from that of a neighboring Community, or Band, each would ensure that
their children learned in the manner that made the most sense to them.

Although most Native Nations did not use literacy in the European
sense, there was a literacy of Nature, that was crucial to survival, and children learned this form of literacy well. In addition, listening and remembering were vitally important. So important was remembering, that later, as
the colonists came, the most minute details could be recalled from memory of a particular event that had been recorded in writing. Their recollec-
tions could be checked against the verbatim records, and much to the
surprise of many Whites, even though a generation may have passed, the
next generation could recite the exact details of the event from memory.
As Four Guns (Oglala Lakota) stated,

Many of the white man's ways are past our understanding.... . They put a
great store upon writing; there is always a paper.

The white people must think paper has some mysterious power to help them
in the world. The Indian needs no writings; words that are true sink deep
into his heart, where they remain. He never forgets them. On the other
hand, if the white man loses his papers, he is helpless. (Nerburn & Mengelkoch, 1991, p. 65)

So, from a Native perspective, Native children received the education they
needed to be active adults within their respective communities.

However, along with the land hunger, many colonists brought with them a religious fervor that demanded the saving of souls. The saving of souls required a modicum of literacy in order to be able to read the word of God. But ultimately, the goal was complete assimilation.

The first efforts at schooling were done in the Native communities. These efforts were directed at Christianizing the Indians, with the intent of establishing "permanent communities in which so called Praying Indians would settle, giving up their nomadic [sic.]way of life and turning to farming and conventional colonial trades instead" (Waldman, 2001, p. 121). While this strategy was moderately successful, with more than 4,000 Christianized Indians by 1674, it was not a strategy that would last. The Praying Indian towns became a ready target for White colonial distrust. Massacre after massacre of the Praying Indians were documented, with the majority of the whole communities being gruesomely murdered in their sleep, or while praying on their knees (e.g., Jackson 1880/1993; Sipes, 1931/1998).

Other strategies to use schooling to assimilate the Indian began to emerge. As early as 1568, the Jesuit Missionaries built the first school for Indians (Bowker, 1993) but when the Praying Towns seemed to fail, another strategy was employed. Instead of moving the Indians into Praying Towns, Native boys would be taken away from their homes/cultures and languages, to learn how to preach the word of God. Then, they could be returned into their own Native communities in order to create more converts. For example, Samson Occum, a Mohegan, was one of the first to be Christianized in this way. Eleazar Wheelock used Occum to recruit Indian children for the Moor's Indian Charity School he had started. Later, he sent Occum to England to raise money for another school, this time, Dartmouth College,[9] which was to be solely for the purpose of educating Indians.

Because Occum was a Native, and was "civilized," he was literally a walking, talking advertisement in the quest for monetary benefactors. But when Occum returned with the money, he became disillusioned with Wheelock, and lived out his years working with other Christianized Indians (Waldman, 1999, p. 270). "Wheelock became Dartmouth's first president, and though he continued to direct his Indian education program, as the president it received less and less of his attention, and after he died Dartmouth College soon became a college of and for Whites" (Metcalf, 1988, p. 695).

Another Native, William Apess (Pequot), was also a Christianized Indian. Born in 1798, he had a difficult childhood, where he was sold into indentured servitude, several times. Still, one of the families where he was indentured, taught him to read and write (O'Connell, 1997).

As an adult he became a preacher to African American and American Indians in a variety of churches. Eventually, in 1829, he published a book, *A Son of the Forest,* an autobiography, which was an unusual literary form at the time. He published three more works before his death, and the second was an effort to engage in critical analysis of the treatment of Indians by whites. It was called, *The Experiences of Five Christian Indians; or, An Indian's Looking-Glass for the White Man*, and was published in 1833. Both the second and third works went into second editions before his death in 1839 (O'Connell, 1997).

Christianizing Indian boys through missionary schools, boarding schools, and by recruiting Indian students to become preachers continued. Eventually, Indian girls were also removed from their families and taken to these religious boarding schools, as well. Even today, religious boarding schools continue on several reservations.

The practice of removing Indian children, as Canassatego mentioned in the quote, from all they knew—their families, their languages, their ways of living, their diets—was deemed a necessary part of the assimilation process. If Indian children were to be successfully "saved from their savage ways" (Reinhardt, 2000, p. 384), they must not be influenced by their "primitive" backgrounds.

Captain Pratt, a retired military officer, raised this method of stripping the Indian child of all that was familiar, to a high art form. Pratt "was authorized by the War Department to establish a school at the abandoned military barracks in Carlisle, Pennsylvania, [and was] the first federally funded, nonreservation boarding school for Indians" (Waldman, 2001, p. 306). Pratt's work in the Carlisle Indian Industrial School, which began in 1879, became the model for a succession of military style, residential boarding schools.

The school had many military aspects to it. Drill, routine, and uniforms were all required. His stout philosophy was that civilizing the Indian was to be akin to a baptism, where the Indian child was to be "held under until thoroughly soaked" (Witmer, 1993).

Students attended classes for the first half of the day, and attended to chores and trade skills in the afternoons. Due to limited funding support, the school needed to be somewhat self-supporting. Indian children were made to do the chores that maintained not merely the school grounds, but also made the uniforms, laundered them, made the shoes, built some of the buildings, maintained the livestock, grew gardens and crops, prepared meals, baked the bread, maintained the dormitories.

Trades were learned as a perquisite to becoming "model members" of White society. For example, in the bakery, young Indian men made "cakes, pies, cinnamon buns, rolls and approximately 216,000 loaves of bread per year" (Witmer, p. 88). For the sewing class, the work "was divided into four grades. First, darning class for small girls and beginners. Second, repairing of clothing plus simple sewing. Third, "plain" sewing where about 3,000 shirts for boys were made each year plus gowns, aprons, curtains and drawers. Fourth, dressmaking class" (p. 94). Boys not only learned basic construction, they also dug trenches, fit pipes for boilers, made bricks, performed masonry, worked in the print shop, shoed the horses, and so forth.

However, as the students got better at what they did, their work financially profited the school. So, for example, the horse drawn carriages they built were sold as far away as Africa. The U.S. government was the largest buyer of the wagons they built. And at one point in the history of Carlisle, sixty-eight Indian boys were sent to work at the Ford Plant in Detroit, Michigan (Witmer, 1993).

In the evenings, besides homework, students had a variety of extracurricular activities to keep them from straying from the path of becoming White. In addition, his philosophy was to keep the students so busy that they would have no time to plot an escape, or to get into mischief. So, students were expected to join evening activities. Students might join singing classes, speech or debate classes, band, football, Shakespearean theater, baseball, fire drills, or parade drills. The Carlisle Indian School Band became quite famous, playing all across the eastern seaboard. They were even slated for travel to Europe. Their fame was only rivaled by that of their football team.

Jim Thorpe (Sac and Fox) was one of the students who played football there. The Carlisle Indian School was only a trade school, yet, when it came to football, they played against Army, Syracuse University, University of Pennsylvania, Brown University, with fair consistency, and beat their more collegiate opponents.

School plays often had the Indian students in ironic roles. For example, Indian students dressed as Pilgrims for Thanksgiving plays. Miles Standish, John Smith, and other White American heroic icons were characters that the Indian students were expected to portray. There are even photographs of some of these students dressed in costume.

Pratt had left few stones unturned. He even had a summer "outing" program, where the Indian children could be "outed" to a White family from as far away as Maine, Maryland, or Virginia, or as close as a community in Pennsylvania. The outing program was designed to prevent Indian children from going home in the summer, where they might "go back to the blanket" and return to their "savage" ways. They would do chores and receive room and board and sometimes, they would earn a little money, but more often than not, they were more like indentured servants for the summer. Both girls and boys were outed in this way.

Even though the students did most of the maintenance and upkeep at the school, money was still needed to pay teachers (who lived on the premises), and to buy the food that could not be cultivated. One of the ways the school earned money was to have the boys in the print shop, print a little weekly newsletter that was sent all over the country as a form of propaganda. Non-Indian people, then, sent cash donations.

In addition, Pratt made famous the "before and after" photographs that would become his trademark. These photographs, of Indian children right after they got off the train, often after days of hard travel, with limited to no English, were the "before" shot. They looked exhausted, forlorn, hungry, and cold. Later, he would take another photograph of the same children. Now they would be dressed in uniforms and hard leather boots, with their hair cropped short, and they would be posed in various ways. He would then make post cards out of these photographs to sell. His main purpose was a form of market exploitation. What better way for a potential benefactor to see the "virtues" of assimilating Indian children, than to see them dressed as Whites?

There was even a drug store and a hospital at the school. However, Pratt's policy was that if a child became seriously ill, they were to be sent home. The idea was that they should not die at the school, if possible, as it was bad publicity. It was bad for recruitment of more Indian children from as far away as Alaska, California, Oregon, and Arizona. If children were dying, then it would be harder to convince Indian parents of the educational value of sending their children. And it was bad for recruitment of financial benefactors. Still, more than 134 children are buried in the cemetery there.

Pratt truly believed that if the Native children could assimilate enough, they would be accepted into White society. For the most part, he underestimated two things; one, that the children would want to stay among White society. Although some did either marry or settle in the east, many returned to Indian country. And two, he underestimated White society's prepareness to accept *Indian* "White people." He had grossly miscalculated the intensity of racism and prejudice that was deeply rooted within the White community. His underestimations, however, did not prevent his continual recruitment. Ultimately, more than 8,000 Indian children, from every part of the lower 48 states and Alaska, came to Carlisle from 1879–1918.

Many boarding schools would follow Pratt's militaristic model. The Hampton Institute, alone, was the exception to the assimilation practice.

A unique chapter in American history unfolded at Hampton Institute between 1878 and 1923. During this forty-five-year period, the school conducted an unprecedented biracial educational program. Hampton Normal and Agricultural Institute had been founded in 1868, in the post-Civil War America in response to the demand by newly freed African Americans for educational opportunities. Ten years after its founding, Hampton opened its doors to American Indian students, who then composed a significant portion

of the student body for nearly a half-century. Over 1,300 Indian students
from sixty-five tribes attended Hampton. (Zeidler, 1989, p. 6)

There, Indian students were encouraged to take pride in their heritage,
and to embrace their past, rather than reject it. They were even allowed to
maintain their Native languages. Unfortunately, Hampton was the rare
exception.

Often when we are taught about Indians and schooling, much of the
information presented above is omitted. For most White Americans,
"schooling" has been equated with "education," and schooling has signaled
increased "opportunity."

Schooling was so prized by White Americans that in order to maintain
the unequal power and social relations of the economic slavery system,
most African Americans within that system, were denied the privilege of an
education. African American disenfranchisement from educational opportunities was a means for White Americans within that system to perpetuate
the status quo of unequal relations. Therefore, with the abolition of slavery,
access to education was often seen by African Americans as a means to a
better life.

For Native Nations the circumstances were different. Native peoples
already had a system of education. While it differed enormously from the
educational structure and system of the White Americans, it was a valued
means of being a viable citizen within a Native community.

The efforts of White Americans to take Indian children away, with the
express purpose of removing them from their lifeways and world views, and
to "kill the Indian, and save the child," introduced Native peoples to the
structure of "schooling." This schooling was neither positive, nor viewed by
many who survived it, as an "opportunity."

While education and schooling were deliberately withheld from African
Americans, it was forced upon American Indian children in ways that
hardly reflected a "better life." Those who eventually did succeed, often
did so at the sacrifice of their cultural heritage and identity. There was no
middle ground. The objective of this form of schooling was cultural genocide. Seize the children, and the future of a Peoples' is limited. This type of
schooling for American Indians created enormous mistrust, reinforcing
previous betrayals of trust through broken treaties, land thefts, and forced
removals.

But few who are not Indian, understand the genocidal aspects or implications of this history of schooling. Some may know that there *were* boarding schools for Indian children, and that these schools were restrictive, but
may not fully grasp how White Americans used these schools as a means of
further disrupting Native existence. They may not see the historic benefits

of such a system to White Americans, who could gain lands and/or resources from the further destruction of Native Nations.

Many may not know that boarding schools still exist today. They have, for the most part, shed the military style. Although many do follow the assimilationist paradigms, there are differences. Some Bureau of Indian Affairs' [BIA] boarding schools have adopted or developed tribally appropriate curricula for the school's Native population contingent on the school's location.[10] They may have Indian teachers and/or staff, as well. And today, Indian children often have more choices. They might go to a boarding school, either BIA or religious, or they might attend public schools. In fact, over half of all American Indian children attend public schools.

The Twentieth Century

Since I was in high school, I have been involved in my tribe's fight to protect our reservation and the environment of southeastern Montana. It was during this time, the early 1970s, that the Cheyenne people learned the horrifying news that our federal trustee, the BIA [Bureau of Indian Affairs], had leased over one-half of our reservation to the coal companies for strip-mining. Cheyenne coal was sold for 11 cents a ton, and no environmental safeguards were on the coal leases. The fight was on, and every resource our small tribe had was committed to this battle. I was with a group of young Cheyenne whom the tribe sent to the Navajo coal mines and then on to the coal fields of Wyoming. The enormity of our situation frightened and angered us. After college, I served on the tribal negotiating committee charged with voiding these coal leases. I was 21 years old, the youngest on my committee, and the only one with a college degree. We were fortunate to find a very capable young attorney with a passion for Indians and for justice because we were suing our federal trustee and the coal companies, both formidable opponents. [Gail Small, Northern Cheyenne Mother of four children & Leader of Native Action (nonprofit environmental organization] (LaDuke, 1999, p. 85)

One of the biggest omissions in how American Indians are portrayed in history is the omission of Indians in the twentieth century (Rains, 2002). While many are familiar with the last of the Indian Wars, in the late 1800s, few think about Indians existing beyond that time frame. Omitted are the Pan Indian movements (from 1911 to the 1920s), where Native peoples, educated in the boarding schools, politically organized across tribal affiliation, for the very first time, to fight for treaty rights, water rights, and citizenship (Hertzberg, 1971). Too, such reports as the Merriam Report, "undertaken by the private Brookings Institution, which, in 1928, after a two-year study, released its report on Indian conditions—declaring the allotment system a dismal failure" (Waldman, 2000, p. 218). The General Allotment Act, also known as the Dawes Act of 1887, had divided up many of the reservations, in particular in Oklahoma, which had been designed to be Indian Territory as long as the 'grass grows and the water flows." The Dawes Act was a policy to eliminate reservations, by offering individual Indians small acreages of land, thereby leaving the rest of the land open for White development. The Merriam Commission found that the system had failed the Indians, and their poverty and conditions were deteriorating rapidly.

The Indian Reorganization Act of 1934 was an effort to remedy that to some extent. But it also authorized a reorganization of political structures of traditional Native Nations. By many traditionalists, it was seen as a time of puppet governments, created as a vehicle for large developers and mining interests to more easily gain access to reservations where resistance to these interests had traditionally been high.

By far one of the most devastating federal policies of the twentieth century, however, was the 1953 Termination Resolution, which literally, by an act of Congress, began to simply terminate entire Native Nations (Deloria & Lytle, 1983; Waldman, 2000).

> From 1954 to 1962, Congress terminated the federal relationship with 61 tribes, bands, and communities.... Although termination was presented as freedom from further federal intervention, an underlying motive for various private non-Indian interests and congressional allies centered around the acquisition of timber on Indian lands. (Waldman, 2000, p. 221)

Urbanization was the newest plan to deal with the "Indian problem." Termination and urbanization went hand in hand (e.g., Fixico, 2000; Kelly, 1988; Waldman, 2000). Native people were given bus tickets by the federal government to such cities as Los Angeles, San Francisco, and Denver and promised housing and jobs (Ketcheshawno, 2002). But lack of jobs, and lack of affordable housing, coupled with the devastation of the loss of land and the affect it had on their cultural survival, took its toll.

This was another failure in Indian policy, but the damage was done for most of the terminated Native Nations, their homelands were gone. The Menominee were, after years and years of effort, able to be reinstated. In 1974, through the hard work of many lawyers, tribal leaders, and such concerned Menominees as Ada Deer, who went before Congress to present their case, Congress passed the Menominee Restoration Act. In 1978, the Ottawa, Wyandot, Peoria, and Modoc were also reinstated as federally recognized Nations.

There are still 550 federally recognized Native Nations today. One of which is the Northern Cheyenne. Gail Small, whose quote is above, offers a small window of insight into the sorts of "resource" wars that pit small Native Nations against large, and often, multinational corporations.

The modern day "explorers" carry brief cases, and represent the nuclear industry, oil companies, toxic waste firms, timber operations, cattle barons, commercial fishing industries, resort/tourist developers, mining interests, hydroelectric power companies, and land developers to name a few (e.g., Burger, 1990; LaDuke, 1999; Voices of Indigenous Peoples, 1994). Native Nations in Florida, North Carolina, Rhode Island, New York, Mississippi, Oklahoma, South Dakota, North Dakota, Montana, Arizona, New Mexico, Utah, Nevada, Washington, California, and Alaska are among those that have been asked to be the national dumping grounds for this country's waste, in recent years.

> According to the Worldwatch Institute, 317 reservations in the United States are threatened by environmental hazards, ranging from toxic waste to clearcuts.
>
> Reservations have been targeted as sites for 16 proposed nuclear waste dumps. Over 100 proposals have been floated in recent years to dump toxic waste in Indian communities.... . Over the last 45 years, there have been 1,000 atomic explosions on Western Shoshone land in Nevada, making the Western Shoshone the most bombed nation on earth.
>
> Over 1,000 slag piles and tailings from abandoned uranium mines sit on Diné [Navajo] land, leaking radioactivity into the air and water. Nearby is the largest coal strip mine in the world, and some groups of Diné teenagers have a cancer rate 17 times the national average. (LaDuke, 1999, pp. 2–3)

These modern day "explorers" represent the second coming of Manifest Destiny. Many of the Native Nations are being bombarded on multiple fronts, from resource extraction to the damming of rivers by energy companies. Often limited, and precious financial resources are drained by efforts to stop or prevent the latest wave of Manifest Destiny upon the small remaining Homelands of many Native Nations.

I have not even skimmed the surface, nor done adequate justice to the quantity and depth of the policies, deeds and misdeeds that have affronted Native Nations during this past century. My effort here is merely to offer a small glimpse into the sorts of facts that are omitted by leaving Indians out of the 20th century. While, to be sure, Native People are not simply victims, and have worked hard, resisted, sacrificed much, and continue to struggle and fight the big fights, they do so, invisibly. They do so, with little support, minimal financial backing, and must often "work without a net."

Nevertheless, what impact does the omission of such information have upon the understandings students are able to glean about the contemporary existence of Native Peoples? How does the omission of such information cripple the ability to make connections between the past and present?" How does the omission of such information affect the "get over it, the past is the past" beliefs that many potential future teachers may harbor? How does the residual guilt create a blind spot so large as to engulf an entire century of missing history?

IMPLICATIONS FOR TEACHER EDUCATION

The elders say, "the longest road you're going to have to walk in your life is from here to here. From the head to the heart." But they also say you can't speak to the people as a leader unless you've made the return journey. From the heart back to the head. [Phil Lane, Jr. Yankton Sioux, 1992] (Hill, 1994, p. 51)

Native Peoples have never been two-dimensional stereotypes. We should not have to dress as our ancestors did 100 years ago, in order to be recognized as "real." White Americans do not have to dress as Pilgrims to be thought of as "real" White people.

The misrepresentations of American Indians in social studies need to change. The time has come to take the journey from the head to the heart, and back. As we stand on the cusp of the new millennia, the time has come for a more accurate and honest history.

Future teachers will benefit from such a history, but only if the teacher educators who help prepare them are knowledgeable. What responsibility do we have to prepare graduate students, who will become the next generation of teacher educators in universities and colleges?

It is often teachers, who go on to graduate school, to become teacher educators. If, as teachers, they have been weaned on a benign history that omits a more honest portrayal, then unless there is effort made at the graduate level to introduce a more accurate past and present, then the hegemonic cycle of blind allegiance to the stereotypes and misinformation will continue.

Granted, the misinformation and stereotypes are not merely in the social studies, as they abound in popular culture as well. However, that is true of all information. The media and the society do play a role in perpetuating myths of all kinds. Still, isn't one of the purposes of education to break down the myths and offer students opportunities to develop richer, deeper, more complex understandings of their world? Social studies should not perpetuate myths, stereotypes, or offer a history so narrow as to obscure reality.

When a narrow and guilt-free history is offered, it may feel good. But, then when the United States defends freedom and fights injustices abroad, there is risk that the rest of the world will view this country as hypocritical, when our own children are not taught the past with accuracy, honesty or integrity.

There is fear. Fear that if we teach about the atrocities committed by heroes like Columbus and Andrew Jackson (e.g., Bigelow & Peterson, 1998; Churchill, 1997; Rains, 2002; Stannard, 1992; Weatherford, 1988) then we will destroy the icons that are the foundation of all that is held dear in this country. Fear that we will destroy people's faith in our foundation. Fear. Fear and guilt.

However, I posit that there is another way to think about this. First, I have faith that the American people are hardy, and can withstand more than the fear may allow us to take into account. Second, and more important, I think that there is a different way to go about this. If, for example, we dare to expose the history in a more accurate way, revealing the omissions, revealing the "good, the bad, and the ugly" so to speak, then I assert that this can be done in a way to lessen our fears. Imagine teaching our children with honesty. If it is true that children learn by example, then isn't "honesty" a core value that we should elicit, that we should model and not merely expect?

Imagine teaching about the deeds and misdeeds of our "heroes," not to destroy them necessarily, but to reveal human actions, as an opportunity to inquire on what motivated these individuals to do what they did? Imagine children taking the more challenging task of analyzing not only motivation, but the consequences of actions taken. Imagine children developing alternative actions, or developing a variety of decisions to investigate the consequences of each, for a particular situation past or present.

The conquest and the consequences of colonial occupation, Manifest Destiny, and westward expansionism are not discussed in terms of consequences. Actions are viewed benignly or in isolation. This denies students the opportunity analyze, or to come to their own conclusions grounded in a deeper inquiry into how events and actions not only have consequences, but also connect to the notion of responsibility and ownership. If we fail to teach our students this, then we deny them the opportunity to reflect on the nature of consequences, on the nature of different sorts of solutions to potential problems, and we fail to provide them with the knowledge and history that readily could offer a multitude of examples. If we truly believe that we can learn as much from mistakes, as from doing things well, then couldn't our children learn from the mistakes in our own history? If, because of fear, guilt, and maybe even embarrassment, we choose not to teach about past misdeeds, past and present mistakes, then isn't the underlying message to children that we should hide our mistakes, or that lying by omission is acceptable? If we really believe that we want our children to understand justice and freedom, then when we, or they see injustice, dare we sit back and do nothing to change it?

CONCLUSION

> The lesson which seems so hard to learn is that of dignity and respect ... [Native voices complain about] the continuing propensity of the white man to change the terms of the debate to favor himself. But deep down these are cries about dignity, complaints about the lack of respect. 'It is not necessary,' Sitting Bull said, 'that eagles should be crows.'[11] [Vine Deloria, Jr., Standing Rock Sioux, 1991] (Hill, 1994, p. 48)

What I have learned over time is that the stereotypes and misinformation are so implanted, they have become the truth for many. But truth rarely comes with a capital "T." As a Native educator, I have witnessed resistance to a more accurate history by those whose sense of guilt over the past, and whose dysconscious (King, 1993) recognition of the unearned benefits of privilege grounded in this history, have kept them in a perpetual state of denial. But as a wise, Black, sister scholar once told me, "guilt is a useless emotion." And I would add that denial is also useless. They only serve to perpetuate the status quo.

My personal experience at the National Council of the Social Studies conference recently, served to remind me of how strong the status quo remains. My culture was assaulted, when I dared to raise a question in a presentation on Manifest Destiny that portrayed it as an exciting "adventure," where Indians were only mentioned in the context of a noble savage in a painting, and then again, at the Battle of the Little Bighorn. The Native representations for this battle were savage and bloodthirsty. No context was offered for why the battle was so fiercely fought by the Lakota. Then, in the ever forward advance of Western civilization on the wings of Manifest Destiny, the Indians were made invisible.

I was gravely concerned, since the White majority audience seemed to be very enthusiastic about the presentation. So much so that when copies of the presentation were distributed, and there were not enough for the large number that had packed into the room, many people were very verbally disappointed. No one appeared to be troubled by the stereotypes and narrowly presented history. Instead, it appeared that their disappointment at not being able to obtain a copy, indicated how much they had hoped to utilize it, if they had acquired it.

Since questions and comments were being entertained from the White audience, as the session progressed, I mustered the courage, as the only Native person in the standing-room-only crowded meeting room, to question the gaps and quality of Native representation. After entertaining White questions, my comments and question were dismissed by the presenters, and I was told that if I wanted to address this, I should wait until after the presentation was over. Like Charlene Teeters before me, I had felt that despite the odds, and despite the overarching enthusiastic support for the topic at hand, I needed to speak up. As a Native person, as a Native educator, I needed to offer accuracy that was missing. But like Charlene, I was dismissed.

It took me by surprise. I had not anticipated that at the biggest social studies conference, on the brink of the new millennia, that there would be such resistance to accuracy. But it taught me a powerful lesson on how deeply engrained are the issues of White privilege and residual guilt, and the maintenance of the status quo.

The beauty of Social studies is that we have the ability to investigate, to inquire, to examine, to analyze, and to reflect as a means of enriching our own understanding. In social studies we have an opportunity to invite students to rethink things, to offer alternatives, even of past events, as a means of learning. As citizens of a country that prides itself on justice and democracy, we have an opportunity to help students understand the consequences of when justice and/or democracy fails. By doing so, we offer students opportunities to question what happened to whom, why, and to question who benefitted and who did not. We offer students an opportunity to reflect on how a different action, a different deed, could result in a different consequence-a tool for learning about possibilities.

And eventually, one day, perhaps, students will see themselves as agents of change, as active participants in social justice, and for social action. We cannot change the past, but we can create a better future, one that is truly just, one where extermination, exploitation, and termination are no longer policies for more greed, devastation and destruction. What a world it would be if Whites and Indians could finally sit down at the table to *work together* for the real betterment of all who share the same water, the same air, and the same land.

As an educator, I want to be optimistic. But as an American Indian woman, I wonder if most non-Indians are really ready to greet the dawn with open eyes? Still, I have been fortunate to meet White colleagues who have been true allies. And I have been graciously invited to write this chapter.[12] That teaches me that things can change, even if the process is slower than I would hope. Five hundred years feels like a long time to wait for justice, and as Vine Deloria would say, is a long time to wait for respect and dignity.

NOTES

1. Someday I hope it will no longer be necessary to clarify this, but for now, I know that many, especially the politically correct, prefer the term "Native American"—as I am corrected by non-Indians when I make presentations. However, the term "Native American" comes from the academy, the ivory tower. Native peoples more often use their tribal affiliation (their tribal name—like Mohawk, Choctaw, and so on) first, or often just plain "Indian." There are many reasons for this, which are too long to go into here, but briefly, Indian children have typically had the same curricula that non-Indians have. And we have been weaned on the label "Indians" in the curricula. Nevertheless, another reason is that many of the treaties use the language of "American Indian" or "Indian," and so, to honor our treaty rights, we often still use these labels. For the purposes of this chapter, I use Native Nation(s), and I capitalize it deliberately, to give honor to the sovereignty that we hold. I also use the word Native or Native People(s) at times. I try to avoid using the word "tribe" (although it is a commonly used word among most Natives) because "tribe" was used by non-Natives as a means of wielding the power of language to delegitimize our nationhood and sovereignty.

2. "Indian Territory" refers historically to an ever dwindling region of land that in the 1820s lay between the Missouri and Red Rivers, covering most of what eventually became the states of Nebraska, Kansas, and Oklahoma. Because of the "ever-expanding non-Indian population, the boundaries kept changing. Time and again, settlers violated treaties..." (Waldman, 2000, p. 206) and Native Nations from the East and Midwest, in particular, but also from the West, were forced to live on smaller and smaller parcels of land. Their weapons for hunting were taken away, and instead they were offered plows. Much of the land was not fit for farming, and the Native Peoples often were starving. By the 1850s, the lands of Indian Territory were further reduced to only include what is now Oklahoma. In 1887, the last of the Indian Territory was eliminated by the Dawes Act. Through this Allotment Act various Native Nations were forced from the lands to make way for White settlement.

3. "Iroquois" comes from the Algonquian language, but has come to mean the larger language family that the Six Nations share with several other Native Nations such as the Huron/Wyndot, Erie, and Cherokee.

4. For a broader sense of the numerous Native Nations that once existed, Carl Waldman has two texts that may be useful to peruse. See the References for full bibliographic information. In addition, such texts as the one by Alvin M. Josephy, Jr. may offer other insights as well.

5. For a Native inquiry into the theory of the Bering Straits, see Vine Deloria, Jr.'s text, cited in the References. It has an entire chapter devoted to an investigation into the land bridge theory.

6. When I heard Charleen speak, I thought I heard her say she was Colville, but in the documentary, they also mention that she is Spokane. I apologize to Charleen for the offense I may cause.

7. I place the name America in quotes because America, the land mass, actually includes Canada and Mexico. And that is just to the North. Depending on how folks learn geography, they may learn about Central America as a separate entity, or they may not. As a country, we do not have sole owner-

ship of the name, and there are certainly people in Canada and Central and South America that find the use of the name "America" as a referent to the United States alone as arrogant at best. Hence, the use of the quotation marks.

8. This was often a reoccurring theme in my classes while I was an assistant professor at the University of Colorado at Boulder.

9. So, Dartmouth College, founded in 1769, only served Indian students until 1779, when Eleazar Wheelock died, and his son John became the president. Under John Wheelock's presidency, Dartmouth stopped serving Indian students, even though the mission statement of the College was explicit. It remained a strictly White, elite institution for almost 300 years, until the late 1960s, when young Native activists, who had read the mission statement and were familiar with the history, demanded that Dartmouth honor its mission as an institution and accept Indian students. Despite these protests, Dartmouth remains a predominantly White institution, with only a token representation of Native students.

10. I say contingent upon location because there is no universal Native culture. Since there are 550 different sovereign Native Nations, depending on where the school is, it may rely on culture that is appropriate to the Native Nation or Nations that it serves.

11. The longer quote from Sitting Bull (Teton Sioux) goes like this:

> If the Great Spirit had desired me to be a white man he would have made me so in the first place. He put in your hart certain wishes and plans; in my heart he put other and different desires

> Each man is good in the sight of the Great Spirit. It is not necessary for eagles to be crows. Now we are poor but we are free. No white man controls our footsteps. If we must die, we die defending our rights. (Sitting Bull, Hunkpapa Lakota)

12. Here I want to acknowledge Dr. Gloria Ladson-Billings. She is one of my true sheroes. She is a courageous woman, who has modeled integrity in the face of odds. She has done so with tact, grace, and yet has not shied away from the difficult battles. As a more advanced scholar, she has given mentorship and encouragement to many budding scholars. She has consistently extended her hand across the color line to me, and I am humbled by her generosity, and grateful for her invitation to write a chapter in this book.

REFERENCES

Blaut, J.M.(1993). *The colonizer's model of the world: Geographic diffusionism and Eurocentric history.* New York: The Guilford Press.

Bowker, A. (1993). *Sisters in the blood: The education of women in Native America.* Newton, MA: WEEA Publishing Center.

Brown, D. (1971). *Bury my heart at Wounded Knee: An Indian history of the American west.* New York: Bantam Books.

Burger, J. (1990). *The Gaia atlas of First Peoples: A future for the Indigenous world.* New York: Anchor Books.

Churchill, W. (1997). *A little matter of genocide: Holocaust and denial in the Americas, 1492 to the present.* San Francisco: City Lights Books.

Cocker, M. (1998). *Rivers of blood, rivers of gold: Europe's conquest of Indigenous peoples.* New York: Grove Press.

Deloria, V., Jr. (1997). *Red earth, white lies: Native Americans and the myth of scientific fact.* Golden, CO: Fulcrum Publishing.

Deloria, V., Jr. & Lytle, C. M. (1983). *American Indians, American justice.* Austin: University of Texas Press.

Fixico, D.L. (2000). *The urban Indian experience in America.* Albuquerque: University of New Mexico Press.

Hertzberg, H.W. (1971). *The search for an American Indian identity: Modern Pan-Indian movements.* Syracuse, NY: Syracuse University Press.

Hill, N.S. Jr. (1994) (Ed.). *Words of power: Voices from Indian America.* Golden, CO: Fulcrum Publishing.

Hurst Thomas, D., Miller, J., White, R., Nabokov, P., & Deloria, P. J. (1993). *The Native Americans: An illustrated history.* Atlanta, GA: Turner Publishing, Inc.

Jackson, H.H. (1880/1993). *A century of dishonor: A sketch of the United States government's dealings with some of the Indian tribes.* New York: Indian Head Press.

Jackson, M. (1992). A legal overview: The case in context. In D. Monet & A. Wilson (Eds.), *Colonialism on trial: Indigenous land rights and the Gitksan and Wet'suwet'en sovereignty case* (pp. x-xi). Gabriola Island, BC: New Society Publishers.

Jennings, F. (1993). *The founders of America: From the earliest migrations to the present.* New York: W.W. Norton & Co.

Josephy, A.M. Jr. (1994). *500 nations: An illustrated history of North American Indians.* New York: Alfred A. Knopf.

Kelly, L.C. (1988). United States Indian policies, 1900–1980. In W.E. Washburn (Vol. Ed.), *History of Indian-White relations: Vol.4. Handbook of North American Indians.* Washington, DC: Smithsonian Institution.

Ketcheshawno, M. (Producer), & Fortier, J. (Director). (2002). *Alcatraz is not an island.* [Documentary film]. (Available from Media Marketing & Sales, University of California, Center for Media and Independent Learning, 2000 Center Street, Fourth Floor, Berkeley, CA 94704-1223, ucmedia@ucxonline.berkeley.edu).

LaDuke, W. (1999). *All our relations: Native struggles for land and life.* Cambridge, MA: South End Press.

Macedo, D., & Bartolome, L.I. (1999). *Dancing with bigotry: Beyond the politics of tolerance.* New York: St. Martin's Press.

McIntosh, P. (1992). White privilege and male privilege: A personal account of coming to see correspondences through the work in Women's Studies. In M. Andersen & P.H. Collins (Eds.), *Race, class, and gender: An anthology* (pp. 70–81). Belmont, CA: Wadsworth Publishing Company. (Original work published 1988).

McLuhan, T.C. (1971). *Touch the earth: A self-portrait of Indian existence.* New York: Simon and Schuster.

Metcalf, P.R. (1988).Wheelock, Eleazar 1711–1779: Non-Indian biographies. In W.E. Washburn (Vol. Ed.), *History of Indian-White relations: Vol.4. Handbook of North American Indians.* Washington, DC: Smithsonian Institution.

Nies, J. (1996). *Native American history: A chronology of a culture's vast achievements and their links to world events.* New York: Ballentine Books.

Nerburn, K., & Mengelkoch, L. (1991). *Native American wisdom.* San Rafael, CA: New World Library.

O'Connell, B. (Ed.). (1997). *A son of the forest and other writings by William Apess, a Pequot.* Amherst: University of Massachusetts Press.

Rains, F.V. (2002). From the eyes of the colonized: Rethinking the legacy of colonization and its impact on American Indians. *Journal of Philosophy and History of Education, 52,* 125–130.

Rains, F.V. (1998). Is the benign really harmless? Deconstructing some "benign" manifestations of operationalized white privilege. In J.L. Kincheloe, S.R. Steinberg, N.M. Rodriguez, & R.E. Chennault (Eds.), *White reign: Deploying whiteness in America* (pp. 77–101). New York: St Martin's Press.

Rains, F.V., Archibald, J.A., & Deyhle, D. (Eds.). (2000). Introduction: Through our eyes and in our own words. [Special issue]. *International Journal of Qualitative Studies in Education, 13*(4), 337–342.

Reinhardt, M. (2000). Saved from our savage ways. [Special issue]. *International Journal of Qualitative Studies in Education, 13*(4), 385.

Robinson, R. (2000). *The debt: What America owes to Blacks.* New York: Plume.

Roesch Wagner, S. (1992). The Iroquois influence on women's rights. In J. Barreiro (Ed.), *Indian roots of American democracy* (pp. 115–134). Ithaca, NY: Akwe:Kon Press.

Roesch Wagner, S. (2001). *Sisters in spirit: Haudenosaunee (Iroquois) influence on early American feminists.* Summertown, TN: Native Voices Book Publishing Co.

Rose, W. (1992). The great pretenders: Further reflections on white shamanism. In M.A. Jaimes (Ed.), *The state of Native America: Genocide, colonization, and resistance* (pp. 403–422). Boston: South End Press.

Rosenstein, J. (Producer & Writer). (1996). *In whose honor? The use of Indian mascots in sports* (Television broadcast, July 15, 1997). Public Broadcast Service.

Sipes, C.H. (1931/1998). *The Indian wars of Pennsylvania: An account of the Indian events, in Pennsylvania, of the French and Indian War, Pontiac's War, Lord Dunmore's War, The Revolutionary War and the Indian uprisings from 1789 to 1795* (2nd ed.). Lewisburg, PA: Wennawoods Publishing.

Stannard, D.E. (1992). *American holocaust: The conquest of the new world.* New York: Oxford University Press.

Venn, S.H. (1998). *Our elders understand our rights: Evolving international law regarding Indigenous rights.* Pentiton, BC: Theytus Books, Ltd.

Voice of Indigenous Peoples: Native People address the United Nations. (1994). Santa Fe, NM: Clear Light Publishers.

Waldman, C. (2001). *Biographical Dictionary of American Indian history to 1900* (rev. Ed.). New York: Checkmark Books.

Waldman, C. (2000). *Atlas of the North American Indian* (rev. ed.). New York: Checkmark Books.

Waldman, C. (1999). *Encyclopedia of Native American tribes* (rev. ed.). New York: Checkmark Books.

Weatherford, J. (1988). *Indian givers: How the Indians of the Americas transformed the world.* New York: Crown Publishers.

Wilson, A. (1992). Invisible people? The hidden history of Canada. In D. Monet & A. Wilson (Eds.), *Colonialism on trial: Indigenous land rights and the Gitksan and Wet'suwet'en sovereignty case* (pp. 3–17). Gabriola Island, BC: New Society Publishers.

Witmer, L.F. (1993). *The Indian industrial school: Carlisle, Pennsylvania, 1879–1918.* Carlisle, PA: Cumberland County Historical Society.

Zeidler, J. (1989). Foreword. In M.L. Hultgren & P. Fairbanks Molin (Eds.), *To lead and to serve: American Indian education at Hampton Institute, 1878–1923* (pp. 6–8). Virginia Beach, VA: Virginia Foundation for the Humanities and Public Policy & Hampton University.

part IV

THE TECHNOLOGY

CHAPTER 11

LEARNING FROM BLACK FOLK(S)

Race, Technology, and Society

Jamel K. Donnor

ABSTRACT

The objective of this chapter is to use critical race theory's tenets of the centrality of history and context, and the rejection of objectivity and neutrality to understand the relationship between race, technology and society. That said, this chapter looks at three specific incidences in the history of African Americans with technology to support this objective. These incidences are: (a) the introduction of the mechanized cotton picker to the Southern region of the United States, (b) the automation of the workplace; and (c) the contemporary uses of computers in educational settings that are predominantly African American.

It is suggested that the examination of some recent experiences of African Americans with technology provides one with the opportunity to identify how technology can perpetuate racial inequity. In other words, the manner in which technology tends to be infused into racial settings suggests that it is a tool that can continue to perpetuate racism.

Critical Race Theory Perspectives on the Social Studies, pages 231–246
Copyright © 2003 by Information Age Publishing

231

> *From the caravels, compasses, navigational techniques, and firearms of the first Portu-guese explorers who reached the coast of West Africa in the 1440s to the never-ending expansion of microchip computing power and its implications for our society, the [B]lack community has had one negative encounter after another with the technologi-cal innovations of the mainstream. Within American history this aspect of [B]lacks' experience is unique.*

—Walton (1999)

INTRODUCTION

The National Council for the Social Studies' (NCSS)(1994) science, tech-nology, and society thematic strand acknowledges:

> Technology is as old as the first crude tool invented by prehistoric humans, but today's technology forms the basis for some of our most difficult social choices. Modern life as we know it would be impossible without technology ... [Y]oung children can learn how technologies form systems and how their daily lives are intertwined with a host of technologies. (p. 1)

NCSS (1994) further asserts, "social studies programs should include expe-riences that provide for the study of relationships among science, technol-ogy, and society" (p. 1).

If NCSS is serious about their assertion to include experiences that elu-cidate the relationships between science, technology, and society; I argue that one possibility would be to look at the experiences of African Ameri-cans' with technology. The justification for such an approach is not only to illustrate the complexity of issues that are involved in the creation, imple-mentation, and use of technological devices. More important, the exami-nation of the social impact of technology through the lived experiences of African Americans would show how significant a role race plays with respect to the type of access and use, and consequences of technology one has of technology. The inclusion of the experiences of a racialized group serves as an analytical lens to better understand the consequences of the "difficult social choices" that are made with technology. These conse-quences include creating, maintaining, and reification of existing unequal social (e.g., educational), and economic relationships.

As Walton's (1999) quote illustrates, access to technology for non-White racial groups has never been an issue. Rather, what has and continues to be of import is the impact technology has on those whose knowledge and experiences have not been integrated into the design and implementation of technological devices. According to Skinner and Rosen (2001) we need to "analyse how exchanges around science and technology take place in the context of structured inequalities between racialised groups" (p. 291).

Such an analysis may help to explain why it is some racial groups have never embraced or experienced the "benefits" of the technology as promised by its proponents.

The overarching goal of this chapter through use of critical race theory and other various sources is to put forth a more critical understanding of technology as it relates to issues of race and society. The examination of some recent experiences of African Americans' with technology provides one with the opportunity to identify how technology both as a concept and as an artifact perpetuates racial inequity. I will be specifically looking at three incidences in the history of African Americans and technology: (a) the introduction of the mechanized cotton picker to the Southern region of the United States, (b) the automation of the workplace; and (c) the contemporary uses of computers in educational settings that are predominantly African American. The rationale of this approach is twofold; the first is to reject the notions of objectivity and neutrality that dominates the discourse surrounding technology. The second is to incorporate the "absolute centrality of history and context" (Crenshaw et al., 1995).

Two final points, one I deem it necessary to first briefly identify which of the six tenets of critical race theory I will be using in this chapter to supply the reader with the racial logic that guides the author's line of reasoning. Lastly, I will also locate the ideological and social positions of technology as a concept within Western civilization to assist me in what I believe has been missing from most comments and discussions about technology-history and context.

CRITICAL RACE THEORY AND A CONTEXTUALIZATION OF TECHNOLOGY

Critical race theory (CRT) is a contemporary theoretical framework that critiques the dominant White hegemonic discourse and power, analyzes the social disparities between races, and challenges popular notions of the construction and employment of race, racism, and racial power in American society by doing the following: (1) incorporating the "absolute centrality of history and context" (Crenshaw et al., 1995), (2) rejecting notions of objectivity and neutrality, (3) recognizing that racism is endemic in U.S. Society (Bell, 1995), (4) employing a variety of theoretical traditions including Feminism, Marxism, post-structuralism, and critical legal studies to provide a more complete analysis of raced people (Tate, 1997), (5) incorporating one's "experiential knowledge" which posits "reality" is situational and socially constructed (Ladson-Billings, 1998, p.11), and (6) working toward the elimination of racial oppression with the goal of ending all forms of oppression (Lawrence III et al., 1993). For the purposes of this chapter I will be using tenets of the centrality of history and context, and rejecting notions of objectivity and neutrality in this discussion of race, technology and society.

TECHNOLOGY IN WESTERN CIVILIZATION(S)

The way that America currently thinks about technology can be traced back to its Ancient Western civilization roots (Buchanan, 1972; Cowan Schwartz, 1997; Klemm, 1959; Pippin, 1999). Technology as a concept is specifically grounded in Ancient European Christian ideology. Ani (1994) writes,

> [T]he general emphasis on technology as a social goal all go hand in hand with an assumption of and belief in the "idea of progress" in which the continued intensification of these facts constitute absolute value. The Judeo-Christian formulation is based on precisely the same concept. Within this tradition "religion" is seen almost as a technological advance, and, therefore, is aided by and aids the growth of the technical order. (p. 184)

It is the belief in the "idea of progress" is where proponents of technology have continued to draw their support. According to Custer (1996) at the heart of the "idea of progress" is a "profound sense of optimism, that a rapidly expanding base of knowledge would contribute to an increase in the quality and virtue of the social and human condition" (p. 66).

Encapsulated within the ideology of progress are multiple themes that are in continuous interplay with one another. For instance, at the philosophical level progress signifies a shift from "inferior to superior; from undesirable to desirable; from ignorance and malaise to wisdom. It is the embodiment of hope in a better future" (Custer, 1996, p. 68). Whereas at the ontological level, Western civilizations posit an essentialist idea of progress premised on: "(a) a high valuation of European history, (b) belief in the nobility of Western civilization, (c) support for economic and technological growth [via capitalism], (d) faith in reason and knowledge, and (e) belief in the intrinsic worth of life on this earth" (Custer, 1996, p. 70). In short, progress as a concept in ancient Europe was powerful because it comprised multiple components that were also being supported by a "super ideology" (i.e., science) (Sanmartín, 1992, p. 72). For in addition to the multiple components that are packaged within the discourse of progress, technology was also being systematically conjoined with science (Ada, 1989). As a result, technology was now expected to scientifically construct a better world in which "human well being is continuously increasing" (Sanmartín, 1992, p. 73).

Technology in American Society

It is the belief in progress as the constant pursuit of improvement in the "human" condition, which also serves as the foundation for America's outlook on technology. However, unlike Europe which interpreted progress on moral and spiritual grounds, North America on the other used capitalism, democracy, and "technical development and industrialization" to conceptualize progress (Klemm, 1959). According to Meier (1978) democracy

[B]ecame consciously and elaborately associated with American progress in the applied science ... this association came to emphasize the special role of technology in providing the physical means of achieving democratic objectives of political, social, and economic equality, and it placed science and invention at the very center at the age's faith in progress. (p. 80)

The two most influential proponents of this redefinition of progress in the United States were Benjamin Franklin and Thomas Jefferson (Smith, 1996). According to Smith (1996) Franklin and Jefferson were both "avid proponents of the cause of liberty, they looked to the new mechanical technologies of the era as [a] means of achieving the virtuous and prosperous republican society that they associated with the goals of the American revolution" (p. 3). For both men, progress in and through the pursuit of technology meant the betterment of "human interests" and "material prosperity" (Smith, 1996, p. 3). What this meant is that progress in America was to be measured materially through the production of objects and artifacts.

In summary, technology in Western civilizations has been constructed in a very racialized manner. By racialized I mean that it promulgates a Western epistemological system.[1] This way of thinking about technology helps to explain the essentialist, and deterministic perspectives that surround its existence. More important, these articulations of technology establish both an ahistorical and an acontextual understanding of its purpose and impact on society. Thus, what ends up happening is a focus on social adaptation to technology, instead of how technology may be designed to fit society, because technology has been socially constructed as an autonomous entity guided by a distinct set of values outside the influence of humans.

This would explain why it is extremely difficult to think of technology in any other way. As a result, it is necessary to engage in critical discussions of technology that address historical and contemporary experiences of non-Whites as a way to better understand the relationship between technology and society.

THE MECHANIZED COTTON BLACKS IN THE SOUTH

Prior to the First World War the economy of Southern states in the United States was still agriculturally based, because they relied heavily on planting crops such as cotton, tobacco, rice, and sugar cane (Willhelm, 1970). Also, up until this time the level of technology used by Southerners in agriculture was low. Overall very little had changed in the way the South was structured socially. For example, although slavery had been abolished in 1862, the bulk of the African American population still resided in the Southern portion of the US but was involved in agriculture as their primary source of employment. In other words, "from the American Revolution until the eve of World War I, about ninety percent of all Black people lived in the South ... [t]he majority of Black male workers ploughed and planted the fields"[2] (Marable, 1983, p. 33).

Sharecropping was the dominant arrangement in which the majority of Southern African Americans in agriculture labored under. Under this arrangement African American farmers occupied land and shelter furnished by White landowners, as well as borrowed "fuel, work stock, stock feed, seed, farm implements, and one-half the necessary fertilizers" from stores operated by White landowners (Low & Clift, 1981, p. 90). In return the farmer was expected to supply his labor, the other half of fertilizer, and 40% of the harvest as payment for use of the land and house. In principle this pact appears amicable, however it was not considering that most of the Black sharecroppers fell into "heavy debt." This debt was accrued as a result of the exorbitant interest rates White land owners charged for the rented housing and field equipment, and provided them with credit from their stores (Christian, 1995, p. 321). Of the crops that were planted the majority of African American sharecroppers farmed the labor-intensive cotton crop (Marable, 1983; Rifkin, 1996). According to Rifkin (1996):

> [P]icking cotton bolls at harvest was a grueling intensive field. Laborers had to crawl on their knees or stoop over as they worked the cotton fields. The soft puff of cotton was surrounded by a tough stem that constantly pierced the hands ... [and] lasted from sunup to sundown, (p. 70)

However, by 1920 the number African Americans involved in agriculture was on the decline. The factors responsible for this decline include the boll weevil, an increase in the number of floods that were occurring in the region, crop diversification, and the Northern states demand for industrial labor (Low &Clift, 1981). Low and Clift (1981) put this decline in perspective by noting that in 1920 there were 882, 850 African American farmers (which constituted 14% of all farmers); whereas just ten years prior there were 893, 370. They continue by pointing out that by 1940 the number had declined markedly to 681, 709 (Low & Clift, 1981). In spite of this decline the majority of African Americans remained in the South. Yet, there would be another factor that would be responsible for the near complete removal of Blacks from agriculture all together.

On October 2, 1944, the mechanical cotton picker was introduced in the South. From a productivity perspective, the mechanical cotton picker could pick approximately one thousand pounds of cotton whereas a field hand could only pick twenty pounds in an hour (Christian, 1995; Rifkin, 1996). What this meant was that instead of relying on a larger number of Black hands to pick cotton, White landowners now only needed roughly three to four workers. In short, one mechanical cotton picker could do the work of fifty people. Almost immediately African Americans became obsolete in the area of agriculture, because of the infusion of a new technology into an economic system that already favored Whites. In 1949 only 6% of all the cotton harvested in South was done mechanically, where by 1964 it soared to 78%[3] (Rifkin, 1996). It is for that reason, in addition to the ones previously mentioned, Black southerners were forced to migrate to the North.

This new advancement in technology now served to only further disenfranchise African Americans of the South. The mechanized cotton picker had furnished Southern white landowners with the power to evict African American sharecroppers from their land.

Thus, the introduction of technology as it pertains to African Americans during this time period was ironic. On the one hand, the mechanical cotton picker had "freed" African Americans from the exploitative system of sharecropping and debt peonage.[4] On the other hand, by being a significant contributor to Black unemployment in the South, the mechanical cotton picker became a "push" factor responsible for Southern African Americans migration to Northern racially segregated inner-city ghettos.

AUTOMATION OF THE WORKPLACE

As previously mentioned, the introduction of a new technology (e.g., mechanical cotton picker) in the Southern states of America had played a significant role in "pushing" its African American residents to migrate to the North. Conversely, technology (e.g., the manufacturing industry) also served as a factor in pulling Southern African Americans to the North. Similar to the mechanized cotton-picker, automation of the workplace would disrupt and displace African Americans both socially and economically. Also similar to the mechanical cotton picker, the automation of the manufacturing industry (e.g., mass production) affected a significant number of exploitable low-skilled and non-educated workers to work in repetitive jobs. For example, with the advent of automation in the manufacturing industry, "skilled" industries such as shipbuilding and aircraft production became divided into "simple components that could readily be taught to inexperienced, low-skilled workers who had never before seen an airplane or a ship" (Killingsworth, 1968, p.).

Unlike mechanization where the emphasis was placed on the creation of a device or object to replace people that work, automation focuses on the process of how work is done. Automation as a process is premised on the following four principles: (a) control, (b) feedback, (c) the viewing of economic activity and work as a process, and (d) the application of the first three principles through electronic devices (Buckingham, Jr., 1961a, 1961b/1955; Diebold, 1969; Drucker, 1961/1955; Rifkin, 1996; Solow; 1961/1956).

The application of these principles however is very specific. For instance, in terms of control, the machine not only replaces the person doing the work, but through its employment it also establishes a "standardization of equipment and specialization of tasks" (Buckingham, 1961a, p. 6). Feedback refers to the inputting of information automatically into the system to "control" (Solow, 1961/1956, p. 24). In other words, the "machines start and stop themselves and regulate quality and quantity of output automatically" (Buckingham, 1961a, p. 11). Computers play an essential role in this because it is programmed with the information upon which the machines are to act on.

The third principle, viewing economic activity and work as a process encompasses "the engineering aspects of automation to the economic, social, and managerial aspects" (Buckingham, 1961a, p. 13). This is considered to be either the "rationalization," or a "philosophy of organizing any work as a system" where the entire production process is "carefully analyzed so that every operation can be designed to contribute in the most efficient way to the achievement of clearly enunciated goals of the enterprise" (Buckingham, 1961a, p.13; Solow, 1961/1956).

Finally, the application of the first three principles through electronic devices allows for a continuous flow of production without human interference. The most salient example of this application is the assembly line, where a device handles, positions, performs a function, and transfers it to the next station in the production process. This process is repeated electronically until the desired product in desired quantity has been created. Drucker (1961/1955) points out:

> early industry ... the integrating principle of work was skill. For instance, in Henry Ford's concept of mass production the organizing principle was the product. With automation, however, the entire activity of the business is a whole entity which must be harmoniously integrated to perform at all. (p. 33)

Automation's Impact on African Americans

African Americans in the automobile industry were profoundly impacted negatively by automation. On the topic of the automotive industry Buckingham (1961a, 1961b/1955) states, "between the world wars the assembly line spread to a host of industries while the automobile industry, where it was used first and effectively, mushroomed into one of the largest industries in the world" (p. 10). With regards to African Americans Rifkin (1996) writes, during the 1950s they had comprised 25.7% of the workers at Chrysler, and 23% of the workers at General Motors. On the surface these numbers may look insignificant, however they become enormous considering that Blacks made up the majority of the unskilled laborers first let go because of automation. Another way to better contextualize this situation is to note that of the 7,425 skilled workers at Chrysler in 1960 only twenty-four were African American; while at General Motors of the 11, 000 skilled workers on the payroll a mere sixty-seven were Black (Rifkin, 1996).

The massive displacement of African Americans by automation is the result of the general failure to see its short comings, and to overstate its benefits. In short, automation eliminates more jobs than it creates. Snyder (1965) supports such a position by positing that there is a duality in automation's displacement of workers; he asserts that people are not only removed directly, but they are indirectly placed on the "*silent firings* in relation to workers who would have been hired for jobs eliminated by automation" (p. 47). Rifkin (1996) notes that from the late 1940s through 1957 the Ford Corporation spent more than 2.5 billion dollars on automation and plant modifications. Noble (1984) points out that in 1948 the Ford Automation Department, which had been in operation for eighteen months "approved the use of five hundred devices, costing a total of $3 million, and expected to increase production by 20% and eliminate one thousand jobs" (p. 67).

At first glance these figures make it appear as if upgrading to automation does not make good business sense. However, if one thinks about it over a ten-year period the issue becomes clearer. Corporations are able to recoup their initial investment in automation and increase their profit margins by not only reducing their payroll through layoffs, but also in reducing their retirement payouts. These companies are also able to weather the financial shocks of introducing new technology because they are no longer responsible for having to pay for the training of new employees.

Automation as a concept and as an application succeeded in modernizing the "routine" elements of manufacturing. However, it came at the expense of the majority of African Americans that worked in the manufacturing industry who tended to occupy jobs within the sector that were either semi or low skilled (Buckingham, 1961a; Killingsworh, 1968; Rifkin, 1996; Willhelm, 1970). According to Rifkin (1996):

> In the md-1950s, automation began taking it toll in the nation's manufacturing sector. Hardest hit were the unskilled jobs in the very industries where [B]lack workers were concentrated. Between 1953 and 1962, 1.6 million blue-collar jobs were lost in the manufacturing sector. Whereas the unemployment rate for [B]lack Americans had never exceeded 8.5% between 1947 and 1953, and the White rate of unemployment had never gone beyond 4.6%, by 1964 [B]lacks were experiencing an unemployment rate of 12.4% while White unemployment was only 5.9%. (p. 73)

Another point to keep in mind is that once these jobs are gone, they are never reinstated. Supporters of automation insist workers that are displaced as a result of its introduction will be absorbed into a self-adjusting labor market (Buckingham, 1961a). However, there is a lack of sufficient data to support this insistence.

Willhelm (1970) insightfully points out "when machines operate machines, man becomes dispensable in the production of goods and performance of services ... man frees himself from man to the extent that technology eliminates even human decision making" (p. 136). In speaking on the effect on Blacks and issues of race, technology and society the:

> [I]ntroduction of automation announces an entirely new perspective by posing the possibility of an alternative available for *Whites* to cope *with [B]lacks*. [Because] The fundamental process of race relations within America society persists whereby economic values set the range of racism by White toward Negroes, but the new technology portends a sharp modification. (Willhelm, 1970)

Finally, the automation of the workplace has further rendered African Americans obsolete. The increase of material productivity in manufacturing through "*Niggermation*"[5] also is responsible for the continued social powerlessness of Black Americans.

PEDAGOGICAL USE OF COMPUTERS IN THE EDUCATION OF URBAN AFRICAN AMERICANS

Presently, the United States has reached a stage in its development where everyone can say computers and related information technologies occupy an important social and economic position. The U.S. Department of Commerce (1999) exclaimed that America is entering an *Information Age*. The information age is characterized by the entire economy will rely on digital technologies, and workers who can create, apply and use information technology in diverse settings including education. According to then U.S. Secretary of Commerce William M. Daly (1999):

> [W]ith the emerging digital economy becoming a major driving force of our nation's economic well-being we must ensure all Americans have the information tools and skills that are critical to their participation. Access to such tools is an important step to ensure that our economy grows strongly and that in the future no one is left behind.

Schools in particular have responded to this call for technological preparedness by trying to ensure access and use of computers in the education of students. For example, the U.S. Department of Education (1999) noted Internet access in public schools had risen from 35 to 89% between the Fall of 1994 and the Fall of 1998. Similarly, the percentage of public schools with instructional rooms with access to the Internet increased during the same time period from "three percent in 1994 to fifty-one percent in 1998" (U.S. Department of Education, 1999, p. 60).

However, what is perhaps most telling about this "booster"[6] discourse are the pedagogical approaches schools employ to use computers in the education of African American students. Of the various educational uses of computer-assisted instruction drill and practice is by far the most dominant approach (Harper, 1987; Kosakowski, 1998; Streibel, 1998). Within educational settings with a student body that is predominantly African American drill and practice is the primary mode of computer use (Carver, 1999). Becker and Ravitz (1998) suggest that in working class schools there tends to be an emphasis on "punctuality, neatness, obedience, and structure because these are the attributes conducive to subordinate labor" (p. 2). When juxtaposed with more affluent educational settings they indicate that creativity, independence, and higher level thinking skills are taught in order to prepare students from middle class and elite schools to maintain their socioeconomic status (Becker & Ravitz, 1998).

As a pedagogical method drill and practice employs the principal of trial and error (DeVaney, 1998). This principle is premised on two assumptions: (a) "students usually learn more, and learn more rapidly" (Kosakowski, 1998, p.1); and (b) students can "master" the class material when allotted sufficient time (Streibel, 1998). The learner in this pedagogical paradigm is constructed as a consumer of information, because of the learning process is viewed as something that can be rationally managed.

Drill and practice programs pedagogically are based on behaviorist theories of learning, which emphasize "stimulus, response, and reward" (Healy, 1998). Learning is framed in very individualistic terms that presume the following: (a) the student has received previous instruction in the subject, (b) instruction is to follow a controlled, step-by-step linear sequence of sub-skills according to an algorithm embedded in the computer program (rote skill building, and pattern skill building; Streibel, 1998), (c) there is a right-wrong answer binary that exists within the logic of the context, (d) instructional interaction occurs in the form of a question-answer format, (e) immediate feedback on the student's response is considered positive; and (f) this approach "frees" the instructor from the more routine aspects of teaching (e.g., grading papers, and recording student progress; Cuban, 1986). As a result, the student's are not active participants in the learning process. Instead they are told by the machine that their way of learning does not "compute." More important, this consumer-relationship emphasizes the students' dependency on the machine because the computer supposedly knows more than the students do. Thus the "relationship" between the student and the computer is one that is grounded in consumption, because the individual students' abilities are judged against a set of predetermined expectations and outcomes.

Drill and practice approaches in computer-assisted instruction are meant to be a supplement to the teacher and the curriculum. They are designed to be responsive to the student in that they elicit a response from the student by putting forth a query. The educational goal of drill and practice courseware is meant to provide practice for basic low-level skills the student has already learned. If new skills or learning are to occur, they are the result of trial and error instead of directed instruction (Gagné, Wager, & Rojas, 1981).

CONCLUSION

By adhering to critical race theory's two tenets of the centrality of history and context, and the rejection of objectivity and neutrality. I have been able to illustrate a distinct connection between race, technology, and society in two ways. The first was by locating the historical position of technology within Western civilizations ideologically. This historical positioning not provided the reader with an understanding of how technology came into existence, but also why it is taken for granted by society. The second illustration was fleshing-out the connections between technology and society as it specifically relates to issues of race and racism. The three examples of African Americans' experiences with technology used here makes one better able to conceptualize the material effects of technology on already marginalized groups. These three examples suggest that the manner in which technology as it is conceived and employed are not neutral.

Instead, the way in which technology tends to be infused into racial settings suggests that it is a tool that can perpetuate racism. In other words, using race as an analytical lens to understand why it is that racial groups, such as African Americans, have a historical pattern with technology in which their social condition continuously worsens, is very informative. Thinking and looking at technology through a critical race lens not only exposes the link between technology and racism ideologically and ontologically. More important, it can show how groups of people are materially affected.

For instance, Kelley (2000) argues that computers can have a profound "negative impact on justice" (p. 48). In discussing the matter of police departments' creation and use of databases Kelley (2000) states,

> If your name appears, you are guilty unless proven innocent. And given the backlog of cases and racial prejudice among police, juries, and judges, public defenders tend to plea-bargain for Blacks and Latinos even when a client appears innocent, because it *reduces* jail time and speeds the process. In the long run, however, it means that a young person just beginning his or her adult life now has a conviction, whether or not he or she has ever, in fact, been convicted. And when one is convicted, one is practically unemployable, and it is difficult to rent an apartment or obtain insurance. (p. 48)

Finally, I believe if NCSS seriously wants to include experiences that make clear the relationships between science, technology, and society. Then NCSS could learn a lot from Black Folk(s).

NOTES

1. Ladson-Billings (2000) states that "epistemology is more than a way of knowing ... [it] is a system of knowing that has both an internal logic and external validity" (p. 257).

2. Marable (1983) wrote that in terms of gender in "1910, 57% of all men and 52% of all Black women workers were farmers" (p. 33).

3. For a more thorough demographic break down by state see Wilhelm's (1970) *Who needs the Negro* (p. 140).

4. Low and Clift (1981) define debt peonage as a "system under which many insolvent black farmers, unable to pay their debts from year to year, were legally bound to work for landlords until their debts were paid. This condition, is equivalent to involuntary servitude" (p. 90).

5. The author came across this term in his reading of Marable (1983) *How capitalism underdeveloped Black America*, he borrows it from D. Georgakas, & M. Surkin (1975), Niggermation in auto: Company policy and the rise of Black caucuses, *Radical America, 8*, 31–57.

6. The booster discourse promotes a "strong sense of inevitability about computers in schools and demonstrate an unshakable faith in the capacity of computer technology to solve, if not all, of the problems of schooling" (Bigum, 1998, p. 590).

REFERENCES

Ada, M. (1989). *Machines as the measure of men: Science, technology, and ideologies of Western dominance*. Ithaca, NY: Cornell University Press.

Ani, M. (1994). *Yurugu: An African-centered critique of European cultural thought and behavior*. Trenton, NJ: Africa World Press.

Becker, H.J., & Ravitz, J.L. (1998). The equity threat of promising innovations: Pioneering internet-connected schools. *Journal of Educational Computing Research, 19*(1), 1–26.

Buchanan, S. (1972). Technology as a system exploitation. In M. Kranzenberg & W.H. Davenport (Eds.), *Technology and culture: An anthology*. New York: Schocken Books.

Buckingham, Jr., W.S. (1961/1955a). The four major principles. In R.P. Weeks (Ed.), *Machines and the man: A sourcebook on Automation*. New York: Appleton-Century-Crofts.

Buckingham, Jr., W.S. (1961b). *Automation: Its impact on business and people*. New York: Harper & Brothers.

Carver, B.. (1999). The information rage: Computers and young African American males. In Polite, V. C., & Davis, J. E. (Eds.), *African American males in schools and society: Practice and policies for effective education* (pp. 20–33). New York: Teachers College.

Christian, C.M. (1995). *Black saga: The African American experience. A chronology*. Washington, DC: First Civitas.

Cowan Schwartz, R. (1997). *A social history of American technology*. New York: Oxford University Press.

Crenshaw, K.W., Gotanda, N., Peller, G., & Thomas, K. (Eds.). (1995). *Critical race theory: The key writings that formed the movement*. New York: The New Press.

Cuban, L. (1986). *Teachers and machines: The classroom use of technology since 1920*. New York: Teachers College.

Custer, R.L. (1996). Examining cultural ideologies. In R.L. Custer & A.E. Wiens (Eds.), *Technology and the quality of life* (pp. 43–84). Glencoe, NY: McGraw-Hill.

Cutcliffe, S.H., & Reynolds, T.S. (1997). Technology in American context. In S.H. Cutcliffe & T.S. Reynolds (Eds.), *Technology and American history: A historical anthology from technology and culture* (pp. 5–26). Chicago: The University of Chicago Press.

DeVaney, A. (1998). Can and need educational technology become a postmodern enterprise? *Theory Into Practice, 37*(1), 72–80.

Diebold, J. (1969). *Man and the computer technology as an agent of social change*. New York: Frederick A. Praeger.

Drucker, P. (1961/1955). The logic of automation. In R.P. Weeks (Ed.), *Machines and the man: A sourcebook on automation*. New York: Appleton-Century-Crofts.

Gagné, R.M., Wager, W., & Rojas, A. (1981). Planning and authoring computer-assisted lessons. *Educational Technology, 21*(9), 17–26.

Harper, D.O. (1987). The creation and development of educational computer technology. In R.M. Thomas & V.N. Kobayashi (Eds.), *Educational technology: Its creation, development and cross-cultural transfer* (pp. 35–3). Oxford: Pergamon.

Harris, C.I. (1995). Whiteness as property. In K.W. Crenshaw, N. Gotanda, G. Peller, & K. Thomas (Eds.), *Critical race theory: The key writings that formed the movement* (pp. 276–291). New York: The New Press.

Healy, J.M. (1998). *Failure to connect: How computers affect our children's minds-and what we can do about it.* New York: Touchstone.

Kelley, R.D.G. (2000). "Slangin' rocks ... Palestinian style:" Dispatches from the occupied zones of North America. In J. Nelson (Ed.), *Police brutality: An anthology* (pp. 21–59). New York: W. W. Norton & Company, Inc.

Killingsworh, C.C. (1968). *Jobs and income for Negroes.* Institute of Labor and Industrial Relations.

Klemm, F. (1959). *A history of western technology.* New York: Charles Scribner's Sons.

Kosakowski, J. (1998). *The benefits of information technology* (ERIC Digest). Syracuse, NY: ERIC Clearinghouse on Information and Technology. (ERIC Identifier No. ED 420302).

Lacy, D. (1972). *The White use of Blacks in America.* New York: Atheneum.

Ladson-Billings, G. (2000). Racialized discourses and ethnic epistemologies. In N.K. Denzin & Y.S. Lincoln (Eds.), *Handbook of qualitative research* (pp. 257–278). Thousand Oaks, CA: Sage.

Ladson-Billings, G. (1995). Toward a theory of culturally relevant pedagogy. *American Educational Research Journal, 32*(3), 466–491.

Lorde, A. (1984). *Sister outsider: Essays and speeches.* Freedom, CA: The Crossing Press.

Low, W.A., & Clift, V.A. (1981). *Encyclopedia of Black America.* New York: Da Capo.

Marable, M. (1983). *How capitalism underdeveloped Black America.* Boston: South End Press.

Matsuda, M., Lawrence, C.R. III, Delgado, R., & Crenshaw, K.W. (1995). *Words that wound: Critical race theory, assaultive speech, and the first amendment.* Boulder, CO: Westview Press.

Meier, H.A. (1978). The ideology of technology. In E.T. Layton, Jr. (Ed), *Technology and social change in America.* New York: Harper & Row.

National Council for the Social Studies 1994, Two: Ten Strands. (n.d.). *Science, Technology and Society.* Retrieved May 14, 2002, from http://www.socialstudies.org/standards/2.8html

Noble, D.F. (1984). *Forces of production: A social history of industrial automation.* New York: Alfred A. Knopf.

Pippin, R.B. (1999) On the notion of technology as ideology. In A. Feenberg & A. Hannay (Eds.), *Technology and the politics of knowledge.* Bloomington, IN: Indiana University Press.

Rifkin, J. (1996). *The end of work: The decline of the global labor force and the dawn of the post-market era.* New York: Tarcher/Putnam.

Sanmartín, J. (1992). The new world of new technology. In S.H. Cutcliffe, S.L. Goldman, M. Medina, & J. Sanmartín (Eds.), *New worlds, new technologies, new issues* (pp. 72–84). Bethlehem, PA: Lehigh University Press.

Smith, M.R. (1996). Technological determinism in American culture. In M.R. Smith & L. Marx (Eds.), *Does technology drive history? The dilemma of technological determinism* (pp. 2–35). Cambridge, MA: The MIT Press.

Solow, H. (1961/1956). "Automation": News behind the noise. In R.P. Weeks (Ed.), *Machines and the man: A sourcebook on Automation*. New York: Appleton-Century-Crofts.

Streibel, M.J. (1998). A critical analysis of three approaches to the use of computers in education. In L.E. Beyer & M.W. Apple (Eds.), *The curriculum: Problems, politics, and possibilities* (pp. 284–313). Albany: SUNY Press.

Tate, W.F., IV. (1997). Critical race theory and education: History, theory, and implications. *Review of Research in Education, 22*, 195–247.

U.S. Department of Commerce (1999). *Falling through the net: Defining the digital divide*. Washington, DC: U.S. Government Printing Office.

U.S. Department of Education. (1999). *Education Statistics Quarterly, 1*(4), 60.

Walton, A. (1999, January). Technology versus African-Americans. *The Atlantic Monthly*, 1–9. Retrieved March 18, 1999, from http://www.theatlantic.com/issues99jan/aftech.htm

Willhelm, S.M. (1970). *Who needs the Negro?* Cambridge, MA: Schenkman Publishing.

Willhelm, S.M. (1983). *Black in a White America*. Cambridge, MA: Schenkman Publishing.

CHAPTER 12

RACE, SOCIAL STUDIES, AND THE WORLD WIDE WEB

Anand R. Marri

ABSTRACT

Social studies education organizations possess the capacity to promote lesson plans that expose students to multiple and critical viewpoints on race. Students must be exposed to such viewpoints on race to become informed and participatory citizens in these diverse United States. The World Wide Web can potentially facilitate this process through easy access to a worldwide library of resources. However, research conducted for this chapter demonstrates that the three most commonly referenced lesson plan websites neglect multiple and critical viewpoints on race. I suggest teaching about and for multicultural democracy may incorporate the necessary multiple and critical viewpoints on race.

INTRODUCTION

The inventor or introducer of the system deserves to be ranked among the best contributors to learning and science, if not among the greatest benefactors of mankind.

Critical Race Theory Perspectives on the Social Studies, pages 247–269
Copyright © 2003 by Information Age Publishing

While it may seem as if this quote is referring to computer-based technology in classroom today, it is in fact describing the "system" of the blackboard (Tyack & Cuban, 1995). Interestingly, enthusiasm for the blackboard was similar to the excitement seen today for the use of the World Wide Web in classrooms. "Reformers have turned to machines when they were concerned about the competence of teachers, or the high cost of schooling, or some external threat to American security or prosperity that gave special urgency to education" (Tyack & Cuban, 1995, p. 121). Thus, the implementation of computer-based technology, such as the World Wide Web, is currently being prescribed to help solve problems (i.e., ineffective teaching, low test scores, inefficiency, etc.) in today's classrooms. This takes on particular significance since teachers and students, for the most part, have access to computers and related technologies available in both their homes and their schools (Cuban, 2001).

For the social studies teacher, the World Wide Web has four potential benefits. First, it enables easy access to documents and resources previously unavailable to educators to use in the classroom. Examples include primary documents and foreign newspapers. Cuban (2001) found that many teachers who use the Internet view access to information via the Internet as a "phenomenal enhancement" to their teaching (Cuban, 2001, p. 94). Second, the Web is a low-cost source of information. In most cases lesson plan websites are free to educators. Third, the Web facilitates access to current and updated materials for social studies educators to use in their classrooms. Finally, in part due to the first three benefits, the Web provides a venue for lesson plans promoting diverse perspectives.

This last potential benefit, the possibility of accessing instructional materials that meaningfully integrate critical and multiple perspectives, presents an exciting opportunity for social studies educators. Unfortunately, even a cursory examination of the most commonly referenced social studies websites reveals that most posted lesson plans neglect to do so. By critical and multiple perspectives, I am, for the purposes of this chapter, limiting myself to race. Most of these websites re-inscribe the dominant ideas found in traditional textbooks, which traditionally ignore critical and multiple perspectives on race. As a result, despite the opportunity for marginalized perspectives to be presented in a low-cost and easily accessible format, dominant viewpoints on race are still privileged.

METHODOLOGY

I aimed to discover how social studies education organizations addressed race through the World Wide Web. Instead of focusing on organizations' general mission statements, I analyzed the promoted lesson plan websites because they would generally reflect the importance of addressing race for the organizations. Furthermore, since the promoted websites served as resources for social studies teachers, these websites had received a "seal of approval." I wanted to see how these "approved" websites addressed race. The goal of this study is not to criticize the individual websites; Instead, I use these websites as a proxy for how social studies curriculum material found on the World Wide Web fails to address race through critical and multiple viewpoints.

I chose to focus on three frequently referenced secondary United States History lesson plan websites for two reasons. First, U.S. History is a course required in all U.S. public high schools and the most commonly taught social studies subject. I wanted a course that all public high school students take, regardless of other factors, in order to increase the generalizability of the findings from my study. Second, I wanted to control for the subject matter of these websites. Choosing U.S. History allows me to pick a commonly taught subject thereby minimizing subject matter variables in my study.

A review of the literature in social studies and technology did not yield studies or other resources examining the most commonly used secondary social studies websites. In order to formulate a list of the three commonly referenced secondary United States History lesson plan websites, I examined six relatively current issues of *Social Education* (September 2001–May 2002), the official publication of the National Council of the Social Studies (NCSS) for social studies educators, and the NCSS website (accessed June 7, 2002).

An examination of *Social Education* and the NCSS website yielded many secondary U.S. History lesson plan websites. To narrow this lengthy list, I chose lesson plan websites that were not limited to specific topics, such as websites on the Bill of Rights, the Civil War, or the presidents. Instead, I focused on websites that included content from a general secondary school U.S. History course. A search for such websites generated a much smaller list. Of these remaining websites, I looked for the websites that were referenced most often.

After selecting these three secondary United States History websites, I analyzed their content to examine if and how critical and diverse perspectives were included. I generated four criteria using two main notions of Critical Race Theory that could be best addressed through the curriculum.

1. Racism is "normal, not aberrant, in American society" (Delgado, 1995, p. xiv), and because it is so enmeshed in the fabric of our social order, it appears both normal and natural to people in this culture. As a result, this necessitates a strategy, as Ladson-Billings (1998) suggests, of unmasking and exposing racism in its various permutations.

2. Storytelling enables analysis of "the myths, presuppositions, and received wisdoms that make up the common culture about race and the invariably render Blacks and other minorities one-down" (Delgado, 1995, p. xiv). In addition, stories are deemed important because they add necessary contexts to the "objectivity" of positivist perspectives (Ladson-Billings, 1998).

Based on these two notions, I used the following criteria to analyze the lesson plans on the websites: Are race and issues surrounding race, such as racism, addressed? If so, are these issues considered as ongoing and current phenomena? Are stories and narratives used in the lessons? If so, are stories by people of color that show how our society is "deeply structured by racism" (Ladson-Billings, 1998, p. 13) included?

After selecting the three websites, I examined secondary U.S. History lesson plans found on each website: 45 lesson plans on website 1, 55 lesson plans on website 2, and 33 lesson plans on website 3. I analyzed and examined each lesson with the above four criteria.

FINDINGS

An examination of the three websites led to three conclusions. First, race is only addressed in lessons that examine the experiences of people of color. Thus, minimalizing the importance of race in all aspects of U.S. History. Second, race and issues surrounding race, such as racism, are treated as historical events and not as ongoing and current phenomena. Third, stories and narratives that capture the continual struggle against racial discrimination in a society deeply structured by racism are missing from the lesson plan websites.

Race and People of Color

First, in all three of websites, race and issues surrounding race, such as racism, are only addressed in lessons that examine the experiences of people of color. The subject of race is not examined in lesson plans that do not focus on people of color, such "American Dreams" and "United We Stand." The following is an example from the most referenced lesson plan website.

In this site, the subject of race is directly addressed in only six of the forty-five lessons available. Interestingly, in each of the six lessons, the experiences of people of color are the focus. Unfortunately, the other lessons found on this site do not address race and issues surrounding race, such as racism. In other lessons, the subject of race is rendered silent even though

Website 1 (45 lessons)	Lessons in Which Race is Directly Addressed (6 lessons)	Description of Lesson from the Website
	After Reconstruction	Students identify problems and issues facing African Americans immediately after Reconstruction using text based sources
	From Jim Crow to Linda Brown	Students explore the era of legalized segregation. The unit culminating activity is the creation of a meeting similar to the Afro-American Council prior to the Brown case in 1954
	Jackie Steals Home	Students engage in close reading of two documents relating to Jackie Robinson's breaking of the racial barrier in professional baseball, which leads to a deeper exploration of racism in the United States, both in and out of sports.
	Reservation Controversies	Students engage in a two part experience using Problem Based Learning (PBL), in which they are confronted or faced with two different, but related real world problems regarding Native Americans, which have no preconceived right or wrong answers.
	Rounding the Bases	Students use primary sources focused on baseball to explore the American experience regarding race and ethnicity.
	To Kill a Mockingbird	Students are guided on a journey through the Depression Era in the 1930s. They become familiar with Southern experiences through the study of the To Kill a Mockingbird, and African American experiences through the examination of primary sources.

the lessons present a good opportunity to address it. Lessons such as "American Dreams," "Images of Our People," "Immigration Through Oral History," and "Immigration/Migration" can be created in which the subject of race can be the foreground. For example, accounts that capture the experiences of people of color can be integrated in these lessons. However, this does not occur. Rather, traditional mainstream academic knowledge, which neglects critical and multiple perspectives on race, is presented (i.e., highlighting the experiences of Irish and Italian immigrants). The silencing of race beyond lessons that focus on people of color also extends to the other two websites as well, as can be seen below.

Website and Number of Lessons	Number of Lessons in Which Race is Directly Addressed	Titles of Lessons in Which Race is Directly Addressed
Site 2—55 lessons	14	The Amistad Case, The Sioux Treaty of 1868, The Fight for Equal Rights: Black Soldiers in the Civil War, Maps of Indian Territory, the Dawes Act, and Will Rogers' File, Affidavit and Flyers form the Chinese Boycott Case, Photographs of the 369th Infantry and African American Soldiers, Documents and Photographs Related to Japanese Relocation during WWII, Memorandum Regarding the Enlistment of Navajo Indians, Documents Related to *Brown v. Board of Education,* Jackie Robinson, Court Documents Related to Martin Luther King, Jr., and Memphis Sanitation Workers, The Civil Rights Act and the Equal Employment Opportunities.
Site 3—33 lessons	6	Bad Blood: The Tuskegee Study of Untreated Syphilis, Back Towns in the West: A Case Study of the Exodusters, Freedom's Children: An Oral History on the Civil Rights Movement, Internment of Japanese Americans in World War II: *Toyosaburo Korematsu v. United States,* Prelude to the Trial of Tears: *Worcester v. Georgia*

Race as a Historical Event

The second conclusion is that race and racism are treated as historical events and not as ongoing and current phenomena in the three websites. The lesson plans on the websites do not address the subject of race and racism as continuing issues in the United States. I will use a lesson from Site 2 on teaching about the Civil Rights Act of 1964 and the Equal Employment Opportunity Commission as an example. The lesson plan follows.

Standards Correlations for This Lesson	*Teaching Activities for This Lesson*

Correlation with the National History Standards:

Era 9—Postwar United States
(1945 to early 1970s)

- Standard 4B—Demonstrate understanding of the women's movement for civil rights and equal opportunities.

Era 10—Contemporary United States
(1968 to the present)

- Standard 1A—Demonstrate understanding of domestic politics from Nixon to Carter.

Correlation with the National Standards for Civics and Government:

- Standard II.C.2—Describe the character of American political conflict and explain factors that usually tend to prevent it or lower its intensity.

- Standard II.D.3—Evaluate, take and defend positions on what the fundamental values and principles of American political life are and their importance to the maintenance of constitutional democracy.

- Standard II.D.4—Evaluate, take, and defend positions on issues in which fundamental values and principles may be in conflict.

- Standard II.D.5—Evaluate, take, and defend positions about issues concerning the disparities between American ideals and realities.

Introductory Exercises

1. Ask students what they think the term "affirmative action" means. Share with them the information from the Historical Background about President Johnson's use of the term.

2. Locate and bring to class examples of job applications, student handbooks, and college applications. Distribute them to students and direct each student to examine the items for any statement related to the implementation of affirmative action. Ask 4 or 5 students to describe the items and read any statement of affirmative action. Ask students if they know why such statements appear on the forms. Inform them that prior to July 2, 1964, such items would not have contained such statements.

Document Analysis

3. Divide students into 8 small groups and provide each group a copy of one of the pages of the featured document. Ask each group to read its page and record the main points. Lead a class discussion on the Civil Rights Act of 1964 by directing one representative from each group to report to the class on the contents of that page. Ask students what the act did and what provisions were included for its enforcement. Also ask students if they think Congress was overly careful in defining terms and why Section 702 included specific definitions.

Standards Correlations for This Lesson	*Teaching Activities for This Lesson*
	Research and Discuss

Research and Discuss

4. Divide students into 4 groups, one to focus on the 1960s, one on the 1970s, one on the 1980s, and one on the 1990s. Require each group to research and design a table "Toward Gender Equality: Public Policy Milestones." Direct them to include congressional, presidential, and judicial actions. Ask students to post tables to each other electronically, using e-mail, or ask one representative from each group to present the table to the class. Conclude this activity by either a. Directing student groups to write an essay, using information from the tables, about how congressional, presidential, and judicial actions taken during the past four decades have influenced gender equality in the workforce, or b. Leading a class discussion on the issues and actions students expect will dominate the next decade. A possible example is women in the military.

Design and Construct a Poll

5. Divide students into two groups and assign each the task of drafting questions for a public opinion poll to determine public attitudes toward affirmative action. Lead a discussion of the questions. Ask: Is each question clear? Is there more than one interpretation? Is there bias? Select the five best questions. Require each student to poll 10 people. For a sample of a poll on this subject, see Gallup, March 1995. Annual published editions of Gallup polls are available in most public and college libraries. Ask students to report their findings to the class.

Standards Correlations for This Lesson	*Teaching Activities for This Lesson*
	Research and Jigsaw Activity
	6. Inform students that in addition to enforcing the Civil Rights Act of 1964, the Equal Employment Opportunities Commission (EEOC) enforces other federal statutes prohibiting discrimination. Provide them a list of the statutes listed in the background essay. Divide students into 8 groups. Direct each group to research their assigned statute and find out what it requires of employers. Direct them to share their information using the jigsaw method.

The writers of this lesson take advantage of the opportunity to examine the affect of the Equal Employment Opportunities Commission (EEOC) by asking students to examine how governmental actions have affected gender equity today and implications for the future. The writers skillfully make clear that gender equity continues to be a major issue. Incidentally, this idea is not applied to the issue of race even though standards cited for this lesson also provide a good opportunity for an in-depth examination of race in contemporary times. For example, the lesson could analyze the consequences of the Civil Rights Act of 1964 in light of current racial relations and the issue of race in the United States. However, the lesson plan does not contain a single direct reference to race. Subsequently, they do not apply the same skill in making obvious that racial discrimination continues to oppress people of color in our society. For example, students are asked to examine affirmative action as a historical event and the poll activity focuses on creating a good poll rather than on the current state of affirmative action policies.

Absence of Struggle

Finally, the three websites neglect to include the stories and narratives that capture the continual struggle against racial discrimination in a society deeply structured by racism. Today people of color and Whites engage in an ongoing battle against racial oppression but evidence of this struggle is missing from the lesson plans on the three most commonly referenced lesson plan websites. Stories and narratives of persons who fought against racial discrimination in the past do exist on the websites. However, these persons are depicted as historical figures and the stories are presented as

historical events limited to that specific time period. The chart below sum-
marizes these figures and stories.

Site	Stories/Persons Directly Presented
Site 1	Reconstruction, Jim Crow, Linda Brown, Immigration, Jackie Robinson
Site 2	The Amistad Case, The Sioux and Treaty of 1868, Henry Garnett and Moses Honner, Black Soldiers in the Civil War, Native Americans and the Dawes Act, Chinese Laborers and the Chinese Boycott Case, 369th Infantry, Japanese Relocation, Enlistment of Navajo Indians, *Brown v. Board of Education*, Jackie Robinson, Martin Luther King, Jr., Civil Rights Act of 1964
Site 3	The Tuskegee Study, Black Towns in the West: the Exodusters, Internment of Japanese Americans: *Korematsu v. United States*, Prelude to Trail of Tears: *Worcester v. Georgia*

The stories and illustrations available do not provide current or recent
accounts of the fight against racism, such as the battles for improved urban
schools and against tracking for special education, Rodney King, and the
OJ Simpson case. This fits within the prevailing thinking among many supporters of racial-neutrality that racial discrimination is a historical event
associated with slavery and Jim Crow legal segregation (Ware, 1996). Furthermore, this line of thinking purports that to the extent racial discrimination exists today, it is isolated and sporadic (Parker, 1998). Consequently,
by omitting current stories and narratives of the struggle, these websites
leave the impression that racial discrimination is a thing of the past.

DISCUSSION

One of the defining elements of Critical Race Theory (CRT) is "racism is
endemic in U.S. society, deeply ingrained legally, culturally, and even psy-
chologically" (Tate, 1997, p. 234). However, the lessons found on the three
commonly referenced secondary United States History lesson plan websites do not reflect this ideology even though race continues to define the
experiences of people of color and racism continues to repress people of
color. Instead, the lessons on these Websites ignore race, except when the
lesson solely focuses on the experiences of people of color. In fact, one
conclusion based on the examination of these websites is that "race matters" (West, 1992), but only for certain topics. The curriculum presented
on these three websites is a culturally specific artifact designed to maintain
a White supremacist master script (Ladson-Billings, 1998). In other words,
people of color are included when we fit into the traditional mainstream

stories. Issues of race are silent for the most part and even when race does come up, it is done within the traditional narrative of United States History. Ladson-Billings states that "this master scripting means stories of African Americans are muted and erased when they challenge dominant culture authority and power" (Ladson-Billings, 1998, p. 18). For example, as Ladson-Billings goes on to state, "Rosa Parks is reduced to a tired seamstress instead of a longtime participant in social justice endeavors and Martin Luther King, Jr., becomes a sanitized folk hero who enjoyed the support of 'good Americans' rather than a disdained scholar and activist whose vision extended to social justice causes throughout the world." In the case of these websites, race is only discussed when race fits into the dominant White supremacist master script. A critical analysis that challenges the White supremacist master script through the lens of race does not occur.

Furthermore, these three commonly referenced secondary United States History lesson plan websites put forth a color-blind or race-neutral premise. This perspective places people of color into a homogenized "we" in celebration of diversity and mistakenly teaches students that the United States is a nation of immigrants (Ladson-Billings, 1998). By putting forth this idea, the varied experiences of groups of color are glossed over and given same status as "every other group" (King, 1992, p. 327). Social studies teachers have the responsibility to challenge this dominant paradigm because traditional interests act to limit and bind the educational opportunities of students of color (Tate, 1997). As the research for this chapter found, the color-blind perspective of the three commonly referenced secondary United States History lesson plan websites fail to challenge this dominant paradigm. Because the websites promote lessons that fail to go beyond the race-neutral premise, teachers have a greater responsibility to dispel this myth. Social studies teachers who understand the pervasiveness of race in education and in society must make racism explicit so that students can recognize and struggle against this particular form of oppression (Ladson-Billings, 1998).

POSSIBLE SOLUTION

The lesson plans available on the Web can serve as invaluable resources for social studies teachers. However, by neglecting critical and multiple perspectives on race, these lesson plans fall short of preparing all students to become active and informed citizens in these diverse United States. I suggest that social studies teachers can overcome this weakness by making race explicit in all lesson plans by teaching about and for multicultural democracy. Before explaining how multicultural democracy can be taught for and about in social studies classrooms, I want to summarize the theory of multi-cultural democracy.

Multicultural Democracy

*They (Americans) are descended from the same ancestors, speaking the same language,
professing the same religion, attached to the same principles of government,
very similar in their manners and customs.*

—John Jay (*The Federalist No. 2*, 1787)

Simply put, this premise is false. The Federalist Papers were papers written by John Jay, Alexander Hamilton, and James Madison, that played an instrumental role, if not the instrumental role, in the ratification of the Constitution in 1789. In these papers, John Jay went on to state that Americans were a "band of brethren." This is not true today nor was it true when John Jay was alive. John Jay, in writing these words, simply chose to ignore the invisible Americans of the time period, such as Native Americans, women, and African slaves. His goal was not to intentionally ignore the status of these groups. Instead, his aim was to approve a document that would overcome the defects of the Confederation and establish a firm national government (Parker, 1996a). Jay accomplished his goal, but at the same time his comments created a misconception that democracy in the United States includes the voices of all Americans. Unfortunately, this misconception still prevails even though such a democracy does not exist. Perry and Fraser (1993) summarize the reality of U.S. liberal representative democracy by stating:

> It is a reality that for most of America's history, women and people of color were not included as full participants in the vision of democracy enunciated by many of the nation's most prominent voices. Our democracy has never been defined effectively as a democratic nation state predicated on a diversity of racial and ethnic origins. (p. 12)

Multicultural democracy, on the other hand, does not ignore diversity. This theory, developed over the last three years, aims to incorporate socioeconomic, cultural, and political democracy. It embraces individual difference, group difference, and political community all at once (Parker, 1996b).

Multicultural democracy begins with the following questions (Parker, 1996b): Who is and is not participating in democracy and on whose terms? And how wide is the path (to participation)? The goal is to ascertain how effectively democracies have resolved the problems posed by socioeconomic and cultural diversity. The questions, respectively, examine the nature of citizens participation and investigate the formal and informal social structures that affect participation. Together they serve as the foundation for the three tenets of multicultural democracy: democracy as a shared path, membership in both large and little publics, and diversity as a strength.

Democracy as a shared path.   Democracy, viewed as a path rather than a destination, is "an ongoing, creative struggle to work out a way of living together fairly, freely, and equally" (Parker, 2001, p. 109). This view welcomes the constant effort that must be put forth and the constant disagreement encountered to move forward on this path. Multicultural democracy holds that citizens share this difficult path of democracy and citizens must be encouraged to work together on that path.

Membership in both large and little publics.   Dewey (1927) recognized the large public as a normative grid that binds citizens together in a broad political, not cultural, comradeship, such as the state. Conversely, little publics are the associations based on religion, sexual orientation, ethnicity, language, race, hobbies, labor, and interests of all sorts (Parker, 1996a). In a multicultural democracy, the large public not only tolerates the little publics but also actively fosters them as a democratic necessity. Multicultural democracy recognizes the importance of its citizens having the liberty to belong to both large and little publics.

Diversity as a strength.   Diversity is a central tenet of multicultural democracy for two simple reasons. First, as Machiavelli claimed, diversity protects liberty and, thereby, is causal in reproducing it (Berlin, 1998). Diversity enables liberty by preventing tyranny of the majority. Factions, as James Madison called them in *The Federalist No. 10*, are groups of citizens "united and actuated by some common impulse of passion or of interest" that is adverse to the rights of other citizens or the common good. They serve to prevent the majority from dominating because they serve as obstacles to uniform goals and actions, thus assuring liberty. Second, diversity challenges the status quo. Groups on the margins serve and continue to serve to criticize current democracy for its unfair policies and actions. By becoming critics, these groups serve to challenge the normative practices and policies of the United States. Diversity among groups helped to create and maintain public spaces of lively debate, boycotts, protests, and dicussions that contested an entrenched status quo (Parker, 2001). This criticism of the dominant viewpoint helped spur changes to improve the lives of all citizens in the U.S. democracy.

Potential Shortfall of Multicultural Democracy

While multicultural democracy holds potential as a more equitable type of democracy, it does have one major potential shortfall. Multicultural democracy is a process that does not have an implementation plan. As a result, other shortcomings are yet to be discovered. However, the promise of multicultural democracy is an improvement on the alternative types currently found.

Even with this potential shortfall, the concept of multicultural democracy holds tremendous promise and must be taught with and about in order to lay the groundwork for such a democracy through multicultural democratic education. In this view, schools have a mission to prepare students for democratic citizenship and are a vehicle for social transformation.

Multicultural democratic education is a combination of democratic *and* multicultural education and aims:

> to improve race relations and to help *all* students acquire the knowledge, attitudes, and skills needed to participate in cross-cultural interactions and in personal, social, and *civic* action that will help make our nation more democratic *and* just. (Banks, 2003, p. x, emphasis added)

Classroom-based Multicultural Democratic Education

Multicultural democratic education begins in the classroom through classroom-based multicultural democratic education. I begin with the classroom based on the idea that true long-lasting change must start in the classroom (Cuban, 1984). Classroom-based multicultural democratic education, a framework I have developed over the last several years, contains three elements: critical pedagogy, building of community, and thorough disciplinary content. These three elements do not exist in isolation of each other. Instead, classroom-based multicultural democratic education requires these elements be incorporated together. The first and third elements, critical pedagogy and thorough disciplinary content, may be used by teachers to foreground race if they choose to incorporate the Web into their teaching.

Critical pedagogy.   Critical pedagogy engages students in social problem solving by enabling them to think about which problems are worth solving, according to whom, to what ends, and in whose favor (Parker, 2001). This critical approach, the first essential principle of classroom-based multicultural democracy, is best suited for teaching about multicultural democracy because this approach lends itself to exploring the essential questions of multicultural democracy, as previously cited: Who is and is not participating and on whose terms? And, how wide is the path (to participation)?

This critical approach begins with the teacher. Students may more easily learn about multicultural democracy if the teacher starts with a critical reconceptualization of democracy. For this to occur, the teacher must allow the lives, histories, and experiences of the diverse socioeconomic and cultural groups, especially those who have been "shortchanged" to play a critical role in the study of multicultural democracy. Socioeconomic and cultural diversity must be studied along with political diversity. This does not mean the simple addition of the voices from various little publics. "This approach is merely additive and leaves the primary stories unchanged" (Perry & Fraser, 1993, p. 19). Instead, critical stories must be told that provide "a much clearer picture of the society's already unequal cultural, economic, and political dynamics" (Apple, 1993, p. 26). Teachers must work to engage students in provocative thinking about the contradictions of U.S. ideals and lived realities. This is important because even though students have a general sense that there have been multiple histories, they seldom hear multiple voices or examine multiple perspectives on events (Hahn, 2001). Teachers must provide students with a critical account of U.S. democracy and, more important, aid students to gain critical thinking skills to learn about multicultural democracy. It is important to note that an additional goal of this critical approach is not to disparage current U.S. democracy but to help students see that U.S. democracy has positive characteristics of its own and these characteristics must be retained in moving toward multicultural democracy.

Finally, the critical approach stresses the importance of conflict, disagreement, and struggle in the path toward multicultural democracy. Students need to learn that this process cannot be achieved without personal and social struggle. This critical approach will best show students that "democracy in its fullest meanings and manifestations is still in the process of being constructed and some degree of conflict is inherent to its continuing development" (Gay, 1997, p. 6). The struggle becomes more crucial in learning about multicultural democracy because, as Dewey (1916) stated, it is by associating and resolving issues with people whose views are different from one's own that democracy is learned.

Social studies teachers, through critical pedagogy, have the ability to use the Web to foreground race. The available lesson plans could serve as resources for teachers. The three commonly referenced secondary United States History lesson plan websites contain numerous invaluable primary documents and other resources that teachers can use as starting points for critical pedagogy. Social studies teachers can use these documents to ask different questions than the ones prescribed on the lesson websites. Instead of asking questions that ignore the racism and its ubiquitous nature, social studies teachers can examine the same documents to focus on what is being privileged, what perspectives are missing, and why. The goal of asking these questions is to encourage students "to consider openly confronting wrongs that afflict their lives, and the lives of others" (Bell, 1994, p. xi).

Unfortunately, this is not an easy task because "the overwhelming majority of teachers employed the technology to sustain existing patterns of teaching rather than to innovate" (Cuban, 2001, p. 134). This fits into the historical pattern of how technology affects teachers and their pedagogy. However, because teachers do use the Web extensively to prepare their work, communicate with their parents, colleagues and students, maintain records, and carry out research (Cuban, 2001), social studies education organizations have a responsibility to create easy to access and implement lesson plan websites that promote critical pedagogy, especially about race.

Building community. This second element of classroom-based multicultural democracy is a participatory approach facilitates teaching about multicultural democracy because students are able to continue their participation in little publics working toward a national civic culture, a large public. Students, for example, are encouraged to engage in discussion and interact socially with other students from different racial, ethnic, cultural, and language groups. Teachers structure interracial cooperative groups that enable students from different racial and ethnic groups to become acquainted as individuals (Banks et al., 2001). Even in homogenous classrooms, based on either race, class, or gender, teachers create cooperative groups that allow students to be seen as individuals, rather than as representatives of a specific group. Furthermore, the building of community begins in the classroom but extends beyond it to the school and the community. There are means of structuring discourse at school in such a way that parents, teachers, students, and administrators are asked to seriously engage a vision of school as a multicultural democracy, asking what this vision means for the total life of the community (Perry & Fraser, 1993). Clearly, the school as a whole goes beyond the context of the individual social studies classroom, but this approach encourages the participation of students and teachers in this process.

Thorough disciplinary content. Thorough disciplinary content element contains two complementary parts. First, this element emphasizes teaching the mainstream academic knowledge, behaviors, and values that reflect views accepted by the subject area or discipline. "Most of the knowledge that constitutes the established canon in the nation's schools, colleges, and universities is mainstream academic knowledge" (Banks, 1995, p. 393). Such knowledge privileges a Euro-centric curriculum. "This approach is politically conservative, valuing stability and common standards of thought and behavior" (Ross, 1997, p. 7). Examples of this approach are the work of Paul Gagnon (1996) and of the committee that produced the *National Standards for Civics and Government* (Center for Civic Education, 1994). Advocates of this approach believe that children should know the past because "historical knowledge is the precondition for political intelligence" (Gagnon, 1996). Quoting Thomas Jefferson,

> History, by apprising them (citizens) of the past, will enable them to judge of the future; it will avail them of the experience of other times and other nations; it will qualify them as judges ... and enable them to know ambition under every disguise it may assume; and knowing it, to defeat its views (p. 243)

Mainstream academic knowledge provides students with the "codes of power" that students need to thrive in schools, colleges, and universities (Delpit, 1989). This belief is a twist on Audre Lorde's notion that one cannot dismantle the master's house with the master's tools (Ladson-Billings, 1998). Thorough disciplinary content is firmly based on the notion that the master's house can only be dismantled with the master's tools.

The most commonly referenced secondary United States History lesson plan websites are ideal for helping students learn mainstream academic knowledge because the lessons are closely aligned to national standards documents, such as the National History Standards and National Standards for Civics and Government, that serve as proxies for mainstream academic knowledge. "The standards that have been created by teams of teachers, administrators, content-level specialists, and policymakers are either too ambitious in what they expect teachers to teach and students to learn, or they are primarily made of factual information—lists of names of historical figures, dates, place names, and cognitively low-level concepts" (Risinger, 2002, p. 233). However, students must learn the content from these proliferating national and state curriculum standards because these standards serve as a basis of high-stakes testing. More and more high stakes tests are being used to determine promotion and graduation, and if teachers want their students to succeed these exams, students should be armed with the necessary mainstream academic knowledge.

In addition to mainstream academic knowledge, thorough disciplinary content also incorporates transformative academic knowledge. "Transformative academic knowledge consists of concepts, paradigms, themes, and explanations that challenge mainstream academic knowledge and that expand the historical and literary canon" (Banks, 1995, p. 394). Students are exposed to multiple perspectives and multiple cases on the subject matter. Content is presented that challenges the notion that traditional interpretations are "universalistic and unrelated to human interests" (Collins, 1990). Teachers provide students with the content that illustrates more the traditional viewpoint. Transformative academic knowledge emphasizes the content that question and critique the standard views accepted by the dominant society.

The "ambitious" nature of these standards, along with vague language used in many of the standards, provide an opportunity for social studies educators to incorporate transformative academic knowledge with mainstream academic knowledge. Educators may use the worldwide library available on the World Wide Web to access lesson plans that foreground multiple viewpoints and perspectives on historical events because the latest research confirms that teachers do use it extensively to prepare their work (Cuban, 2001). One way to accomplish this is through providing lesson plan websites that allow stories, from multiple perspectives, to be told along with the mainstream academic knowledge.

Stories from people of color are an example of transformative academic knowledge that challenges the universal nature of traditional mainstream academic content. Unlike mainstream academic knowledge, stories give "voice" to the experiences of ordinary people. In addition, such stories provide "a way to communicate the experience and realities of the oppressed, a first step in understanding the complexities of racism and beginning a process of judicial redress" (Ladson-Billings, 1998, p. 14). Through this "voice" people of color speak with the experiential knowledge about the fact that our society is deeply structured by racism (Delgado, 1990). As a result, social studies education organizations, such as NCSS, have a responsibility to create lesson plans that incorporate multiple stories, especially from people of color, and promote these websites. Because teachers use the World Wide Web for lesson planning, lesson plans that include multiple stories will make it easier for teachers incorporate these stories into their teaching.

CONCLUSION

Historically educators have turned to new technologies to help solve problems in schools, such as improving pedagogy. The World Wide Web has this potential because it can serve as an information resource for classroom teachers as they transform their pedagogy to better meet the needs of all of their students. The Web can aid educators by facilitating the publication of excellent ready-to-use lesson plans. Unfortunately, based on the research for this chapter, this has not occurred. For example, the most commonly referenced secondary U.S. History lesson plan websites on the Web, while providing access to a wide-range of teaching activities, do not provide excellent lessons because they neglect to include critical and multiple perspectives on race. By neglecting to incorporate critical and multiple perspectives on race, these lesson plans do not adequately prepare students for active democratic citizenship in the diverse United States. As a result of the shortcoming of these websites, teachers become responsible in addressing this fault if they wish to help prepare students to become effective democratic citizens. Teaching about and for multicultural democracy may aid teachers as they guide students for active democratic citizenship.

For this chapter, I turned to the work promoted by social studies education organizations because they aim to help teachers accomplish the goal of "fulfilling the duties of citizenship in a participatory democracy." For example, the mission statement of NCSS, as it appears on the website, states:

> Social studies educators teach students the content knowledge, intellectual skills, and civic values necessary for fulfilling the duties of citizenship in a participatory democracy. The mission of National Council for the Social Studies is to provide leadership, service, and support for all social studies educators. (www.ncss.org)

One way that NCSS and other social studies education organizations can "provide leadership, service, and support for *all* social studies educators" is to promote lesson plan websites which incorporate critical and multiple perspectives on issues, such as race, that affect *all* students. By neglecting critical and multiple perspectives on race, social studies education organizations, unfortunately, are also neglecting to capture the experiences of all groups historically and currently in the United States.

REFERENCES

AAUW. (1992). *How schools shortchange girls.* Washington, DC: American Association of University Women.

Apple, M. (1993). Constructing the "other": Rightist reconstructions of common sense. In C. McCarthy & W. Crichlow (Ed.), *Race, representation and indentity in education.* New York: Routledge.

Apple, M., & Beane, J. (Ed.). (1995). *Democratic schools.* Alexandria, VA: Association for Supervision and Curriculum Development.

Appleby, J. (1992). Recovering America's historic diversity: Beyond exceptionalism. *The Journal of American History, 79*(2).

Banks, J. (1995). Multicultural education and curriculum transformation. *Journal of Negro Education, 64*(4).

Banks, J. (2001). Citizenship education and diversity. *Journal of Teacher Education, 52*(1), 5–16.

Banks, J., Cookson, P., Gay, G., Hawley, W., Irvine, J., Nieto, S., Schofield, J., & Stephan, W. (2001). *Diversity within unity: Essential principles for teaching and learning in a multicultural society.* Seattle: University of Washington Press.

Banks, J. (2003). Series foreword. In W. Parker (Ed.), *Teaching democracy: Unity and diversity in public life.* New York: Teachers College Press.

Barr, R., Barth, J., & Shermis, S. (1977). *Defining the social studies.* Arlington, VA: National Council for the Social Studies.

Bell, D. (1987). *And we are not saved: The elusive quest for racial justice.* New York: Basic Books.

Bell, D. (1992). *Faces at the bottom of the well.* New York: Basic Books.

Bennett, C. (2001). Genres of research in multicultural education. *Review of Educational Research, 71*(2), 171–217.

Berlin, I. (1998). *The propers study of mankind.* New York: Farrar, Straus and Giroux.

Campbell, D. (1996). *Choosing democracy: A practical guide to multicultural education.* Englewood Cliffs, NJ: Prentice-Hall.

Center for Civic Education (1994). *National standards for civics and government.* Calabasas, CA: Center for Civic Education.

Cherryholmes, C. (1980). Social knowledge and citizenship education: Two views of truth and criticism. *Curriculum Inquiry, 10,* 115–151.

Cremin, L. (1989). *Popular education and its discontents.* New York: Harper & Row.

Cuban, L. (1984). *How teachers taught: Constancy and change in American classrooms, 1890–1980.* New York: Longman.

Cuban, L. (2001). *Oversold and underused: Computers in the classroom.* Cambridge, MA: Harvard University Press.

Dahl, R. (1998). *On democracy.* New Haven, CT: Yale University Press.

Delgado, R. (1989). Symposium: Legal storytelling. *Michigan Law Review, 87,* 2073.

Delgado, R. (1990). When a story is just a story: Does voice really matter? *Virginia Law Review, 76,* 95–111.

Delgado, R. (1991). Brewer's plea: Critical thoughts in common cause. *Vanderbilt Law Review, 44,* 1–14.

Delgado, R. (Ed.). (1995). *Critical race theory: The cutting edge.* Phildelphia: Temple University Press.

Delpit, L. (1988). The silenced dialogue: Power and pedagogy in educating other people's children. *Harvard Educational Review, 58,* 280–298.

Democracy's century: A survey of global political change in the 20th century. (1999). New York: Freedom House.

Dewey, J. (1916). *Democracy and education.* New York: Macmillian.

Dewey, J. (1927). *The public and its problems.* Chicago: Swallow.

Diamond, L. (1996). Is the third wave over? *Journal of Democracy, 7*(3), 20–31.

Dietz, M. (1992). Feminism and theories of citizenship. In C. Mouffe (Ed.), *Dimensions of radical democracy* (pp. 62–85). London: Verso.

Dillon, J. (1994). *Using discussion in classrooms.* Buckingham: Open University Press.

Engle, S. (1988). *Education for democratic citizenship: Decision making in the social studies.* New York: Teachers College Press.

Fraser, N. (1993). Rethinking the public sphere: A contribution to the critique of actually existing democracy. In C. Calhoun (Ed.), *Habermas and the public sphere* (pp. 109–142). Cambridge, MA: MIT Press.

Gagnon, P. (1996). History's role in civic education. In W.C. Parker (Ed.), *Educating the democratic mind* (pp. 241–262). Albany: State University of New York Press.

Gay, G. (1997). The relationship between multicultural and democratic education. *The Social Studies, 88*(1), 5–11.

Gould, C. (1996). Diversity and democracy: Representing differences. In S. Benhabib (Ed.), *Democray and difference* (pp. 171–186). Princeton, NJ: Princeton University Press.

Grant, C., & Tate, W. (1995). Multicultural education through the lens of multicultural education research research literature. In J.A. Banks (Ed.), *Handbook of research on multicultural education* (pp. 145–166). New York: Macmillan.

Grossman, P., Wineberg, S., & Woolworth, S. (2001). Toward a theory of teacher community. *Teachers College Record, 103*, 942–1012.

Gutmann, A. (1999). *Democratic education* (2nd ed.). Princeton, NJ: Princeton University Press.

Hahn, C. (1998). *Becoming political: Comparative perspectives on citizenship education.* Albany: State University of New York Press.

Hahn, C. (2001). Democratic understanding: Cross-national perspectives. *Theory Into Practice, 40*(1), 14–22.

Hursh, D. (1997). Multicultural social studies: Schools as places for examining and challenging inequality. In E.W. Ross (Ed.), *The social studies curriculum: purposes, problems, and possibilities* (pp. 107–120). Albany: State University of New York.

Jacobs, J. (1961). *The death and life of great American cities.* New York: Vintage.

King, J. (1992). Diaspora literacy and consciousness in the struggle against miseducation in the Black community. *Journal of Negro Education, 61*, 317–340.

King, J. (1995). Culture centered knowledge: Black studies, curriculum transformation, and social action. In J. A. Banks & C.M. Banks (Ed.), *Handbook of research on multicultural education.* New York: Macmillian.

Ladson-Billings, G. (1995). Toward a theory of culturally relevant pedagogy. *American Educational Research Journal, 32*(465–491).

Ladson-Billings, G. (1997). Crafting a culturally relevant social studies approach. In E.W. Ross (Ed.), *The social studies curriculum: purposes, problems, and possibilities* (pp. 121–136). Albany: State University of New York Press.

Ladson-Billings, G. (1998). Just what is critical race theory and what's it doing in a nice field like education? *Qualitative Studies in Education, 11*(1), 7–24.

Ladson-Billings, G. (2000). Racialized discourses and ethnic epistemologies. In N. Denzin & Y. Lincoln (Ed.), *Handbook of qualitative research* (2nd ed.). Thousand Oaks, CA: Sage.

Ladson-Billings, G., & Tate, W. (1995). Toward a critical race theory of education. *Teachers College Record, 97*, 47–68.

Lowe, L. (1996). *Immigrants acts: On Asian American cultural politics.* Durham, NC: Duke University Press.

Macedo, S. (2000). *Diversity and distrust: Civic education in a multicultural democracy.* Cambridge, MA: Harvard University Press.

National Council for the Social Studies. (2002). *www.ncss.org.* [2002, June 7].

National Council for the Social Studies. (2001). *Social Education, 65*(5), 258–326.

National Council for the Social Studies. (2001). Teaching about technology. *Social Education, 65*(6), 330–392.

National Council for the Social Studies. (2001). Reflections in a time of crisis. *Social Education, 65*(7), 394–464.

National Council for the Social Studies. (2002). Cases, controversy, and the court. *Social Education, 66*(1), 2–72.

National Council for the Social Studies. (2002). *Social Education, 66*(2), 74–136.

National Council for the Social Studies. (2002). Teaching with tech. *Social Education, 66*(3), 138–190.

Newmann, F., Secada, W., & Wehlage, G. (1995). *A guide to authentic instruction and assessment: Vision, standards and scoring*. Madison: Wisconsin Center for Education Research.

Okihiro, G. (1994). *Margins and mainstreams: Asians in American history and culture.* Seattle: University of Washington Press.

Oliver, D., & Shaver, J. (1966). *Teaching public issues in the high school.* Boston: Houghlin-Mifflin Co.

Parker, L. (1998). "Race is … race ain't": an exploration of the utility of critical race theory in qualitative research in education. *Qualitative Studies in Education, 11*(1), 43–55.

Parker, W. (1996). "Advanced" ideas about democracy: toward a pluralist conception of citizen education. *Teachers College Record, 98*(1), 104–125.

Parker, W. (1996b). Curriculum for democracy. In R. Soder (Ed.), *Democracy, education, and the schools* (pp. 182–210). San Francisco: Jossey-Bass.

Parker, W. (1997). Navigating the unity/diversity tension in education for democracy. *The Social Studies, 88*(1), 12–17.

Parker, W. (1997). Democracy and difference. *Theory and Research in Social Education, 25*(2), 220–235.

Parker, W. (2001). Toward enlightened political engagement. In W.B. Stanley (Ed.), *Critical issues in social studies research* (pp. 97–118). Greenwich, CT: Information Age Press.

Perry, T., & Fraser, J. (1993). Reconstructing schools as multiracial/multicultural democracies. In T. Perry & J.W. Fraser (Ed.), *Freedom's plow: Teaching in the multicultural classroom.* New York: Routledge.

Phillips, A. (1993). *Democracy and difference.* University Park: Pennsylvania State University Press.

Risinger, C. (2002). Two different worlds: The dilema facing social studies teachers. *Social Education, 66*(4), 231–233.

Ross, E. (1997). The struggle for the social studies curriculum. In E.W. Ross (Ed.), *The social studies curriculum: Purposes, problems, and possibilities* (pp. 3–20). Albany: State University of New York Press.

Ross, E. (Ed.). (1997). *The social studies curriculum: Purposes, problems, and possibilities.* Albany: State University of New York Press.

Schlesinger, A. (1991). *The disuniting of America.* New York: Norton.

Sen, A. (1999). Democracy as a universal value. *Journal of Democracy, 10*(3), 3–17.

Singer, A. (1997). *Social studies for secondary schools : Teaching to learn, learning to teach.* Mahwah, NJ: L. Erlbaum.

Singer, A. (1999). Teaching multicultural social studies in an era of political eclipse. *Social Education, 63*(1), 28–30.

Stanley, W., & Nelson, J. (1994). The foundations of social education in historical context. In R. Martusewicz & W. Reynolds (Ed.), *Inside/out: Contemporary critical prespectives in education* (pp. 266–284). New York: St. Martin's Press.

Survey on democracy. (1996, December 12, 1996). *The Economist, 341,* S1-S14.

Tate, W. (1997). Critical race theory and education: History, theory and implications. *Review of Research in Education, 22,* 191–243.

Torres, C. (1998). *Democracy, education, and multiculturalism.* Lanham, MD: Rowman & Littlefield Publishers, Inc.

Touraine, A. (1998). *What is democracy?* (D. Macey, Trans.). Boulder, CO: Westview Press.

Tyack, D., & Cuban, L. (1995). *Tinkering toward utopia: A century of public school reform.* Cambridge, MA: Harvard University Press.

Valli, L. (1997). Listening to other voices: A description of teacher reflection in the United States. *Peabody Journal of Education, 72,* 67–88.

Ware, L. (1996). Tales from the crypt: Does strict scrunity sound the death knell for affirmative action in higher education? *Journal of College and University Law, 23,* 43–90.

West, C. (1992, August 2). Learning to talk of race. *New York Times Magazine, 24,* 26.

CHAPTER 13

TECHNOLOGY, RACE CONSCIOUSNESS AND THE OPPRESSOR

A Plea for the Performative[1]

Michael J. Zambon

ABSTRACT

Oppositional narratives by people of color are intended to challenge the mind-set members of the dominant group have toward issues of injustice and social inequity. Pre-service teacher education students often respond to the lived experiences of these counterstories by using technology such as email, listservs, or online journals. Definitions of technology in education courses continue to exclude alternative practices for majority-race readers to use when examining the relationship between racial privilege and oppression. A performative approach to technology, with its emphasis on the visual and performing arts, offers educators a new set of resources to critique narratives that maintain the status quo.

Critical Race Theory Perspectives on the Social Studies, pages 271–290
Copyright © 2003 by Information Age Publishing

In a graduate course on multicultural education, an audiotaped interview of an African American man discussing his life's experiences was played for the class. Students were also provided with a written transcript of the recording to read while they listened to the tape. What I remember most vividly about this activity was the profound silence that engulfed the classroom at the end of the recording. What could one say after experiencing such an emotional, and often painful recounting of the injustices this man witnessed as a person of color? For the White students in the class, myself included, at that moment, it seemed that there were no words or responses that could adequately address a perspective of society in the United States that "we" could only imagine, yet never truly comprehend. I left the class that day struggling to find a way to express my emotions and feelings where words, both spoken and written, failed me. In the years since, I have often wondered how my reaction to this powerful narrative would have differed had the class been presented with only the transcript, and not the taped recording.

INTRODUCTION

For critical race theorists and scholars, narratives by people of color are the *sine qua non* to challenge legal and academic discourses that perpetuate oppression and social inequity in the United States. It has been more than a decade since Delgado (1989) first made his plea for narratives as a means by which individuals of historically marginalized groups could document and circulate their experiences and realities of oppression. These narratives, whether in the form of stories, chronicles, or counterstories, were intended to provide alternative perspectives to societal injustices regularly elided from mainstream analyses of legal discourses. While attempting to create shared understandings and meanings between outgroups and aiming to subvert reality, oppositional stories were also meant to challenge the "mindset by which members of the dominant group justify the world as it is" (Delgado, 1995, p. 64). Directed at a group not accustomed to examining the relationship between privilege and oppression, stories by people of color are meant to effect the "oppressor" by "catelyze[ing] the necessary cognitive conflict to jar dysconscious racism"[2] (Ladson-Billings & Tate, 1995, p. 58). After reading a narrative, the intended effect upon the majority-race reader is suggested to occur as follows:

> The story invites the reader to alienate herself or himself from the events described [and] enter into the mental set of the teller, whose view is different from the reader's own. The oppositional nature of the story, the manner in which it challenges and rebuffs the stock story, thus causes him or her to oscillate between poles. (Delgado, 1995, p. 73)

The dissonance or conflict generated from the "oscillation" between the world of the dominant group and that of the storyteller will hopefully lead the reader to re-evaluate, question, and challenge those narratives that maintain the status quo and social inequity. While critical race theorists (Delgado, 1989; Ladson-Billings & Tate, 1995) have emphasized the importance of narratives by people of color and alluded to their potential effect on the majority-race reader, for individuals who cannot operate from "a standpoint epistemology that sees the world from the point of view of oppressed persons of color" (Denzin, 2000, p. 910), critical race theory has not offered a "space" by which members of the dominant group can create/perform/construct/respond to the powerful voices in these narratives.

In pre-service teacher education programs, an undergraduate student's initial experience with oppositional narratives often occurs in courses that recognize voices of people of color as crucial for "a more complete analysis of the educational system" (Ladson-Billings & Tate, 1995, p. 58). In response to these articles, students are often required to write or "post" a reflection using email, listservs, or on-line reflective journals (Bennett & Pye, 1998). These responses can be either incorporated into class discussions or used by the instructor to assess the degree of oscillation and critical consciousness on the part of the reader. This practice, which has not changed significantly in its basic premise despite rapid advances in computer hardware and software, appears to be associated with a belief that these stories are in themselves the "cure" to "shatter the complacency" majority-race students have toward issues of race and injustice (Delgado, 1995). Even where technology was used to support a methods course entitled "teaching for social justice," there continued to be a disproportionate emphasis on the use of email, listservs, web searches, and videoconferencing as technologies students use to respond to class readings (Beyerbach & Russo, 2001). In having students respond to these voices via text, the assumption embedded in this practice is that over the duration of a course or a pre-service teacher education program, students, particularly majority-race readers, will develop a more acute awareness and critique of societal inequities. However, given the often-defensive reactions on the part of readers to these stories (Delgado, 1995), an examination of the practices by which majority-race readers address the lived experiences and perspectives of these stories, is required.

In addition to narratives, people of color have used "performative" practices, with their emphasis on the non-narrative and nonverbal ways of knowing, to create a critical race consciousness in which to implement critical race theory. Through a range of performative practices, such as film, photography, music, and dance, Denzin (2000) argues that a feminist, Chicano/a and black performance-based aesthetic can be used to criticize and resist racist cultural practices. Despite Blocker's (1999) caveat that "in the rush to visibility, minorities and women can become victim to their own public representations, which contributes to, rather than subvert, dominant ideologies," oppressed groups have employed a variety of technologies, whether in paintings by Basquiat[3] (Hoban, 1998), documentary film (Riggs, 1989; Tajiri, 1991), sound portraits (Isay, Jones, & Newman, 1993) or performance ethnography (Smith, 1993, 1994) to "make visible" their impressions and perspectives of oppression and inequity. This shift from the narrative to the performative has also been used to broaden the dialogue and debate surrounding postcolonialism and multicultural theory (Dimitriadis & McCarthy, 2001), where the visual arts are seen as offering educators "a rich new set of resources for thinking about issues and concerns that seem ever more beyond their grasp and control" (p.16). However, even where the performative is viewed as "a complement, alternative, supplement and critique of inscribed texts" (Conquergood, 1991, p. 191), little attention has dealt with the issue of how educators and students are to respond to the issues and concerns embedded within these performances.

In this chapter, I argue that the next step on the road to justice requires a more "active" role for all readers of oppositional narratives, particularly majority-race readers, in pre-service teacher education programs. The disproportionate emphasis on the practice of having students in undergraduate courses respond to these oppositional stories with email or listservs has muted a more profound examination of issues related to race and social inequity on the part of the reader. In addition, viewing technology through principally a "narrative" lens by instructors has precluded the exploration of alternative, non-discursive practices that students may use to communicate their awareness of the complex issues associated race and education in the United States. In the same manner that Delgado (1989) made his plea for narratives by people of color, this chapter makes a plea for the use of the performative as a practice by which majority-race readers can respond and be held accountable to the voices of the oppressed as a means to develop a more critical race consciousness.

THE PERFORMATIVE: AT THE INTERSECTION OF PERFORMATIVITY AND PERFORMANCE

Most readily associated with performance studies, the term performance began to float "free of theater precincts" (Diamond, 1996) and circulate within critical and academic discourses during the 1970s as a way "to name a new visual art form and to distinguish dramatic scripts from performances on-stage" (McCall, 2000, p. 421), where it is seen to embrace a myriad of practices, ranging from the stage to festival and everything in between, which could include film, photography, television, computer simulation, music, performance art, political demonstrations, health care, cooking, fashion, and shamanistic ritual. For ethnographers, where "texts-as-performances" challenge the meanings of lived experience, performance is an interpretive event grounded in the presence of live bodies and that consists of a rehearsed or improvised creative set of activities, with a beginning, middle, and end, and which are performed for the benefit of an audience and the performers (Denzin, 1997). These performances, according to Phelan (1993) are "ontologically nonreproductive" and can only implicate the "real" through the presence of living bodies:

> In performance art spectatorship there is an element of consumption: there are no left-overs, the gazing spectator must try to take everything in. Without a copy, live performance plunges into visibility—in a manically charged present—and disappears into memory, into the realm of invisibility and the unconscious where it eludes regulation and control. (1993, p. 148)

Any attempt to document or reproduce these events, whether through video, photographs, or multimedia technology, would cease to render the event as a performance. This paradox between performance and reproducibility is reflected in performative documentary, which is intended to "generate a distinct tension between performance and document, between the personal and the typical, embodied and disembodied" (Nichols, 1994, p. 97). By their deflection away from "traditional" documentaries, with their emphasis for persuasive arguments about the historical world, performative documentaries such as Sari Red[4] (Pratibha, 1988), Tongues Untied[5] (Riggs, 1988), and History and Memory[6] (Tajiri, 1991), are characterized by a shift of emphasis toward the poetic, the expressive, and the rhetorical. With their departures from the search for a master narrative and questioning of realist epistemologies via their stylized and evocative nature, these documentaries promote a social subjectivity within the viewer that remains unattached to a logical explanation, invoking "an epistemology of moment, memory and place, more than of history and epoch" (Nichols, 1994, p.102).

In contrast to the poetic and rhetorical, Butler (1990) views performance as not acting, but as a repetition of disempowered acts, gestures, enactments which are performative in the sense that the essence or identity that they otherwise purport to express are "fabrications" created by normative and/or regulatory discourses (1990, p. 60). Gender is seen as a stylized repetition of acts through time and not a seemingly seamless identity. Identity is an illusion of repeated performances, which must be understood as a process, an ongoing discursive practice that produces the appearance of substance and the illusion of origins that break down the dichotomy between culturally intelligible and unintelligible identities.

Gender, and therefore identity, is "performatively constituted by the very expressions that are said to be its results" (p. 25). Butler's notion of performativity, with its emphasis on repetition, has also served as a foundation for an examination of the construction of racial identities (Fuller, 1996; Mirón & Inda, 1997) and more recently, to examine the "postcolonial" relationship between ideology and English language policy (Pennycook, 2000). In order to begin the process of defining the term performative, it is necessary to examine its relationship to, and intersection with, notions of performance and "performativity."

While the term *performative* has been associated with linguistics and cultural studies (Austin, 1962), "communication" (Derrida, 1986), a political prevision (Bourdieu, 1991), cultural difference and the nation state (Bhabha, 1994), the Holocaust (Patraka, 1999), hypertext environments (Odin, 1998) and the pedagogical (Giroux & Shannon, 1997), since the 1980s and early 1990s, the term has become increasingly associated with a genre of qualitative research, termed performative ethnography, which involves the process of turning ethnographic field notes and interviews into poems, short stories, scripts and dramas that are read and performed before audiences (Denzin, 1997). However, the development of additional theoretical relationships with the performative, as evidenced from the preceding examples, provide a number of interesting perspectives from which to conceptualize a rationale for the use of performative practices as they relate to the presentation of oppositional narratives in teacher education programs and courses. For example, in terms of the pedagogical, performative practices are viewed as "transgressive, interdisciplinary, and oppositional" and as "connected to a wider public project to increase the scope of racial, economic, and social justice" (Giroux & Shannon, 1997, p. 2). More than simply opening up texts that have occupied a "formalistic space," the performative is the process of creating/performing/constructing that involves the "negotiation between a doing (a reiteration of norms) and a thing done (discursive conventions that frame our interpretations)," and in so doing, gives "access to cultural meanings and critique" (Diamond, 1996. p. 5). By having students use a range of technologies and performances that emphasize "artworks as social practice of the performances of everyday life and culture," where "liminality is emphasized over legibility and change over fixity," the actions of the performative, in a similar manner to critical race theory, may be plotted "within a grid of power relationships" (Blocker 1999, p. 24). In doing so, analysis and critique of the power relationships that maintain and perpetuate social inequity can be explored through the creation of documentary films, photographs, paintings, theater, political protests, and performance art in a way that differs from narrative and offers the majority-race reader the possibility for an examination of the relationship between the "self" and the "other" (Phelan, 1993, p. 4).

Just as importantly, as Patraka (1999) has noted in her exploration of the Holocaust performative, where theater and performance texts work to situate the event, performative practices must also be accountable to the "struggle between history and its representation, between desire and loss, and between the unmanageable and the manageable" (1999, p. 7). In an analogous way, a "critical race performative" would demand and expect a notion of accountability on the part of majority-race readers to the challenges of racial inequity and just as importantly, to the lived experiences and struggles of people of color in the narratives they read. These performative acts, as hooks (1994) notes, in providing a space for "everyone to become more and more engaged, to become active participants in learning" (hooks, 1994, p.11), enable educators to "engage audiences" in ways currently not available within current notions, definitions and uses of technology in teacher education programs.

TECHNOLOGY AND UNIVERSITY METHODS COURSES

The decision to incorporate the use of multimedia technology in a social studies methods class was based on a review of the literature on information technology in teacher education programs. The emphasis in undergraduate courses on word-processing, email, listservs, Internet searches, educational software analysis, and the evaluation and design of web sites (Bennett & Pye, 1998; Beisser, 1999; Beyerbach & Russo, 2001) is primarily to facilitate the distribution and communication of information, such as responses to class reading, online discussions about topics relevant to the teaching environment or to share lists of web sites compiled by students. This current use of technology, however, has not changed significantly since similar examples were documented in a review of technology and teacher education in the early 1990s (Brooks & Kopp, 1991). While examples of the use of technology in methods courses have included the integration of computer simulations and databases in social studies or hypermedia/multimedia programs to create teaching materials or support instruction in science (Willis & Mehlinger, 1996, pp. 496–497), no examples were found in the literature were students used technology to create a presentation documenting their understandings and experiences with critical social issues.[7]

In addition, this enhanced role of information technology in the course was in response to surveys of teacher education programs which found that "methods courses seem be particularly tough to integrate technology" (Bruder, 1989, p.33) and to the statements that "most pre-service teachers know very little about effective uses of technology in education" and that "there is a pressing need to increase substantially the amount and quality of instruction teachers receive about technology" (Willis & Mehlinger, 1996, p. 978). Informal conversations with teacher education students prior to the start of the course revealed that their experiences with technology were generally limited to the use of email and word-processing, despite the availability of free workshops on instructional technology on campus and the wide range of software for graphic, video and multimedia production.

The goal of using the Microsoft's PowerPoint® in a social studies methods course was to not only complement the use of Blackboard®, an online course management system which allows students to access course information and document, view announcements and participate in class discussions on course readings, but more importantly, to have students begin to view technology from a different aesthetic and framework. This shift in approach, where students were being required to use technology to create or construct with, rather than respond to, initially resulted in a majority of students becoming somewhat anxious about the assignment. Although the experience of "letting go" of a narrative approach to technology in order to design a presentation that emphasized visual and auditory was a novel experience for most students, the majority of the class expressed a keen interest in acquiring the necessary skills to use the software effectively. Not surprisingly, there were also a few students who were already familiar with the software and were able to share their expertise with their peers.

The presentations were based on information students had acquired in the design of literature sets and units on a topic relevant to the social studies. In addition to the requirement of demonstrating a minimum level of competency with PowerPoint®, students had to structure a presentation with a minimum of 10 slides that included text, but just as importantly, images and video from a range of sources where available. Each presentation also had to be accompanied by a piece of music to be played when the projects were shared with the entire class. Although more than 150 presentations were produced over the course of three semesters, for the purposes of this chapter, a qualitative analysis of only three presentations by three majority-race readers is included.

PRESENTATIONS AS A PERFORMATIVE PRACTICE

I think we have to come prepared to look at an issue and say, there are more things happening.... (Matthew, undergraduate student)

Toward a More Perfect Union?

As the title of the presentation appears, "Toward a More Perfect Union?" set against a blue background, the United States Flag waves and a rendition of the Star-Spangled Banner by Jimi Hendrix begins to play. With red, white, and blue as text and background colors, images of early America, including the signers of the Constitution, are presented. As the anthem starts to deviate from a "traditional" playing, the background colors become less patriotic as images and text begin to focus on the disparity between the words in the Constitution and the treatment of historically marginalized groups. When the playing reaches its most dissonant, the presentation returns to the Constitution and looks at Article V, which allows for amendments to be made. On a black background, the final slide highlights the 13th, 15th, and 19th amendments. As the title reappears, "Toward a More Perfect Union?", this time without the question mark, the United States flag is once again visible, but superimposed on the three amendments.

For Matthew,[8] an actor and writer of children's literature who described himself as one of the oldest students in the pre-service teacher education program, the opportunity to create a presentation that was "film-driven" was an experience he had been waiting to do. Given his background in the arts, he immediately saw the potential of this technology, with its capability to animate objects and to make things move, as one that would interest kids. In designing the presentation as part of a 5th grade unit on the U.S. Constitution, he wanted to explore the theme of how language in government documents, such as the Preamble and the Bill of Rights, was contradictory to what was occurring to non-dominant groups in the United States at the time. He sought to highlight the discrepancies between words such as "freedom," "equality," "social welfare," and "domestic tranquility" by demonstrating through images and text that these civil liberties were not extended to all groups. He chose Jimi Hendrix' rendition of the "Star Spangled Banner" since it not only represented an alternative perspective and interpretation of the national anthem in its playing, but also contributed to a dissonance between images and text. The selection not only challenged the "mythological foundations of America," but at the same time conveyed the "fractured" nature of U.S. society as witnessed by an individual outside the mainstream. In examining the intersection between "race" and the Constitution, he sought to move beyond a black/white binary and to "open" up the concept in order to include other historically marginalized groups. More importantly, he wanted to convey a sense of tension embedded in the notion of a "perfect union" and the amendments made in response to political changes. The inclusion of multiple perspectives, for Matthew, is a fundamental component that social studies teachers need to examine when designing presentations for their students, or when having students design and create their own presentation.

During his first year of teaching in a 5th grade classroom, he was able to use the technical and critical skills developed from his initial presentation to work with groups of students to create presentations that compared and contrasted the representation of Columbus in two school textbooks. Through a juxtaposition of images and text, students began to notice that the contemporary textbook included more images and perspectives of indigenous peoples than in the older text. Given more time to examine the issue, he would have had students examine the connection between the change in representations of Native Peoples and the American Indian Movement of the 1960s and 1970s. However, this use of technology to contrast images did open up a "space" for students in which to become sensitive to the representation of non-dominant groups. The presentation was shared at a conference on storytelling, which provided students with the opportunity to discuss and share their critiques and observations of the information in a wider forum with students from different schools.

> I write about them [political and social issues] all the time, but nobody reads what I write.... (Samantha, undergraduate student)

Civil Liberties in Times of Fear and War

The tone of the presentation "Civil Liberties in Times of Fear and War" is established with an opening quote by U.S. Supreme Court Justice William O. Douglas: "Restriction of free thought and free speech is the most dangerous of all subversions. It is the one un-American act that could most easily defeat us." In a bold white font set against a black background, the title of the slide "Then" begins a section that moves from the Sedition Act and Espionage Act passed during World War I, to the founding of the ACLU, the internment of Japanese-Americans during WWII, ending with the McCarthy hearings of the 1950s. The faded, yellow political cartoons contribute to the historicity of the section. Throughout the slides, the words "un-American," "dissent," "unpatriotic," and "un-loyal" stand in sharp contrast to the surrounding text. In leading to the contemporary section, "Now," one immediately notices the sharpness and clarity of the political cartoons after 9/11. The words that stand away from the text focus on the U.S. Patriot Act and its potential adverse effects on civil liberties while suggesting that one should not act blindly to pressure and in the end, "Don't Give Up!" The final slide of the presentation ends with an adaptation of the quote by Rev. Martin Niemoeller.[9]

According to Samantha, a self-described social activist, her primary motivation for using this technology was to design a presentation that would give her the opportunity of directing the topic of civil rights at individuals in the class who had grown "tired of listening to her" analyses and critiques, and that no matter what comments she had to offer, either in class or in responses to journal articles, there were some students who were never going to read what she wrote. Thinking about her fellow students as the audience helped her to not only focus on what content to include, but to structure the presentation in a way to achieve her goal of influencing her peers:

> I think that that's actually where I do most of my political action is in terms of trying to make the people around me, that I have day-to-day contact with, think about things in a different way. I think I'm pretty good at it … you know, that when they see something or they hear something, that in the back of their head, they'll have that idea.

The idea to focus on civil rights as the theme of her presentation arose not only in response to political events in the United States following September 11, 2001, where it seemed that "people were willing to give up their civil rights without any notion of the historical or political context," but from her examining a number of Supreme Court cases dealing with freedom of speech while working on a Master's degree as a graduate student. Yet, having only seen one PowerPoint® presentation, that in her words, "was not very creative," one of her challenges and concerns in the design of the presentation was in making the topic of dissent visual. Having collected a number of political cartoons since graduate school, she decided to use these evocative and informative drawings as a way to communicate an idea in a short amount of time and convey the notion: "Here we go again!" In selecting an instrumental piece to accompany the text and images, she looked for music that would not distract from the text, yet leave the audience with an ominous and sad impression, as though "doom was approaching." Although her initial opinion of the technology was not favorable, while doing the layout of the presentation and deciding on the particular order in which to present images, she discovered that the software could be used in an "evocative and provocative way" and that it was much more communicative than by simply placing pictures on a flat piece of paper.

> It was a perfect format for doing what I was trying to do, which was just to introduce an issue to show how people became angered by it, upset by it, and decided to change it. (Kathy, undergraduate student)

Untitled

With instructions informing us that we are about to go "back into the past" to see images of children working in the United States between 1880 and 1920, the non-titled presentation on child labor begins. The first series of slides contain only a single black-and-white photograph taken by the photographer Lewis W. Hine[10] of children working under various conditions. The next series of slides contain both a single image and a single line of text. This pattern of text and photograph on a series of slides is interrupted and alternates with a short series of photographs without commentary. After almost 40 slides, one is informed that "people" became angry about the working conditions of children and the final set of images highlights the way in which people organized to protest this social problem. The presentation ends with a poster entitled "Making Human Junk" and the audience is asked to think about what the image means.

Despite having little experience with labor movements in the United States, for Kathy, her collaboration on a unit dealing with this issue with another student prompted her to choose this theme. In describing her previous experience with technology as "really difficult," the use of PowerPoint® afforded her the opportunity to create a presentation that was "artistic." By designing slides with the minimum amount of text, one of her goals was to let these powerful images "speak for themselves." Given that her target audience was going to be upper elementary students, and conscious of the presence of second-language learners in the classroom, she wanted to make the text accessible to everyone. The images selected were considered sufficiently thought-provoking that addition of any detailed descriptions to images was felt to detract from the "feeling" and "emotional response" students might have. This awareness to not trivialize the experiences of children represented in the images was also reflected in her choice of music: an instrumental guitar piece, whose tempo changed to coincide with the progressive movement of the images toward activism. When questioned about the lack of a diverse representation in the photographs, she responded that while she found some images with children of color, the ones she did find were not related to the theme, and therefore, not used. One reaction that did surprise her was from two fifth-grade students, originally from Mexico, who began to discuss the living conditions of many children in contemporary Latin America and compare those descriptions to the historical representations of child labor in the presentation.

TOWARD A PEDAGOGY OF PERFORMATIVE PRACTICE

From the presentations and subsequent interviews with these three major-ity-race readers, it became evident that approaching the use of technology from a performative framework offered these students a 'space' in which to address their construct and perform their topic while also providing the possibility for individuals from the dominant group to not speak directly about issues of oppression and social inequity, but as Minh-ha (1982) advo-cates, to "speak" nearby. Given the emphasis of critical race theory on the use of narrative by people of color, for individuals who operate from a standpoint epistemology that see the world from the point of view of the oppressor, there is an inherent limitation in attempting to use text as the only means by which to respond to the lived experiences of the oppressed and for the reader to "make visible" their thinking about complex issues and concerns, such as race and education, that seem ever more beyond their grasp and control (Dimitriadis & McCarthy, 2001). As the presenta-tion on child labor demonstrates, when the ability to speak directly to as issue is limited by narrative, the use of non-discursive forms, such as photo-graphs and images, can "resist, exceed, and overwhelm the constraints and strictures of writing" (Conquergood, 1991, p. 193), and thus give the reader the opportunity of speaking "nearby" an issue that had not been possible with text alone. With their wide variety of visual, aural, and dynamic practices and "polyphonous form of representation" (Jarmon, 1996, p. 11), these performative practices can be viewed as a supplement and alternative to conventional approaches to technology, such as digital or computer technology, which continue to be defined through a predom-inantly narrative perspective. By viewing specific examples of technology through a performative lens, a much wider and varied range of responses becomes available for instructors to use when attempting to gauge the crit-ical consciousness of their students. More importantly, the production of these cultural texts provide spaces that "enable multiple ways of speaking and acting as part of the ongoing engagement with the critical issues of identity, agency, and democracy" (Giroux & Shannon, 1997, p. 5).

While the emphasis of information technology in teacher education has continued to be defined through the use of computers (Brooks & Kopp, 1991; Willis & Mehlinger, 1996) and peripheral hardware and software, such as digital equipment, that support their use (Mehlinger & Powers, 2002), performative practices may also include, but are not limited to, a range of 'older' technologies. Examples of these technologies might include the use of tape recorders to produce an audio documentary (http://www.soundportraits.org/), the use of 16 mm "white-leader" film (Apple, 1993), or analog video camcorders (Juhasz, 1993). Instructors and students should view a performative approach to technology as both "a method of discovery and means of demonstration" (Gray & VanOosting, 1996, p. 37). For those who have traditionally "observed" the oppression of historically marginalized groups, in the process of designing a response to the complex issues of education, they themselves may discover "gaps" and inconsistencies in dominant narratives that maintain the fundamental structural inequalities in society. Additionally, undergraduate students in teacher education programs may discover that the performative offers them the possibility for presenting issues in an "evocative and provocative way" that differs from narrative.

A performative response challenges the belief that the "oscillation" experienced by majority-race readers occurs only in response to narratives by people of color (Delgado, 1989) and that in demonstrating their under-standing of these complex societal issues, majority-race readers can con-tribute to this cognitive conflict or dissonance. By assuming that the depth of critical consciousness does not vary across significantly individuals within the dominant group, critical race theory has limited the opportunity for majority-race readers to impact the perspective and critical conscious-ness of other individuals. As Samantha has demonstrated, her primary motivation in learning how to construct a presentation with the software was to use her experiences and analyses of political institutions in ways to get people around her, in this case other majority-race readers, to "think about things in a different way." While one must recognize that individuals from the dominant group can never transcend the epistemology of the oppressor, the possible impact and contribution similar students can make to the critical race project, cannot be underestimated. Therefore, the project of oscillating the critical race consciousness of majority-race read-ers is one that must be conceived of, and directed from, a multidirectional, rather than unidirectional, approach.

Despite reading and responding to a number of journal articles and oppositional narratives throughout the course, and having taken a course on multicultural education the previous semester, only a handful of stu-dents attempted to examine their issue from a critical race consciousness in their multimedia presentations. In the presentation on child labor, for example, perspectives and images were not included due to the suggestion that such resources did not "fit" or were unavailable. While analogous rep-resentations and examples might have been sought, their absence from the presentation suggests the ease with which issues of race can be elided from the discourses of social injustice. Rather than attributing this to an absence of consciousness about race, given the number of readings, listserv and classroom discussions over the duration of the course, the uncritical way in which the majority of students examined their topic may be indicative of what King (1991) refers to as dysconscious racism, that is "a form of racism that tacitly accepts White norms and privileges. It is ... an impaired consciousness or distorted way of thinking about race as compared to, for example, critical consciousness" (p. 135). Additional factors which may have contributed to this "absence" may have been structural, that is, that the majority of the oppositional narratives were read and discussed at the beginning of the course while the projects were not due, or presented, until the end of the semester. Due to the limited amount of time available at the end of semester, there was often little time after the presentation for students to discuss their reactions to, and readings of, these performances. Yet, the fact that some students were able to demonstrate not only a critical consciousness about race in their presentations, but also make visible to other members of the dominant group the "distorted" ways in which racial privilege is perpetuated, suggests that the "performative" may provide individuals an opportunity to document their "impaired consciousness" that is unavailable to them in a textual form. Although Phelan (1993) would argue against the reproducibility of these performances, these "documents," whether as multimedia presentations, artwork, photographs or dance, can be used for an ongoing analysis and critique of the critical consciousness of the oppressor and their ability to challenge racial inequity. As Becker (1997) notes, "once work is hung on a wall, placed on a floor, projected into a space in public view, performed, its statement becomes part of the public sphere, the public discourse, and is subject to all the strengths and limitations of the society it has entered" (p. 23).

CONCLUSION

I have often thought about how I would have responded as a majority-race reader to the audiotaped interview presented in that graduate course. While this was one of my first encounters with an oppositional story by a person of color from within the boundaries of the United States, I have had numerous experiences in my travels where I have been the privileged recipient of personal stories and realities from marginalized and oppressed peoples in Asia, Latin America and the Caribbean. Always emotional, and sometimes painful, these narratives have also provided me opportunities to examine my own degree of critical race consciousness from both a local and global perspective. In many instances, I have only reflected on the stories. However, there have been opportunities where I have created aesthetic representations of these experiences as a way for me to both work through the issues embedded within these stories and to reflect on my own awareness between oppression and racial privilege. Although the examples of performative practices in this chapter focused only on the use of computers and multimedia authoring software, I envision undergraduate students in teacher education courses one day using a range of technologies, in collaboration with a number of academic disciplines, to create/perform/construct visual representations and performances as responses to the lives and experiences by people of color they have read about. It is hoped that with each brush stroke, shaping of clay, and choreography, the majority-race reader will be in a constant and sustained dialogue between their own race consciousness and the stories of the marginalized and oppressed.

This chapter sought to extend the concept of narratives offered by Delgado (1989) by examining the ways readers in teacher education programs, particularly majority-race readers, use technology to respond to these "authentic voices of people of color" (Ladson-Billings & Tate, 1995, p. 58). While there is value in having students acquire skills with email, listservs, and analyzing software, the lived experiences and realities embedded in these counterstories, revisionist histories, or parables by people of color require and demand a more profound response, a "doing," on the part of the reader. Current approaches to the use of information technology by university faculty, graduate students and instructors in teacher education programs must be supplemented with practices which enable the reader to not only address the alternative perspectives and realities of the oppressed through visual forms, such as photographs, film, or art, but just as importantly, to use these performances to evaluate and critique their own mis/understanding and critical consciousness of issues related to race and inequity in the United States. By viewing students in pre-service teacher education programs as "artists" rather than simply "intellectuals,"[11] these performative practices not only "open up" a space for the use of a wider range of technologies, but more important, offers the majority-race reader alternative practices with which to begin to answer the fundamental question: "How can I reconcile the two worlds, and will the resulting world be a better one that the one with which I began?" (Delgado, 1995, p. 73).

NOTES

1. The title of this chapter was inspired by the article by Delgado (1989) and seeks to continue the challenge of "oscillating" the race consciousness of majority-race readers.
2. Joyce King defines dysconscious racism as "a form of racism that tacitly accepts dominant White norms and privileges. It is not the absence of consciousness (that is, not unconsciousness) but an impaired consciousness or distorted way of thinking about race as compared to, for example, critical consciousness"(King, 1991, p.135).
3. The African-American artist Jean Michel Basquiat's paintings are characterized by the use of paint and crayon on unprimed canvas, featuring crude, angry, and powerful figures and graffiti-like written messages (see "Three

postcolonial painters: The pedagogies of Bennett, Roche-Rabell, and Basquiat" in Dimitriadis & McCarthy, 2001).

4.   Made in memory of Kalbinder Kaur Hayre, a young Indian woman killed in 1985 in a racist attack in England, "Sari Red" eloquently examines the effect of the ever-present threat of violence upon the lives of Asian women in both private and public spheres. In this moving visual poem, the title refers to red, the color of blood spilt and the red of the sari, symbolizing sensuality and intimacy between Asian women. (Retrieved November 15, 2002, from http://www.wmm.com/Catalog/pages/c10.htm).

5.   Using poetry, personal testimony, rap and performance, "Tongues Untied" describes the homophobia and racism that confront Black gay men. Some of the tales are troublesome: the man refused entry to a gay bar because of his color; the college student left bleeding on the sidewalk after a gay-bashing; the loneliness and isolation of the drag queen. Yet Riggs also presents the rich flavor of the Black gay male experience, from protest marches and smokey bars to the language of the "snap diva" and Vogue dancer. It is a benchmark film that speaks for itself. (Retrieved November 15, 2002, from http://www.frameline.org/hv_ce_files/hv_tongues_untied.html).

6.   In "History and Memory" the viewer hears Rea Tajiri narrate her family's history during the time that all people of Japanese ancestry were interned. She say's that she is in "search of an ever absent image and a desire to create an image when there are so few." Her family does not have many photographs or other objects that would serve as a remembrance of that time. All that her mother remembers about that time was "why she forgot to remember." Rea Tajiri made this firm because she was "searching for a history, my own history," because she knew that the story that she had heard was not true and that parts had been left out. (Retrieved November 15, 2002, from http://www.wmm.com/catalog/_makers/fm357.htm).

7.   Examples of teacher education students using multimedia authoring software included Hyperstudio® to create presentations with maps and globes (Bessier, 1999) or PowerPoint® to create "learning journeys" on social justice (Beyerbach & Russo, 2001). However, there were no specific examples of using this software to examine or critique social issues.

8.   The names of students that appear in this chapter are pseudonyms.

9.   Rev. Martin Niemoeller, an outspoken advocate for accepting the burden of collective guilt for WW II as a means of atonement for the suffering that the German nation (through the Nazis) had caused before and during WW II, wrote the following in 1945: "First they came for the Communists, and I didn't speak up, because I wasn't a Communist. Then they came for the Jews, and I didn't speak up, because I wasn't a Jew. Then they came for the Catholics, and I didn't speak up, because I was a Protestant. Then they came for me, and by that time there was no one left to speak up for me."

10.   To view additional images by Lewis Hine, visit the following web site: (http://www.historyplace.com/unitedstates/childlabor/).

11.   Becker (1997) draws her views of the "artist as public intellectual" from Edward Said's (1996) *Representations of the Intellectual.* New York: Vintage. While this notion is extended to only a few 'lofty' individuals, I believe that by viewing pre-service education students we work with as individuals who only engage oppression and injustice from an 'intellectual' standpoint, limits student responses to these issues. Rather, by viewing the students as 'art-

ists' we may begin to see them as individuals capable of "adding something else" by responding creatively to the challenges of racial inequity in the United States.

REFERENCES

Apple, M.W. (2000). *Official knowledge: Democratic education in a conservative age* (2nd ed.). New York: Routledge.

Austin, J.L. (1962). *How to do things with words.* Cambridge, MA: Harvard University Press.

Becker, C. (1997). The artist as public intellectual. In H.A. Giroux & P. Shannon (Eds.), *Education and cultural studies: Towards a performative practice* (pp. 13–24). New York: Routledge.

Beisser, S.R. (1999). Infusing technology in elementary social studies methods. *SITE 99: Society for information technology & teacher education international conference, USA, 10,* 2–8.

Bennett, L., & Pye, J. (1998). Technology: Creating a community of thinkers. *Proceedings of Selected Research and Development Presentations at the National Convention of the Association for Educational Communications and Technology (AECT), USA,* 21–28.

Beyerbach, B.A., & Russo, P. (2001). Using technology to support teaching for social justice in a preservice program. In M. Justice (Ed.), *Diversity and International: SITE 2001 Section* (pp. 4–8).

Blocker, J. (1999). *Where is Ana Mendieta? Identity, performativity, and exile.* Durham, NC: Duke University Press.

Bhabha, H.K. (1994). *The location of culture.* New York: Routledge.

Bourdieu, P. (1991). Description and prescription: The conditions of possibility and the limits of political effectiveness. In J.B. Thompson (Ed.), *Language and symbolic power* (pp. 127–136). Cambridge, MA: Harvard University Press.

Brooks, D., & Kopp, T.W. (1991). Technology and teacher education. In W.R. Houston, M. Haberman & J. Sikula (Eds.), *Handbook of research on teacher education* (pp. 498–513). New York: Macmillan.

Bruder, I. (1989). Future teachers: Are they prepared? *Electronic Learning, 8*(4), 32–39.

Butler, J. (1990). *Gender trouble: Feminism and the subversion of identity.* New York: Routledge.

Conquergood, D. (1991). Rethinking ethnography: Towards a critical cultural politics. *Communication Monographs, 58,* 179–194.

Delgado, R. (1989). Legal storytelling: Storytelling for oppositionists and others: A plea for narrative. *Michigan Law Review 87,* 2411–2441.

Delgado, R. (1995). Legal Storytelling: Storytelling for oppositionists and others: A plea for narrative. In R. Delgado (Ed.), *Critical race theory: The cutting edge* (pp. 64–74). Philadelphia, PA: Temple University Press.

Denzin, N.K. (1997). *Interpretive ethnography: Ethnographic practices for the 21st century.* Thousand Oaks, CA: Sage.

Denzin, N.K. (2000).The practices and politics of interpretation. In N.K. Denzin & Y. S. Lincoln (Eds.), *The handbook of qualitative research* (2nd ed., pp. 897–921). Thousand Oaks, CA: Sage.

Derrida, J. (1986). *Margins of philosophy.* Chicago: University of Chicago Press.

Diamond, E. (1996). Introduction. In E. Diamond (Ed.), *Performance & cultural politics* (pp. 1–12). New York: Routledge.

Dimitriadis, G., & McCarthy, C. (2001). *Reading and teaching the postcolonial: From Baldwin to Basquiat and beyond.* New York: Teachers Columbia Press.

Fuller, L.S. (1996). Disrupting whiteness: Race, queerness and pedagogy. *University of Wisconsin-Madison,* 0-591-13588-4.

Giroux, H.A., & Shannon, P. (1997). Cultural studies and pedagogy as performative practice: Toward an introduction. In H.A. Giroux & P. Shannon (Eds.), *Education and cultural studies: Towards a performative practice* (pp. 1–9). New York: Routledge.

Gray, P.H., & VanOosting, J. (1996). *Performance in life and literature.* Needham Heights, MA: Allyn & Bacon.

Hoban, P. (1998). *Basquiat: A quick killing in art.* New York: Viking Presss.

hooks, b. (1994). *Teaching to transgress: Education as the practice of freedom.* New York: Routledge.

Jarmon, L.H. (1996). Performance ethnography: Creating a mechanism for engagement by the academy. *Paper presented at the Annual Meeting of the Speech Communication Association, USA, 82,* 1–35.

Jones, L. (Producer) Newman, L. (Producer). Isay, D. (Producer) (1993). *Ghetto Life 101* [audio recording] (Available from Sound Portraits Productions, 176 Grand Street, 3rd Floor, New York, NY 10013).

Juhasz, A. (1992). WAVE in the media environment: Camcorder activism and the making of HIV TV. *Camera Obscura, 28,* 135–151.

King, J.E. (1991). Dysconscious racism: Ideology, identity, and the miseducation of teachers. *Journal of Negro Education, 60*(2), 133–146.

Ladson-Billings, G., & Tate, W.F., IV (1995). Toward a critical race theory of education. *Teachers College Record, 97*(1), 47–68.

McCall, M.M. (2000). Performance ethnography. A brief history and some Advice. In N.K. Denzin & Y.S. Lincoln (Eds.), *The handbook of qualitative research* (2nd ed., pp. 421-433). Thousand Oaks, CA: Sage.

Mehlinger, H.D., & Powers, S.M. (2002). *Technology and teacher education: A guide for educators and policymakers.* Boston: Houghton Mifflin.

Minh-ha, T.T. (Director). & Boarder, J.P. (Producer). *Reassemblies: From the firelight to the screen* [video recording]. (Available from Third World Newsreel. 545 Eighth Avenue, 10th Floor. New York, NY 10018).

Mirón, L.F., & Inda, J. (2000). Race as a speech act. *Cultural Studies: A Research Volume, 5*(8), 83–105.

Nichols, B. (1994). Performing documentary. In B. Nichols (Ed.), *Blurred boundaries: Questions of meaning in contemporary culture* (pp. 92–106). Bloomington: Indiana University Press.

Odin, J.K. (1998). *The Performative and processual: A study of the hypertext/postcolonial aesthetic.* (Retrieved November 29, 2002 from http://65.107.211.206/post/poldiscourse/odin/odin1.html).

Patraka, V.M. (1999). *Spectacular suffering: Theatre, Fascism, and the Holocaust.* Bloomington: Indiana University Press.

Pennycock, A. (2000). English, politics, ideology: From colonial celebration to postcolonial performativity. In T. Ricento (Ed.), *Ideology, politics and language policies* (pp. 107–120). Philadelphia, PA: John Benjamins Publishing.

Phelan, P. (1993). *Unmarked: The politics of performance.* New York: Routledge.

Pratibha, P. (Director) (1988). *Sari red.* [video recording]. (Available from Women Make Movies, Inc., 462 Broadway, Suite 500WS New York, NY 10013).

Riggs, M. (Director). (1989). *Tongues untied* [video recording]. (Available from California Newsreel, P.O. Box 2284, South Burlington, VT 05407).

Stern, C.S., & Henderson, B. (1993). *Performance texts and contexts.* New York: Longman.

Tajiri, R. (Director). (1991). *History and memory* [video recording]. (Available from Electronic Arts Intermix, Inc., 535 West 22nd Street, 5th floor, New York, NY 10011).

Willis, J.W., & Mehlinger, H.D. (1996). Information technology and teacher education. In J. Sikula, T.J. Buttery, & E. Guyton (Eds.), *Handbook of research on teacher education* (2nd ed., pp. 978–1029). New York: Macmillan.

ABOUT THE CONTRIBUTORS

Ceola Ross Baber, Associate Dean for Teacher Education and Associate Professor of Curriculum and Instruction, the University of North Carolina–Greensboro. Her research interests include equity education (the relationship between race/ethnicity, class and schooling) and social studies education.

André Branch, Assistant Professor of Education, San Diego State University. His research interests include student ethnic identity development through curriculum development and strategies for increasing the number of ethnically diverse teachers.

Jamel K. Donnor, Ph.D. candidate in Educational Communications and Technology in the Department of Curriculum and Instruction at the University of Wisconsin–Madison. His research interests include the pedagogical uses of technology in education, critical race theory, the education of African American scholarship football student-athletes, and curriculum theory.

Geneva Gay, Professor of Education at the University of Washington–Seattle. Her research interests are general curriculum theory, multicultural education, and the interaction between race, culture, and ethnicity in teaching and learning.

Jessica Gordon Nembhard, economist and Assistant Professor, African American Studies Department and The Democracy Collaborative, University of Maryland–College Park. Her research interests include democratic

Critical Race Theory Perspectives on the Social Studies, pages 291–292
Copyright © 2003 by Information Age Publishing

community-based economic development, urban cooperative economic development, outcome measurement, racial wealth inequality, and popular economic literacy.

Tyrone Howard, Assistant Professor, Urban Schooling Division, University of California–Los Angeles. His research interests include multiculutral education, urban education, and access and equality in schools.

Gloria Ladson-Billings, Professor of Curriculum and Instruction, University of Wisconsin–Madison. Her research interests include the relationship between culture and schooling and critical race theory.

Lisa Loutzensheiser, Assistant Professor of Curriculum Studies, University of British Columbia. Her research interests include education and marginalized students, anti-oppressive education at the K–12 and teacher education levels, queer and gender theories, and research methodologies.

Anand R. Marri, Ph.D. candidate in Curriculum and Instruction, University of Wisconsin–Madison. His research focuses on social studies education, multicultural education, and technology in education.

Patricia Marshall, Associate Professor in Curriculum and Instruction, North Carolina State University–Raleigh. Her research interests include African American achievement and social studies.

Valerie Ooka Pang, Professor of Teacher Education, San Diego State University. Her interests include multicultural education, social studies education, and Asian Pacific American youth.

Frances Rains, Faculty member of Native American and World Indigenous Peoples Studies, The Reservation Based Community Determined Program, The Evergreen State College, Olympia, Washington. Her research interests include critical race theory and American Indian educational issues.

Cynthia Tyson, Associate Professor of Social Studies and Global Education, The Ohio State University. Her research interests include critical pedagogy and teaching for social justice in the social studies, and the examination of race/racism in qualitative research.

Michael Zambon, Ph.D. candidate in Curriculum and Instruction, University of Wisconsin–Madison. His research interests focus on the interaction of multicultural education, cultural studies and post-colonial theory.

CPSIA information can be obtained
at www.ICGtesting.com
Printed in the USA
LVHW08s0129300818
588617LV00002B/23/P